MAGNIFICENT
DESOLATION

MAGNIFICENT
DESOLATION

THE LONG JOURNEY HOME FROM THE MOON

BUZZ ALDRIN

with KEN ABRAHAM

HARMONY BOOKS · NEW YORK

Copyright © 2009 by StarBuzz LLC

All rights reserved.
Published in the United States by Harmony Books, an imprint of the Crown
Publishing Group, a division of Random House, Inc., New York.
www.crownpublishing.com

HARMONY BOOKS is a registered trademark and the Harmony Books colophon is a
trademark of Random House, Inc.

Library of Congress Cataloging-in-Publication Data available upon request.

ISBN 978-0-307-46345-6

Printed in the United States of America

Design by Lauren Dong

10 9 8 7 6 5 4 3 2 1

First Edition

To MY FELLOW ASTRONAUTS from the Mercury, Gemini, Apollo, and Skylab eras. Each one of these men possessed special talents that contributed to the success of human space exploration. I am proud that I had the privilege of joining these space pioneers who ventured outward to expand mankind's presence beyond our planet Earth.

To MY PARTNER and great love in life, Lois, who sustains my efforts to chart future pathways to the stars.

Contents

MAGNIFICENT DESOLATION

A JOURNEY for
ALL MANKIND

Wednesday, July 16, 1969, 6:00 a.m. (EDT) Countdown: T minus three hours, thirty minutes to liftoff. Clear Florida sky.

ELEVATED 300 FEET IN THE AIR ON AN UPPER PLATFORM OF Kennedy Space Center's Launch Pad 39-A, I stood alone on the grating of the towering gantry. A few yards away, loaded with more than 2,000 tons of liquid oxygen and hydrogen propellant, the giant Saturn V rocket also stood, primed for liftoff as the countdown progressed. Large shards of frost were already falling off its outer skin from the super-chilled liquid oxygen within.

Hours earlier my Apollo 11 crewmates, Neil Armstrong and Michael Collins, and I had enjoyed a predawn steak-and-eggs breakfast—an astronaut tradition—and had gone through an elaborate suiting-up with NASA's equipment team helping us get into our pressurized suits, helmets, gloves, and boots. Along with our Pad Leader, Günter Wendt, a gray-haired man of German descent who had worked on almost every launch since the early days of the Mercury program, the three of us, carrying our portable air-conditioning ventilators as though we were heading off to work with our briefcases, loaded into the courier van for the short drive out to the launchpad.

Slowly we ascended in the gantry elevator, passing red metal grated walkways at various intervals leading to strategic areas of the rocket. Each of us had trained for his entire life leading up to this moment. As a crew, we had worked together for nearly a year, with Neil and I initially on the backup crew for the gutsy Apollo 8 mission, the first to fly around the moon after only two prior missions with the Saturn V, and then with Mike as the prime crew for the Apollo 11 mission. Because of the seating order in the cramped conditions of the Apollo command module—comparable to the interior of a small van in which the three of us would live and work for more than a week—climbing over one another to enter the craft while wearing our spacesuits was next to impossible. So Günter stopped the elevator about three-fourths of the way up, and dropped me off to wait there on the metal grating while he, Neil, and Mike proceeded two more flights up to where the elevator opened at the "white room," the final preparation area leading to the narrow hatch opening to the spacecraft. In less than three and a half hours, if all went well, the enormous rocket, with the power of an atomic bomb, would release an engulfing fireball and lumber off the pad, slowly gathering speed as it rose majestically into the sky, launching America's first attempt to land human beings on the moon.

The sun had not yet come up and was barely peeking above the horizon as I stood on the grating and peered through the clear bubble helmet I wore. The only sound I could hear came from my ventilation unit. Looking up and down the coastline, my eyes scanned the beaches for miles along the causeway near Cape Canaveral, where more than a million people had started gathering the night before, trekking in cars, motorcycles, pickup trucks, campers, and large motor homes, inching their way through bumper-to-bumper traffic as they sought the perfect launch viewing location. Already people were filling in every available spot of dry ground, and thousands of boats were anchored on the Indian and Banana rivers near the Cape. Without a good set of binoculars, most of the spectators could not see me, and from my vantage point I could barely see them, but I could see the evidence of them in the flickering campfires that dotted the beaches in the pre-dawn darkness. Everyone knew that something big was about to happen.

Because of the danger of explosion should something go wrong, the area immediately near the Saturn V was evacuated except for technicians making their final pre-launch checks. Even if the launch was perfect, no human could stay within several miles of it outside of the Firing Room, the launch control center at the Cape. The hot gases and thunderous noise would consume anyone standing too close to the rocket at ignition. The VIP spectator area—from which former president Lyndon B. Johnson, the astronauts' families, politicians, celebrities, and others with the coveted special pass would watch the launch—was a full three miles away. Even there, the vibrations would be felt, and the roar from the engines would be almost deafening.

I looked to the south, where some of the older launchpads were located, and I couldn't help letting my eyes linger on Launch Pad 34, where, two and a half years earlier, three of my fellow astronauts—Gus Grissom, Roger Chaffee, and Ed White—had lost their lives when they were trapped inside their space capsule in a torrid burst of flames during a pre-launch training test for Apollo 1. Ed had been a year behind me at West Point, where we became friends, and we'd later served together in the Air Force as fighter pilots in Germany, flying F-100s in the "Big 22" Squadron. He was the key person who had kindled and encouraged my efforts to contribute to the space program and ultimately become an astronaut, and now he was gone.

Instinctively my hand moved to a pocket on my spacesuit that contained a special pouch in which I carried an original mission patch honoring the men who had died aboard *Apollo 1*, as well as various medals honoring Soviet cosmonauts Vladimir Komarov, who had been killed on *Soyuz 1*, and Yuri Gagarin, the first man in space. In that same pouch I carried a silicon disk inscribed with wishes from leaders of seventy-three nations of the world, and a gold pin in the shape of the olive branch of peace that we had chosen as a symbol of our mission for all mankind. I planned to leave these tributes on the moon.

Not too far from Pad 34, I could see the remnants of Pad 19, where Jim Lovell and I had crewed the last mission of the Gemini program, for a series of complex rendezvous maneuvers and the world's first successful spacewalk. It was exhilarating to end that program on a high note and pave the way for Apollo. I thought about how far we had come since man's dream of flight was first realized when the Wright Brothers' *Flyer* took to the air on the Outer Banks of North Carolina, at Kill Devil Hill, near Kitty Hawk, in 1903—the very year my mother, Marion Moon, was born. Now, only sixty-six years later, we were aiming for a much longer, more daring, and dangerous flight.

For fifteen minutes I stood on that walkway, suspended from the steadily marching countdown, and enjoying a moment of peace and solitude as I contemplated the journey ahead. I recalled just how wonderful my life had been to get me to this point. All the facets and experiences had worked out along the way to put me in the right place at the right time. Now I was leaving Earth to land on another celestial body, and, if all went as planned, I would return to family and friends, to a full life. Our confidence was high—about 60 percent certain that we would succeed in landing on the moon, the part that had never been done before, and 95 percent that we would make it back home alive. We had trained, tested, and simulated nearly each element of the mission. But there were no guarantees. Even with all the preparation, a myriad of things could go wrong. As astronauts, we were trained to accept such risks, even the risk of not returning.

Finally, Günter was ready for me. I ascended the remaining twenty feet or so, and Günter helped me into the hatch, strapping me into my seat in the center couch, between Neil on my left, strategically situated near the abort handle, and Mike on my right. As we settled in, there was nothing left to do but wait while the countdown continued.

◗　○　◗

AT 9:32 A.M., as the five large Saturn V engines ignited, we heard the final sequence of the countdown in our headsets: "T minus ten, nine, eight . . ." I quickly glanced at Neil and Mike, and we exchanged nervous but confident grins. Outside, at the base of the rocket, gases rushed out of each of the engine nozzles as we built up thrust. "T minus five, four, three . . ." With the engines running at full power, the gantry latches released and for a couple of seconds that seemed like forever, the rocket was standing unsupported, free as an eagle ready to soar.

"Two, one . . . zero . . ." The normally calm voice of Public Affairs Officer Jack King cracked with emotion from the Firing Room. "All engines running!" Even inside the command module with our helmets on, we could hear the mighty rumble. What looked like hundreds of tiny amber lights blinked on the instrument panels in front of us as the controlled but excited voice cried, "Liftoff! We have a liftoff!"

The rumbling sound grew louder and the huge rocket felt as though it swayed slightly as it smoothly inched off the pad. In fact it was so smooth that at first we couldn't detect the exact moment we left the ground. More large shards of frost fell from the sleek metal sides as blue sky seemed to move past the hatch window directly above me. Below us an inferno of flames, steam, and gases billowed all around the launch pad. With 7.6 million pounds of thrust pushing all 3,240 tons of the rocket and spacecraft, we cleared the tower and rapidly accelerated, the g forces dramatically building up and pressing against us. We were on our way to the moon!

Twelve seconds into our flight, shortly after we cleared the tower and were streaking from a straight vertical shot to a gradually changing angle of inclination into the blue sky above, the hundreds of technicians hovering over their displays and consoles in the Firing Room at Cape Canaveral could breathe a little easier. At that point their main job was done and control of our mission moved to the nerve center at Mission Control in Houston, where hundreds of other technicians and engineers manned their consoles and displays, monitoring every aspect of our flight. In the main control room, whimsically known to NASA's engineers as the "bat room" because of the darkened area in the front where large video screens tracking the flight covered the walls, dozens of people worked at separate stations, with each console controller monitoring one specific aspect of the spacecraft and reporting to the

Flight Director if everything was "go," or if anything was wrong. Although the room was filled with experts handling vital information, only one person communicated directly with us in the *Apollo 11* spacecraft: the Spacecraft Communicator, or "Capcom," a fellow astronaut. All the information that we needed to know from the many monitors in Mission Control, and feedback on what we were experiencing in space, flowed through the Capcom.

Three minutes into the flight, the g forces had increased to the highest point, as we felt nearly four times heavier than our normal body weight. We were forty-five miles high, at least six times higher than most commercial jets can fly, traveling at a speed of nearly 6,500 miles per hour. Neil, Mike, and I had all been in space on previous missions, but it was nonetheless thrilling to look out our window and see the curved Atlantic horizon rapidly receding from view as we looked back at Earth. Within four minutes we were approaching the sixty-two-mile mark, the division between Earth's blue skies and the endless blackness of space. By twelve minutes we had accelerated to nearly 17,500 miles per hour, the speed required to maintain an orbital course around the Earth. It was time to get busy; during our one and a half orbits we had to make sure all systems were functioning before we left the bounds of Earth orbit to redirect our course to the moon.

Crucial to the success of our flight navigation were the two onboard guidance computers we had on the mission (one in the command module and one in the lunar module), each with about 74 kilobytes of memory and a 2.048 MHz clock processor. With their small displays and nineteen-button keyboards, the Apollo control system seems archaic by today's standards. Many modern mobile phones have more computing power than we did. But these computers enabled us to measure our velocity changes to a hundredth of a foot per second, determine rendezvous and course corrections, and make minute maneuvers for our descent to the moon. You couldn't do that with a slide rule. NASA made sure the Apollo computers were the most advanced of the day, the first to use integrated circuit technology, and we expected them to work astoundingly well to perform all the complex calculations needed.

Weightless now, we could float around the module as Neil and I began running through our checklists while Mike checked out the equipment bays below. At approximately three hours into the trip, Mike ignited the Saturn V third-stage rocket engines for our Trans-Lunar Injection burn to take us out of Earth's orbit, catapulting us to a speed of nearly 25,000 miles per hour, heading toward the moon. The burn was successful, so it was time to let go of the third stage rocket. But first we needed to extract the lunar module (LM) that had been stored in the third stage, now fully exposed as the protective panels were released. We detached the command module (CM) to move forward and away from the rocket, and then navigated a full U-turn to head back toward the LM. Mike adeptly docked the nose of the CM to the nose of the LM, just as he had done hundreds of times in simulations. With a firm hold on the lunar lander, we practically plucked it out of the third rocket stage as we threw the switch to release the rocket and send it on its way in the direction of the sun. We were now an odd-looking apparatus speeding along, one cone-shaped command module sitting atop its cylindrical service module, nose to nose with what looked like an upside-down, gold-foil-covered cement mixer. We would fly that way until we reached lunar orbit, when Neil and I were safely inside the LM ready to disconnect from Mike and the CM, and descend to the surface of the moon.

The eight-day journey to the moon would take three days outbound, and another three days to get back home, plus two days in lunar orbit, including the day Neil and I planned to be on the lunar surface, so we were happy when we could finally take off our bulky pressurized space suits and stow them after the first five hours. Working in our more comfortable flight suits, we could now move around our weightless environment much more freely, having completed several crucial engine burns and our docking procedures. We ate our first meal aboard—real tasty precooked food from pre-measured packages organized by each meal. We had selections of chicken salad, applesauce, and even freeze-dried shrimp cocktail. It wasn't exactly gourmet cooking, but it was enough sustenance to keep us energized. Some of the meals were ready to eat, and others required hot water, which we could add from a hot water gun in the CM. Eating with a spoon was a much trickier activity without gravity; any crumbs from your pineapple fruitcake could float around just about anywhere in the cabin. But I liked it better than simply squirting food into my mouth, as Jim Lovell and I had done on our Gemini 12 mission.

With the CM starting to feel like home, after dinner it was time for a nap. We pulled down the shades on our windows, and dimmed the cabin lights and the sound from our radio. Mission Control could contact us if necessary, but in the meantime a bit of peace and quiet would be welcomed. I settled into my lightweight sleeping bag and stretched out, floating weightless in the lower equipment bay, while Neil curled up on a couch and Mike moved back and forth between the two areas, keeping a close watch on the instruments on the walls all around the couches. Amazingly, I found it relatively easy to rest in our artificial environment. It hardly occurred to me that just an inch away, outside the thin wall of metallic alloy, was a deadly, vast, airless vacuum.

On the way to the moon, we slept only about five hours each night. Our excitement and adrenaline made sleep elusive; besides, our schedule was full of tasks and preparations. We constantly monitored our progress, and fired small guidance rockets to check and correct our course. We also sent back live television broadcasts to give people on Earth a glimpse of our activities inside the spacecraft, such as making a ham-spread sandwich with the bread floating in zero gravity. We had to coordinate our times with Houston, since there was really no telling day from night in space. The sun was always shining, yet the sky around us was a constant black blanket dotted with millions of stars. One thing was certain: with each passing hour, the Earth was growing smaller and the moon was getting larger when we looked out our windows.

Here and there, we had a few "blank pages" in our flight plan that allowed us the opportunity to reflect. As we moved outward into space, it was an interesting feeling looking back at Earth. Our blue and brown habitat of humanity appeared like a jewel of life in the midst of the surrounding blackness. From space there were no observable borders between nations, no observable reasons for the wars we were leaving behind.

The decade of the 1960s had been a tumultuous one. Camelot had fallen, marred by the 1963 assassination of President John F. Kennedy, and the 1968 assassinations of his brother, Robert Kennedy, during his presidential campaign, and of the Reverend Martin Luther King Jr. A few days after Dr. King's death, I called my pastor in Houston to join me in a "walk"—as we participated in a memorial march through the streets of downtown Houston in honor of Dr. King's life and all he'd fought for in the civil rights movement. There was the weight of global crises during this era as well. The conflict between the United States and the Soviet Union had escalated with the Cuban Missile Crisis. And we were embroiled in an ongoing war in Vietnam, with no clear victory in sight. There arose social unrest and a cry for peace on many fronts, with war protests and civil rights marches, teach-ins at universities, the pacifist message of the Beatles, and the mobilization of the youth movement that would culminate in the Woodstock festival during the summer of 1969.

Our space quests continued through all of this. In the Cold War environment, it had to. The Soviets had jump-started the Space Age with the launch of *Sputnik* in October 1957, and the satellite's strange new beeping sound startled the western world as it orbited the Earth. On April 12, 1961, the Soviets sent the first human into space, cosmonaut Yuri Gagarin, for one full orbit around the Earth. NASA responded by sending America's first astronaut, Alan Shepard, for a fifteen-minute suborbital ride, sixty-two miles up to the edge of space, on May 5. Three weeks after Shepard's fledgling flight, President John F. Kennedy addressed Congress and issued a stunning challenge to the nation to embrace a bold new commitment to land a man on the moon and bring him safely home before the end of the decade. It was May 25, 1961. We didn't have the know-how, the technology, or the rocketry, but we had the willpower. NASA's innovative engineers and rocket scientists, including the indomitable Wernher von Braun, along with the aerospace industry, congressional support, and teams of thousands throughout the country, worked together to bring us to this point of being on the verge of realizing Kennedy's challenge.

We *needed* this first moon landing to be a success to lift America, and to reaffirm that the American dream was still possible in the midst of turmoil. We needed this mission to succeed after eight years of national effort to get us here. Yes, we were determined to win the space race, to beat the Soviets to the moon. In the broadest sense, we hoped this mission would lift and unite the world, and stand as a symbol of peace for all mankind. That's why we included an olive branch in the design of our Apollo 11 mission patch, which we wore on all our spacesuits. Initially, the design depicted an American bald eagle (the inspiration for the name of our lunar landing craft) with its talons stretched out, about to land on the crater-marked surface of the moon. When we added the olive branch of peace to be carried in the eagle's talons, that made it all the more significant to me. In addition, we departed from tradition and chose not to include our names on the patch. We felt the mission had a bigger meaning than that of the individuals involved.

On the third day of our journey, *Apollo 11* flew into the shadow of the moon. We were more than five-sixths of the way to our destination. But for now we marveled at the unusual view ahead of us of a shadowed lunar sphere eclipsing the sun, lit from the back with a bright halo of refracted light. The soft glow of reflected light from the Earth helped us see ever more vividly the moon's protruding ridges and the impressions of craters, almost adding a 3-D sensation to our view.

On the morning of day four, it was time to enter the moon's gravitational influence. We needed two Lunar Orbit Insertion burns to move us into position before the command module could separate from the lunar module so Neil and I could begin our descent to the surface. For the first burn, we strapped ourselves in to swing around the moon's far side, the rugged, dark side never seen from Earth, bombarded by meteoric activity. And for the first time we would lose all communication signals with Mission Control during the forty-eight minutes it would take for us to traverse the far side. The burn had to be precisely orchestrated at exactly the right time for six minutes to slow us down to just over 3,600 miles per hour—the speed at which we would be "captured" by lunar gravity. But we were entirely on our own for this one. This had to go right. Mike punched the PROCEED button to fire the engine, and the timing was perfect—although Mission Control would not receive confirmation for another forty minutes.

Now that we were in lunar orbit, we had two hours to initiate one more burn to transform our wide elliptical orbit into a tighter, more circular one. We carefully aligned our navigation using star sightings. Through a complex series of star positioning checks and alignment of our CM platform, we were ready for our second burn. If we over-burned for as little as two seconds, we would be on a collision course back toward the far side of the moon. Working this time in full coordination with Mission Control, the tricky procedure came off perfectly as we sailed even closer to the moon.

The next morning at 8:50 a.m. (EDT) on Sunday, July 20, 1969, Neil and I floated up through the access tunnel that linked the CM to the LM, the spacecraft in which Neil and I would descend to the lunar surface. We were no longer in flight suits, but fully suited up in our twenty-one-layered extra-vehicular-activity (EVA) spacesuits that we would wear until returning to the CM. We hooked up the hoses from our suits to the oxygen supply on the LM, donned our helmets, and waited while Mike went through his lengthy preparations for separation. Our hearts pounded in anticipation of the "powered descent" to the lunar surface.

As lunar module pilot, I had previously entered the LM on the second day of our journey to check things out and prepare what would now be Neil's and my home away from home for approximately twenty-four hours. The LM was the epitome of bare-bones construction. A technological wonder, it had to be as light as possible, so it was far from luxurious inside. Everything in the interior of the LM had been sprayed with a dull navy-gray fire-resistant coating. To further reduce weight, nothing was covered unless absolutely necessary; all the wiring bundles and plumbing were completely exposed, and there weren't even covers on the walls of circuit breakers and switches. There were no seats in the LM, or sleeping couches. We would sleep in makeshift hammocks hung from the walls, and we would fly the lunar lander while standing up, almost shoulder to shoulder, in our pressurized suits and helmets. We would be tethered to the deck of the LM by elastic cords. Two small upside-down triangular windows, one on each side of the control panels, provided our only sight of the surface. It was going to be an interesting ride.

The time seemed interminable as Mike went through his checklist to make sure every item was carefully set up. If he botched the undocking and damaged the tunnel, Neil and I would have no way to rejoin Mike in the CM. At least not the way we planned. If we found that the tunnel was jammed after attempting to re-dock, then Neil and I would have no other option than to exit the LM for an EVA spacewalk, using our emergency oxygen containers, and follow the handrails outside the LM to the top to manually open the CM's hatch and climb in. As commander of the Gemini 8 mission, Neil had not performed a spacewalk, since no commanders participated in EVA prior to Apollo, but he was well trained to perform one if necessary. My five-and-a-half-hour spacewalk on Gemini 12 had been thrilling, and had set a world record for spacewalking in large part thanks to being the first astronaut to train underwater using scuba gear, and the first to use a system of greatly improved fixed hand and foot restraints I had suggested for the exterior of the Gemini spacecraft. But an emergency EVA was a different story. The timing, owing to the limited supply of oxygen in our emergency packs, would be critical. And if for some reason we could not dock at all with the CM, Neil and I would still need to exit the LM for a spacewalk so Mike could gently maneuver the CM in our direction to pick us up. Although far from ideal, an emergency EVA could be our only means of survival. One way or another, we would need to pass through the narrow tunnel connecting the two spacecraft to return home, or we wouldn't return at all.

On our thirteenth orbit around the moon, we found ourselves on the far side when Mike informed us that we were ready to commence undocking. Until this point, our docked pair of spacecraft had simply been known as *Apollo 11*. Now, as we rounded the moon back toward Earth's side and sealed off the hatches to become two separate entities, the CM would take on the name picked by Mike, the *Columbia*, and the LM became known to Mission Control and the world as the *Eagle*, the name selected by Neil and me. Houston began monitoring the data that was now streaming between the computers of the two spacecraft. Finally we heard the words from Mission Control: "You are go for separation, *Columbia*."

Mike wasted no time. As though he were backing a truck out of a parking space, he pulled the *Columbia* away from the *Eagle*, releasing us with a resulting thump. At 1:47 p.m. (EDT), July 20, the *Eagle* separated from the *Columbia*. "Okay, *Eagle*," Mike said. "You guys take care."

"See you later," Neil replied, as casually as if we were back in Houston, heading home from another day of training.

As one last precaution before setting off on his own solo orbits around the moon—the first man in history ever to do so—Mike visually inspected the LM from his perspective in the *Columbia*, after we had undocked. "I think you've got a fine-looking machine there, *Eagle*, despite the fact that you're upside down."

"Somebody's upside down," Neil quipped in return.

Standing shoulder to shoulder, now it was our turn to focus on our lengthy checklist as we began flying the LM backwards, continuing in our own orbit around the moon. We flew around the moon once and started around a second time while Mission Control monitored all aspects of our progress. Then, with the friendly twinge of a Texas drawl, the voice of astronaut Charlie Duke, who was now serving as Capcom, parted the static. "*Eagle*, Houston. You are go for DOI."

Charlie was telling us that it was showtime. Descent Orbit Insertion (DOI), would take us on an initial coasting descent to within eight miles of the lunar surface, just slightly higher than most commercial aircraft fly over Earth. The DOI burn lasted less than thirty seconds. I looked out the triangular window closest to me and could see the surface of the moon rolling by. The craters were becoming larger and more distinct, their beige color taking on a chalky gray appearance. We continued flying above the terrain until we again heard Charlie Duke. "*Eagle*, Houston," Charlie sounded controlled but excited. "If you read, you're go for powered descent. Over."

Because of the static in our headsets, Charlie's words were garbled, but fifty miles above us, Mike Collins heard them clearly and relayed the message: "*Eagle*, this is *Columbia*," he said calmly. "They just gave you a go for powered descent." With no video monitor onboard, Mike could not see the LM or watch the proceedings, but he could listen in on the radio communications. It was a good thing he was paying attention.

Neil nodded as we acknowledged the implications of Charlie's message. Inside my helmet, I was grinning like we had just won the biggest race of all time. In eleven minutes we were going to set the *Eagle* down for a landing unlike any other.

◐　○　◑

NEIL THREW THE switch to ignite the powered descent burn. Oddly, we could barely hear it or feel any sensation when a hot orange plume poured out of the engine into the black space below us. Had we not seen the change on the instrument panel in front of us, we might not have even known that the engine had ignited and was whisking us downward. But downward we were going, and rapidly, too. Through the window on my right, I could see the moonscape seemingly rising toward us.

I turned on the 16-millimeter movie camera that was located in my window to film our descent to the lunar surface. I also switched on my microphone to voice activated mode (VOX). Neil didn't really care whether or not we were on an open mike as we descended, but I did, so I turned the setting to VOX. There were simply too many things going on to have to worry about a "push to talk" microphone system as we came down. Looking back, I'm glad that I left the mike on. Millions of people on Earth listened in to the static-filled radio transmissions between Mission Control in Houston and us as we descended. Some of our transmissions were barely distinguishable. That was one problem we had not anticipated in our hundreds of hours of working in the simulator back on Earth—it hadn't really occurred to us that we wouldn't be able to hear instructions from Mission Control, but we were catching enough to stay focused and keep going.

Five minutes into our powered descent, everything was looking good as we passed through about 35,000 feet on our altitude readout. Suddenly an alarm flashed on the screen in front of me.

Neil saw it as well. "Program alarm!" he said instantly to Houston.

Even with our transmissions traveling at the speed of light, it took one and a half seconds each way between the moon and the Earth, causing a three-second delay in all our communications. This meant that Charlie couldn't respond immediately, so his response was based on our prior communication. Indeed, he was still quite positive.

"It's looking good to us. Over."

"It's a twelve-oh-two." Neil's voice included a hint of urgency. "What is it?" Neil said to me. We had never seen a 1202 alarm in our simulations, and in the middle of our crucial eleven-minute landing maneuver, we weren't about to take out the thick guidance and navigation dictionary we had brought along. Then to Houston, Neil said, "Give us a reading on the twelve-oh-two Program Alarm."

"Twelve-oh-two," I called out, the seriousness of the alarm evident in my voice as the data screen in front of me went blank. We were now at 33,000 feet above the moon, not a time or place to have an alarm go off, and certainly not a time to have our landing data disappear. Neil and I exchanged tense looks. Something was affecting our guidance computer and causing it to have difficulty in handling the gigantic array of information coming into it from the landing radar.

Nevertheless, we weren't thinking about aborting; we didn't want to get this close to landing on the moon and have to turn back; we were intent on fulfilling our mission. On the other hand, the alarm was ominous. If the 1202 alarm meant an overflow of data in the computer, we might not be able to rely on the very computer we needed to land on the moon. Either the computer's programs were incapable of managing all the landing data coming in to it at once, or perhaps there was a hardware problem caused by all the jostling around since we'd left Earth four days ago. Maybe something inside the computer had broken, just as might happen to a home computer. In any case, we had no time to fix it. The potential for disaster was twofold: first, maybe the computer could not give us the accurate information we needed to land; or, second, if in fact we succeeded in landing, the computer's malfunction could prevent us from blasting off the moon and making our rendezvous with Mike the next day. The demands on the computer then would be even greater.

While we grappled silently with these possibilities, we continued descending toward the moon pushing through 27,000 feet. The large red ABORT STAGE button on the panel loomed large in front of us. If either Neil or I hit the button, the *Eagle* would instantly blast back up toward *Columbia*, and America's attempt to land on the moon would be dubbed a failure.

"Roger," Charlie's voice broke through the static into our headsets. "We've got you . . . we're go on that alarm." Even from 250,000 miles away, I could hear the stress in Charlie's voice. Yet for some reason the experts at Mission Control judged the computer problem an "acceptable risk," whatever that meant. There was no time to discuss the situation, or to remedy it; we could only trust that Mission Control had our best interests at heart and would guide us in the right decisions. Of the hundreds and hundreds of people who had helped get us here, nobody wanted to abort the mission. Yet at the same time we knew that Mission Control would not jeopardize our lives unnecessarily. Two nights before we launched, NASA's top administrator, Tom Paine, had eaten dinner with Neil, Mike, and me in the crew quarters. "If you have to abort," he said, "I'll see that you fly the next moon landing flight. Just don't get killed."

Just as I was getting over my concern about the first alarm, another 1202 alarm appeared on the display, another computer overload problem. Nearly seven minutes in, we had descended to 20,000 feet. I felt a shot of adrenaline surge through my system. I'd been a fighter pilot during the Korean War and had shot down two Russian-built MiGs that had been gunning for me. I knew instinctively the sense of danger a pilot experiences when he is in serious trouble and knows he needs to head back to his home base. Neil and I were in serious trouble, and we were a long, long way from home.

At Mission Control in Houston, twenty-six-year-old Steve Bales— about the average age of most of the guys in the Mission Operations Control Room—was the expert in the LM guidance systems. When the alarms started flashing in the *Eagle*, they showed up on Steve's computer as well. He immediately realized the problem, but determined that it would not jeopardize our landing. He based his decision on the fact that the computer was receiving an overflow of radar information; it had been programmed to recognize the radar data as being of secondary importance and would ignore it while it did the more important computations necessary for landing—he hoped.

Forty years later, I can now tell you why that computer overloaded, although at the time it never occurred to us. The reason the computer could not handle the data was that Neil and I had purposely left the rendezvous radar in the on position.

At some point after the *Eagle* had separated from the *Columbia*, I should have turned off the rendezvous radar, but I'd chosen not to do so. I hadn't wanted to eliminate an opportunity to check the rendezvous radar before we actually needed it, so I'd simply left it on. I wanted a safety precaution in case we had to make a quick ascent, hightailing it away from the moon's surface and back into space to catch up with Mike Collins and the *Columbia*, our ride back home. As it was, we had no idea that the computers couldn't handle information from the rendezvous radar and the landing radar at the same time, or process the data quickly enough.

About two weeks prior to our launch, the *Apollo 12* astronauts had also been training at the same time as the *Apollo 11* crew, since the missions were quite similar. They had experienced the computer alarms in simulation, so they'd aborted the mission. The simulation trainers in

Houston and Florida said, "You should not have aborted. It was not that serious."

Flight Director Gene Kranz was irate. "Go back and study this matter," he told the *Apollo 12* crew. "We don't want any of these kinds of mistakes in the future."

Unfortunately, the incident was never reported to Neil, Mike, or me. Whatever had been learned about this alarm, and whether it meant a go or no-go, never made it into our mission preparation. Being the systems guy in the LM, I was very much in the dark when this alarm came up during the tense moments of our powered descent. The lack of communication could have proved deadly.

At Mission Control, as the *Eagle* zoomed lower at a velocity of 250 feet per second, Gene Kranz called out to Steve Bales, "GUIDO?" (This was the acronym for Steve's position as Guidance Officer.) "Are you happy?"

Steve Bales knew the computer was still overloaded, but it didn't appear that the problem was hardware-related. Although he couldn't be certain to what extent the software glitch might affect the computer twenty-four hours later, when it came time for us to get off the moon's surface, he had to make a decision now: either go or no-go for landing.

With his eyes glued to his computer screen, Steve called back to Kranz, "Go!"

Charlie Duke passed the word on to us. "*Eagle*, you're go for landing."

We throttled down and continued our descent, closing in rapidly making adjustments to pitch over as we checked our position relative to the surface. Seven and a half minutes in, we were at 16,000 feet. Eight minutes in, 7,000 feet. Nine minutes in, 3,000 feet.

Twenty seconds later, at an altitude of only 2,000 feet, another alarm lit up on the computer display in the LM. Neil and I looked up simultaneously. "Twelve alarm," he said to Houston. "Twelve-oh-one."

"Roger," Charlie acknowledged our concern. "Twelve-oh-one alarm."

At the Mission Control consoles, the ever calm, crewcut Kranz winced. "GUIDO?"

Steve Bales had only a fraction of a second to make up his mind. "Go," he said tersely.

"We're go," Charlie relayed the decision to us. "Hang tight. We're go."

At about 1,000 feet above the surface, Neil began a visual search, looking for a good spot to land. "That's not a bad looking area . . . Okay. One thousand at thirty is good."

Charlie Duke replied, "*Eagle*, looking great. You're go." He must have seen the same thing we did, another alarm, because there was a pause in Charlie's strained voice. Then, "Roger. Twelve-oh-two. We copy it."

While Neil was looking out the window, my gaze was glued to the instrument readings in front of me. With the dropouts in communication, and the dropouts in radar information owing to the computer glitches, it was even more vital that Neil receive accurate altimeter readings. Moreover, our fuel level was becoming a concern. I didn't dare take my eyes off the read-outs for more than a fraction of a second.

Neil was still scanning the surface as we headed to our designated landing site, and he was not happy with what he saw.

"Seven-fifty, coming down at twenty-three," I called from where I was standing beside him, letting Neil know that we were a mere 750 feet above the surface and descending at twenty-three feet per second.

"Okay," Neil said quietly. "Pretty rocky area . . ."

"Six hundred, down at nineteen."

Neil had made up his mind. "I'm going to . . ." He didn't have to finish his statement. I knew that Neil was taking over manual control of the *Eagle*. Good thing, too, since our computer was leading us into a landing field littered with large boulders surrounding a forty-foot-wide crater. Neil made a split-second decision to fly long, to go farther than we had planned to search for a safe landing area.

"Okay, four hundred feet," I let him know, "down at nine." Then, for the first time, I added, "Fifty-eight forward." We were now skimming over the moon's surface at fifty-eight feet per second, about forty miles an hour.

"No problem," Neil responded, but I could tell by the tone of his voice that he still wasn't satisfied with the terrain. I started to be concerned about our fuel. It would be problematic to get this close and run out of "gas."

"Three hundred," I called. "Ease her down. Two-seventy."

"Okay, how's the fuel?" Neil asked without taking his eyes from the surface.

"Eight percent," I responded.

"Okay, here's a . . . looks like a good area here."

"I got the shadow out there," I said, referring to the shadow cast by the *Eagle* as it flew, and thinking it might be some sort of aid to Neil in landing. I might have seen the shadow earlier, but I was staying extremely focused on the instrument panel and calling out the numbers, rather than looking out the window.

"Two hundred fifty. Altitude-velocity lights." I was letting Neil know that the warning lights indicated that the computer was not getting good radar data. "Two-twenty, thirteen forward. Coming down nicely."

"Gonna be right over that crater," Neil said more to himself than to me, Mission Control, and the rest of the listening world.

"Two hundred feet, four and half down," I responded.

"I've got a good spot," Neil said.

I looked at our fuel gauge. We had about ninety-four seconds of fuel remaining, and Neil was still searching for a spot to bring us down. Once we got down to what we called the "bingo" fuel call, we would have to land within twenty seconds or abort. If we were at fifty feet when we hit the bingo mark, and were coming down in a good spot, we could still land. But if we still had seventy to one hundred feet to go, it would be too risky to land; we'd come down too hard. Without wanting to say anything to Neil that might disrupt his focus, I pretty much used my body "English" as best I could in a spacesuit, as if to say, *Neil, get this on the ground!*

"Sixty seconds," Charlie warned. Our ascent engine fuel tanks were filled to capacity, but that fuel did us no good, since the descent engine tanks were completely separate. We had sixty seconds worth of fuel left in the descent tanks to either land or abort. I glanced furtively out my window and saw that we were at eye level with the moon's horizon. Off in the near distance was nothing but blackness.

"Sixty feet, down two and a half." Neil had slowed our descent to two and a half feet per second. "Two forward," I said. "That's good." We wanted to be moving forward when we landed to make sure that we didn't back into something we couldn't see, or some crater shrouded by darkness. "Forty feet . . . Picking up some dust."

We were moving over the lunar surface like a helicopter coming in for a landing, but we were now in what we sometimes referred to as the "dead zone." Any touchdown from higher than ten feet was sure to damage the landing gear. Moreover, if we ran out of fuel at this altitude, we would crash onto the moon before our ascent engine could push us back into space. "Four forward. Drifting to the right a little . . ."

"Thirty seconds," Charlie said, the nervousness evident in his voice.

Neil slowed the *Eagle* even more, searching . . . searching . . . we'd come so far, surely there was a safe place where we could come down.

Then I saw it—the shadow of one of the three footpads that had touched the surface. Although our engine was still running and the *Eagle* was hovering, a probe had touched the surface. "Contact light," I said. Neil and I looked at each other with a stolen glance of relief and immense satisfaction. The LM settled gently, and we stopped moving. After flying for more than four days, it was a strange sensation to be suddenly stationary. "Shutdown," I heard Neil say.

"Okay, engine stopped," I answered.

It was 4:17 p.m. (EDT) on July 20, 1969, and we had less than twenty seconds worth of fuel remaining, but we were on the moon.

Feelings of elation threatened to overwhelm me, but I dared not give in to them. We still had a lot to do before we could breathe easier. I continued rattling off items from our flight-check list. We didn't want to make any mistakes at this point. "ACA out of detent," I said, reminding Neil to take the "Attitude Control Assembly," the joystick with which he had manually landed us on the moon, out of MANUAL and put it back to AUTO for our ascent.

"Out of detent. Auto." Neil replied matter-of-factly.

I continued with our procedures, but just then Charlie Duke's voice broke in. "We copy you down, *Eagle*," he said with obvious relief.

For the first time I paused and glanced out my window. The sun was out, the sky was velvety black, and the surface appeared even more desolate than I had imagined. The gray-ash colored rocks and pock-marked terrain, which now for the first time in its existence hosted human beings, stretched out as far as I could see and then dipped into the horizon. With our engines stopped, the pervasive silence seemed surreal.

At that moment, however, Neil did something that really surprised me. "Houston," he said calmly. "Tranquillity Base here. The *Eagle* has landed."

Neil's statement must have surprised Charlie as well, since he seemed momentarily tongue-tied. "Roger, Twan . . ." he began, and then corrected himself. "Tranquillity. We copy you on the ground. You got a bunch of guys about to turn blue. We're breathing again. Thanks a lot."

"Thank *you*," I offered.

This was no time for celebration, but in the exhilaration of the moment, I reached over and gripped Neil's hand. "We made it!" I whispered, almost as if I didn't want to seem as amazed as I was at that moment. It was all starting to sink in, what we had just accomplished. For the rest of my life I would remember those few seconds after we saw the contact button light up when the first probe on one of the *Eagle*'s legs touched the surface of the moon.

Charlie broke in again. "You're looking good here."

"Okay," Neil said to me. "Let's get on with it." Immediately, we were back to business. Then to Mission Control, he added, "Okay, we're going to be busy for a minute."

Neil and I went back to work. Although we were now perched on the lunar surface, we didn't know yet whether we could stay, and we had only a tiny window of opportunity to find out. If something was wrong—if the *Eagle* was about to tip over, if we had a fuel leak, or if some part of the LM had been damaged upon landing and could impair our liftoff, or if some other dangerous situation existed—now was the time to find out, since we had a discrete time in which blasting back off the moon and catching Mike and the *Columbia* would be more favorable. Otherwise it would take another two hours for him to get around the moon and back to us. Mike would be passing by above us now, but after about two minutes it would be too late. We would need to ignite the ascent engines within those two minutes to rendezvous with him, or he'd be too far ahead of us to catch up. That's why Neil's taking even a few seconds to communicate our status to Houston had surprised me. At this point every second could be crucial.

We ran hastily down through our checklists, preparing as though we were going to lift off within the two-minute window. I had personally included this precaution in our flight plan, just in case of any mishap. Prior to our mission, there had been a lot of discussion and some question about what we should do first after landing on the moon. Because we had so many variables to consider, I had suggested that the first thing we do on the moon should be to go through a simulated ascent. That way, if for any reason we had to make a hasty escape, we'd have already gone through a practice run of lifting off. Moreover, it had been nearly a week since our last simulated liftoff. If there was an emergency ascent required, at least we would have had a recent reminder of what we were supposed to do.

Neil and I went through each step, activating the computer program, assessing lunar gravity alignment, star-sighting to get our bearings for rendezvous with Mike, if necessary. We did everything but push the button to lift off.

Finally, we could relax.

Almost.

The guys back in Houston were concerned about a pressure buildup in one of the descent fuel tanks that should have been venting and wasn't, creating the potential for an explosion. After traveling a quarter million miles and landing with just seconds to spare, we now ran the risk of being annihilated. While the world was ecstatically celebrating our accomplishment, the guys at Mission Control discreetly "suggested" that we throw a switch to vent the tank.

I looked out the window. I had just experienced the most intense, exciting ride in my life. And the real adventure was just beginning. Outside that window, the lunar surface awaited mankind's first footprints.

2

MAGNIFICENT DESOLATION

L ANDING ON THE MOON IS NOT QUITE THE SAME THING AS arriving at Grandmother's for Thanksgiving. You don't hop out of the lunar module the moment the engine stops and yell, "We're here! We're here!" Getting out of the LM takes a lot of preparation, so we had built in several extra hours to our flight plan. We also figured it was wise to allow more time rather than less for our initial activities after landing, just in case anything had gone wrong during the flight.

According to our schedule, we were supposed to eat a meal, rest awhile, and then sleep for seven hours after arriving on the moon. After all, we had already worked a long, full day and we wanted to be fresh for our extra-vehicular activity (EVA). Mission Control had notified the media that they could take a break and catch their breath since there wouldn't be much happening for several hours as we rested. But it was hard to rest with all that adrenaline pumping through our systems.

Nevertheless, in an effort to remain calm and collected, I decided that this would be an excellent time for a ceremony I had planned as an expression of gratitude and hope. Weeks before, as the Apollo mission drew near, I had originally asked Dean Woodruff, pastor at Webster Presbyterian Church, where my family and I attended services when I was home in Houston, to help me to come up with something I could do on the moon, some appropriate symbolic act regarding the universality of seeking. I had thought in terms of doing something overtly patriotic, but everything we came up with sounded trite and jingoistic. I settled on a well-known expression of spirituality: celebrating the first Christian Communion on the moon, much as Christopher Columbus and other explorers had done when they first landed in their "new world."

I wanted to do something positive for the world, so the spiritual aspect appealed greatly to me, but NASA was still smarting from a lawsuit filed by atheist Madalyn Murray O'Hair after the *Apollo 8* astronauts read from the biblical creation account in Genesis. O'Hair contended this was a violation of the constitutional separation of church and state. Although O'Hair's views did not represent mainstream America at that time, her lawsuit was a nuisance and a distraction that NASA preferred to live without.

I met with Deke Slayton, one of the original "Mercury Seven" astronauts who ran our flight-crew operations, to inform him of my plans and that I intended to tell the world what I was doing. Deke said, "No, that's not a good idea, Buzz. Go ahead and have communion, but keep your comments more general." I understood that Deke didn't want any more trouble.

So, during those first hours on the moon, before the planned eating and rest periods, I reached into my personal preference kit and pulled out the communion elements along with a three-by-five card on which I had written the words of Jesus: "I am the vine, you are the branches. Whoever remains in me, and I in him, will bear much fruit; for you can do nothing without me." I poured a thimbleful of wine from a sealed plastic container into a small chalice, and waited for the wine to settle down as it swirled in the one-sixth Earth gravity of the moon. My comments to the world were inclusive: "I would like to request a few moments of silence . . . and to invite each person listening in, wherever and whomever they may be, to pause for a moment and contemplate the events of the past few hours, and to give thanks in his or her own way." I silently read the Bible passage as I partook of the wafer and the wine, and offered a private prayer for the task at hand and the opportunity I had been given.

Neil watched respectfully, but made no comment to me at the time.

Perhaps, if I had it to do over again, I would not choose to celebrate communion. Although it was a deeply meaningful experience for me, it was a Christian sacrament, and we had come to the moon in the name of all mankind—be they Christians, Jews, Muslims, animists, agnostics, or atheists. But at the time I could think of no better way to acknowledge the enormity of the Apollo 11 experience than by giving thanks to God. It was my hope that people would keep the whole event in their minds and see, beyond minor details and technical achievements, a deeper meaning—a challenge, and the human need to explore whatever is above us, below us, or out there.

◗ ○ ◖

SHORTLY AFTER OUR touchdown, both Neil and I tried to describe for the people on Earth what we were seeing on the moon. Looking out the window, I said, "We'll get to the details of what's around here, but it looks like a collection of just about every variety of shape, angularity, granularity, about every variety of rock you could find. The color is . . . well, it varies pretty much depending on how you're looking relative to the zero-phase point (the point directly opposite the sun). There doesn't appear to be too much of a general color at all. However, it looks as though some of the rocks and boulders, of which there are quite a few in the near area—it looks as though they're going to have some interesting colors to them."

Neil wanted Mission Control to know why we had flown over our intended landing area. "Hey, Houston, that may have seemed like a very long final phase," he said. "The auto targeting was taking us right into a football-field-sized crater, with a large number of big boulders and rocks for about one or two crater diameters around it, and it required us going in and flying manually over the rock field to find a reasonably good area."

Charlie Duke summed up what we were all feeling. "It was beautiful from here, Tranquillity."

Neil could hardly wait to describe to Mission Control what he saw out his window. "The area out the left-hand window is a relatively level plain," he reported, "with a fairly large number of craters of the five- to fifty-foot variety, and some ridges which are small, twenty, thirty feet high, I would guess, and literally thousands of little one- and two-foot craters around the area. We see some angular blocks out several hundred feet in front of us that are probably two feet in size and have angular edges. There is a hill in view, just about on the ground track ahead of us. Difficult to estimate, but might be a half a mile or a mile."

Mike Collins chimed in from high above the moon in the *Columbia,* "Sounds like it looks a lot better than it did yesterday . . . It looked rough as a corn cob. then."

"It really was rough, Mike," answered Neil. "Over the targeted landing area, it was extremely rough, cratered, and large numbers of rocks that were probably larger than five or ten feet in size."

"When in doubt, land long," Mike replied.

Charlie Duke wanted us to reset the gravity-alignment circuit breaker, and the mission timer, which for some reason had blown a circuit breaker, so Neil's commentary was momentarily interrupted. When he continued, he attempted to describe the stark, bland landscape. "I'd say the color of the local surface is very comparable to what we observed from orbit at this sun angle—about ten degrees sun angle, or that nature. It's pretty much without color. It's gray; and it's a very white, chalky gray, as you look into the zero-phase line. And it's considerably darker gray, more like ashen gray as you look out ninety degrees to the sun. Some of the surface rocks in close here that have been fractured or disturbed by the rocket engine plume are coated with this light gray on the outside; but where they've been broken, they display a very dark gray interior; and it looks like it could be country basalt."

We wanted to get these descriptions on the record as early as possible, should we for any reason have to make a hasty departure. More than anything, however, we wanted to get out there and explore the moon's surface for ourselves.

● ○ ◐

THE PREPARATION TO go outside was complex; finalizing our suiting-up process from our visor-protected helmets down to our overshoe moon boots would alone take us several hours in the cramped space of the *Eagle*. With just enough room to maneuver, Neil and I helped each other one at a time to put on the 185-pound life-support backpacks, still large and cumbersome even with their lunar-equivalent weight of thirty pounds in the one-sixth gravity. We switched over our life-support connector hoses from the onboard supply of oxygen and electricity to the backpack, fully equipped with its own electrical supply, water connector, communicator, and oxygen inlets and outlets. With no air on the moon, and plenty of heat from the sun and cold in the shadows, our suits and backpacks were truly our life-support system, a 100-percent fully contained living environment. In them, we had cooling provisions in our underwear, thanks to an ingenious system of plastic tubing, about 300 feet worth, that could circulate the ice water that was being produced by the backpack. We had electrical power and enough oxygen for four hours, and antennae connections for radio communications between Neil and me, but also so our conversations could be heard back on Earth. On top of our large backpacks, we had an additional emergency supply of oxygen in a separate container, in case we needed it while on the moon, or for an emergency EVA spacewalk upon re-docking with *Columbia* after liftoff from the moon.

Since we were ahead of schedule, we took our sweet time, making sure that everything was correctly in place. That we weren't rushed helped us to relax as we anticipated venturing out onto the surface. I remember, right before cabin depressurization, a passing thought I voiced as I put on my helmet, which ended up on the transmission to Houston: "Sure wish I had shaved last night." I was about to walk on the moon for a one-night stand on a stage before the world, so appearances were on my mind! In final preparation, Neil glanced at a printed checklist attached on his left wrist and forearm, facing inside just above his gloved hand, that would remind him of the tasks he had to perform during our short time on the moon. I had a similar checklist sewn onto my suit.

When Neil and I had completed connecting all of our life-support equipment, and had made sure all our systems were functioning correctly, we depressurized the *Eagle's* cabin so we could open the door to the outside world. I watched carefully as the gauge eased down to zero. I attempted to reach down and open the hatch, but it wouldn't release. The cabin still wasn't quite empty of oxygen. Amazingly, just a tiny bit of oxygen pressure would keep that hatch from opening inward. I made a mental note of that, since I would be the last man out of the LM. If there was any oxygen remaining in the *Eagle* when I stepped out, and the hatch should close, we'd have a hard time getting back in our ride home. The pressure inside would seal the hatch closed. That's a good thing when you're on the inside; not so good if you're stranded outside, trying to get back in.

Finally, seven hours after we had landed on the surface of the moon, we were ready. Neil opened the hatch and I helped guide him as he backed out on his hands and knees onto the small, shelflike "porch" just above the ladder attached to the forward landing leg, which steadied the LM on the surface.

Neil moved slowly down the ladder, making sure he was securely on each step before allowing his foot to move to the next. He took a strap with him, similar to a clothesline, that was fastened to a pulley, so when he got down to the bottom of the ladder I could put the still camera on the pulley and send it down to Neil. We would later use that same conveyor system to load the lunar samples and the boxes of rocks we collected from the surface and planned to take back to Earth with us. While I guided Neil out, and he was backing down, he reached over to the side of the spacecraft and pulled a lever, causing the equipment-bay side of the lander to open up like a desktop. The desktop fell open, revealing all our tools on it, including a television camera that was pointed at the *Eagle*. I pushed in the circuit breaker, and suddenly Neil was on live TV. "We're getting a picture on the TV," the new Capcom, Bruce McCandless, exclaimed. It was a good thing that the signal went to Mission Control first; as Neil was coming down the ladder, the video image was upside down. The experts at Mission Control quickly righted the image, and beamed it to the television networks, which sent it around the world. I had another 16-millimeter color movie camera loaded with film in my window, so I set that at one frame per second, to capture Neil's first step on the lunar surface and everything that he did, albeit in a herky-jerky old home-movie sort of way. This same camera would shoot the color footage of Neil and me planting the American flag on the moon.

"I'm at the foot of the ladder," Neil said. "The LM footpads are only depressed in the surface about one or two inches." That was an intriguing point, since some scientists had speculated that the lunar surface could house a lot of dust, and that our landing pads might sink deep down into the dirt, possibly even dangerously deep.

"I'm going to step off the LM now," Neil said, confidently but tentatively. It was 10:56 p.m. (EDT), and the world was watching the black-and-white live broadcast on their TV sets. I watched, too, from the window as Neil, with his right hand firmly grasping the ladder, moved his left blue lunar overshoe from the metal dish of the footpad to take the first step onto the powdery gray surface of the moon. He kept his right foot on the footpad until he could tell how the surface might respond to his weight. He paused briefly, and proclaimed those now famous, well thought-out words: "That's one small step for . . . man, one giant leap for mankind." He later said that he intended to say "one small step for a man . . ." but the "a" got lost in transmission. It didn't matter; the world got the message, and it was good.

At first Neil was tethered to the ladder, because no one knew for sure if the surface would be like quicksand, literally sucking a person down into a quagmire of dust. "The surface is fine and powdery," Neil said. "I can kick it up loosely with my toe. It does adhere in fine layers, like powdered charcoal, to the sole and sides of my boots. I only go in a small fraction of an inch, maybe an eighth of an inch, but I can see the footprints of my boots and the treads in the fine, sandy particles." Neil let go of the ladder and put both feet on the moon. He quickly found that it was solid below the immediate layer of dust, and it was relatively easy to walk around on the surface.

One of Neil's first actions after he made those initial steps was to grab some samples of rocks and soil and place them in his thigh pocket. These were our contingency samples in case we had to leave in a hurry and had no time to gather other samples of the lunar surface, or were otherwise unable to complete our full EVA as scheduled. If something went wrong, at least we would have some samples of the moon that we could bring back. Meanwhile, I used the tether strap rigged up as a pulley system to lower the specially designed 70-millimeter Hasselblad camera to Neil.

After Neil had been on the surface for about twenty minutes, it was time for me to join him. It was my turn to ease out of the hatch and back down the ladder. Neil stood on the surface taking photos of my progress and offered watchful comments much like a rock climber relaying helpful hints from below as I commenced my rappel. I arched my back to clear the bulkhead, and continued to the edge of the porch to position my feet on the ladder. I remembered that the checklist said, "Do not leave the hatch wide open." For some reason we never completely figured out, the checklist instructed me to partially close the hatch.

My gloved hand on the hatch door, I attempted a touch of humor to ease the tense moment. "Okay, now I want to back up and partially close the hatch," I said, "making sure not to lock it on my way out."

Watching me from the surface, Neil cracked up laughing. "A particularly good thought," he quipped.

We had just discovered what would happen if that door was shut, with a very small amount of oxygen inside. With no handle on the outside to unlatch the hatch after returning from our EVA, it would take only a trace of cabin pressure to make it nearly impossible to open. We certainly did not want to lock ourselves out by allowing the hatch to seal shut due to a variance in the external pressure on the moon.

"That's our home for the next couple of hours, and we want to take good care of it," I said. "Okay. I'm on the top step . . . It's a very simple matter to hop down from one step to the next." As I descended the ladder, I began to get my bearings, making sure that I knew how to operate in lunar gravity and that I wouldn't roll over with my heavy backpack, and fall off the ladder. There was a distance of about three feet between the bottom rung of the ladder and the surface, so I jumped down from the ladder to the footpad.

Our procedure was that at the bottom of the ladder, we would jump back up again just to be sure we could comfortably make that first step when we returned from our moonwalking EVA. From within the *Eagle* looking outside the window, I had watched Neil when he checked getting back up from the pad onto the ladder, and it didn't look so bad. Now, with my boot down on the *Eagle*'s footpad, I made the small leap. But I underestimated the lunar gravity, thinking it would be pretty easy to bounce back up. I missed by an inch, scraping the bottom rung of the ladder. Feeling pretty awkward, I now had some moon dust on my suit; my shins were smudged. Later people would wonder if I had fallen down, or knelt on the ground, but I had done neither. Just a minor scrape of moon dust that had been deposited from Neil's boots on the ladder.

For a moment, though, I lost a bit of confidence. Maybe it was not quite as easy as it looked to move around in the one-sixth-gravity environment. I decided this would be an excellent opportunity to relieve the nervousness in my bladder. I don't know that history grants any reward for such actions, but that dubious distinction is my "first" on the moon.

I then said to myself, *I'll put a little more oomph in it,* and I jumped up, this time easily reaching the bottom rung. From there I dropped back down to the footpad and turned around to take in the panorama. In every direction I could see detailed characteristics of the gray ash-colored lunar scenery, pocked with thousands of little craters and with every variety and shape of rock. I saw the horizon curving a mile and a half away. With no atmosphere, there was no haze on the moon. It was crystal clear.

"Beautiful view!" I said.

"Isn't that something!" Neil gushed. "Magnificent sight out here."

I slowly allowed my eyes to drink in the unusual majesty of the moon. In its starkness and monochromatic hues, it was indeed beautiful. But it was a different sort of beauty than I had ever before seen. *Magnificent*, I thought, then said, "Magnificent desolation." It was a spontaneous utterance, an oxymoron that would take on ever-deeper dimensions of meaning in describing this strange new environment.

Turning in Neil's direction, I tried out a few steps and a couple of short jumps to test my maneuverability and recovery, and to figure out the best way to maintain my balance. With the heavy backpack altering my center of mass, I leaned slightly forward in the direction I was moving to keep from falling backwards.

Then for the first time since stepping on the surface, I looked upward, above the LM. It was not an easy thing to do in a pressurized suit, inflated as stiff as a football, with a gold sun visor jutting out from my helmet. But I managed to direct my view homeward, and there in the black, starless sky I could see our marble-sized planet, no bigger than my thumb.

I became all the more conscious that here we were, two guys walking on the moon, our every move being watched by more people than had ever before viewed one single event. In a strange way there was an indescribable feeling of proximity and connection between us and everyone back on Earth. Yet we were physically separated and farther away from home than any two human beings had ever been. The irony was paradoxical, even overwhelming, but I dared not dwell on it for long.

Snapping out of my momentary reverie, I noticed some damage to the LM's struts. "Looks like the secondary strut had a little thermal effect on it right here, Neil." I pointed to the blackened area on the strut.

"Yes, I noticed that," Neil agreed. "That seems to be the worst, although there are similar effects all around." Overall, though, at first glance, it seemed that the *Eagle* had landed with surprisingly few bumps and scrapes.

The moon dust fascinated me. "Very fine powder, isn't it?"

"Isn't it fine?" Neil responded.

The lunar dust seemed to go down quite a ways into the surface. Although it was loose close to the surface from the many impacts of asteroid material, it was firm deeper down. Even our spacecraft only pierced the surface ever so slightly, about an inch or two beneath the dust.

Once I set foot on the lunar surface, my first responsibility was to examine and photograph the condition of the *Eagle's* landing gear. So I "borrowed" the Hasselblad camera from Neil and got busy photographing the pad, the thrusters, the slight crater underneath it caused by our landing, and any potentially damaged areas around the ascent stage, as well as the descent. I walked all around the LM, snapping photos as I went, including a couple of Neil. I passed the camera back to Neil, whose responsibility it was to take most of the pictures. We also needed to set up the black-and-white live-feed television camera in a panoramic position out from its stationary location attached to the LM, as far as the camera's cable would allow. As Neil moved out with the TV camera, I fed the cable from the LM, until he reached an area just beyond a freshly made crater about fifty feet out. Perched atop a tripod, it could now record our activities as we moved around within its field of view.

Back on Earth, when we practiced deploying and extending that camera out from the spacecraft, the cable lay flat, but in lunar gravity it was almost floating above the surface, just waiting for some daydreaming astronaut to trip over it, pull over the camera, and really mess up the mission. Not to mention embarrassing himself in front of the world and for all of history. Those were the things that you just didn't want to have happen in front of millions of people watching.

In commemoration of this first landing, we unveiled the plaque that was attached to the leg of the LM, and would remain on the lunar surface for eons to come. Depicting the two hemispheres of the Earth and dated July 20, 1969, the plaque stated our heartfelt desire:

HERE MEN FROM THE PLANET EARTH FIRST SET FOOT ON THE MOON.
WE CAME IN PEACE FOR ALL MANKIND.

Most of our activities took place within a hundred feet or so of the *Eagle*. We were the moon's first explorers, so on this mission we stuck pretty close to home. Just a short distance away from the LM, we found a spot to put up the American flag. But getting the flagpole to stand in the lunar surface was more difficult than we anticipated. The pole itself was hollow, and we were trying to push it down into the lunar "soil" that was made up of millions of years worth of asteroid impacts, all densely packed down into a hard surface. But the soil wouldn't compress, because there was no air or moisture in the dust. Inserting the flagpole was almost like trying to punch a hole in a bunch of tiny rocks. For the first time a shot of panic seared through me. Since childhood I had seen pictures of great explorers planting their flags in their new worlds. Would I be the first to plant the flag and have it fall over?

Finally we secured the pole in the surface, and extended the Stars and Stripes along the telescoping arm so it wouldn't droop down in the airless, breezeless plain of Tranquillity. But the arm would not telescope out all the way, which, by accident, made the flag look furled as though waving in the nonexistent wind. As we raised the flag, almost instinctively I took a few steps back and proudly saluted our brave banner. The camera was still running, so the whole world saw me offer the salute. Neil caught it on the Hasselblad, as well. I still think it's the best-looking flag up there, out of all six that would be planted during subsequent Apollo missions.

While Neil collected an assortment of rock samples, my next task was to test the various modes of locomotion in the lunar gravity. We knew the television camera was aimed at us and sending live pictures from its pedestal, so I moved into the camera's field of view to begin experimenting with a variety of steps. I started jogging around a bit, and it felt like I was moving in slow motion in a lazy lope, often with both of my feet floating in the air. One of the pure joys of being on the moon was our somewhat lightfooted mobility. But on the moon, inertia seemed much greater than on Earth. Earthbound, I would have stopped my run in just one step with an abrupt halt. I immediately sensed that if I tried that on the lunar surface, I would end up facedown in the lunar dust. Instead, I had to exercise a little patience and use two or three steps to wind down to a halt. I cut to the side like a football

player, skipped straight forward, and then tried the two-legged kanga-
roo hop—which looked fun, but proved tiring to do for long with the
extra effort exerted. When I moved my arms more vigorously, I could
nearly lift my feet off the ground with an easy buoyancy.

I almost wished that Neil and I had brought a baseball to test a few
tosses back and forth to further demonstrate the effects of lunar gravity. At the end of our EVA, when we jettisoned some of the materials
from the LM to reduce our weight, we noticed how they fell in a slow,
lazy trajectory as we tossed them onto the surface. Later Apollo missions would engage in a few more experimental pastimes, such as Alan
Shepard hitting a golf ball. The experiments on this first mission, however, had a more serious tone altogether.

About that time, Bruce McCandless, who was communicating to us
from Mission Control, said that President Nixon wanted to speak to
us. *The President wants to talk to us while we're on the moon?* I thought. I
didn't know that was going to happen. My heart rate, which had been
low the entire flight, suddenly jumped. I could not help feeling a tinge
of stage fright, but Neil had a fairly good, albeit short, conversation
with the President. I remember Nixon saying, "Because of what you
have done, the heavens have become a part of man's world. . . . For one
priceless moment in the whole history of man, all the people on this
Earth are truly one." Our commander-in-chief invited us to visit him
in the Oval Office after the mission, an invitation we were delighted to
accept, assuming all went well and we could get off this rock.

◗   ○   ◗

EVERY STEP ON the moon was a virginal experience. Exploring this
place that had never before been seen by human eyes, upon which no
foot had stepped, or hand touched—was awe-inspiring. But we had no
time for philosophical musings. Our time on the surface had been designed by Mission Control to be extremely limited—a mere two and a
half hours outside the LM, and that included getting out and getting
ourselves and our rock samples back inside the lander. There would be
time for philosophizing later. Reflecting metaphysically was contrary

to our mission. We weren't trained to smell the roses or to utter life-changing aphorisms. Emoting or spontaneously offering profundities was not part of my psychological makeup anyhow. That's why for years I have wanted NASA to fly a poet, a singer, or a journalist into space—someone who could capture the emotions of the experience and share them with the world. Neil and I were both military guys, pilots who were accustomed to keeping our feelings reined in. Right now, we couldn't dally; we had a job to do, a mission to accomplish.

It was time to deploy a few scientific experiments that NASA planned to have us leave on the moon: the laser radar reflector, the passive seismometer to measure moonquakes, and the solar-wind experiment to catch particles from the sun. I was to erect the last two with their greater complexities, so I set about putting up the foil flag in the direction of the sun to catch the ions of helium, neon, and argon in the solar wind.

The seismometer experiment was more of a challenge, since it had to be leveled and aligned just right for the readings to be accurate. After moving it around on the uneven surface, pushing dirt aside where necessary, at last it appeared to be level. Apparently the sensors were working just fine. When I made a mistake of walking in front of it, which I shouldn't have done, it registered the data back on Earth. I hoped that the guys monitoring it weren't wearing headphones. It probably would have sounded like King Kong's footsteps in their ears!

Neil was collecting additional rock samples and putting them in the rock box, so I retrieved the camera from him, and moved on to my next task, the "scuff/cohesion/adhesion" activity. With each step, I purposefully kicked up the lunar dust with my boots. I continued to be intrigued by the dust, as fine as talcum powder. It exhibited a most unusual quality. I must have kicked about a half-dozen sprays or more, and each time the dust flew out in front slightly, landing in a perfect semicircle, every grain spraying out uniformly and equidistantly without any rippling effect. I related my observations to Houston, and thought, *This is surreal, how each grain of moondust falls into place in these little fans, almost like rose petals.*

Nearby, with the camera in hand, I searched for a relatively flat area of the surface undisturbed by my dust-kicking, so I could take a photograph of a footprint. Finding a good spot, I first took a picture of the pristine surface; then, right in the middle of that flat area, I put my boot down, and then I moved my boot away and took a picture of that. Framed in the photo was the evidence of man on the moon—a single footprint, showing in perfect detail a reverse mold of the treads from the bottom of my moon boot. *That is kind of lonely looking*, I thought. *So I'd better put my boot down, and then move my boot away from the footprint, but only slightly so it's still in the frame, and take a picture of that.* These were my small contributions to our lunar photography, but that single footprint shot became one of the most famous photographs in history, and a symbol of man's need to explore.

● ○ ◉

NEIL SHOT MOST of the photos on the moon, having the camera attached to a fitting on his spacesuit much of the time while I was doing a variety of experiments. I didn't have such a camera holder on my suit, so it just made sense that Neil should handle the photography. He took some fantastic photographs, too, especially when one considers that there was no viewfinder on the intricate Hasselblad camera. We were basically "pointing and shooting." Imagine taking such historic photographs and not even being able to tell what image you were getting. Unlike the digital camera era of today, in 1969 we were shooting on film, typically looking through a small optical opening on the back of the camera that corresponded with what the camera's lens was "seeing." But with our large space helmets, such a viewfinder would have done little good anyhow. So, similar to cowboys shooting their sixguns from their hips, we aimed the camera in the direction of what we wanted to photograph, and squeezed the trigger. Given that ambiguity, it is even more of a credit to Neil that we brought back such stunning photographs from the moon.

One of the most striking photos he took has come to be known as the "visor shot." It is probably the one photo from our adventure seen more than any other. Indeed, it may be the most familiar photo from any lunar landing, and perhaps one of the most famous photos in history. It is a simple picture of me standing on the rough lunar surface with my left hand at my waist, with the curve of the horizon easing into the blackness of space behind me. But if you look more carefully at the reflection in the gold visor on my helmet, you can see the *Eagle* with its landing pad, my shadow with the sun's halo effect, several of the experiments we had set up, and even Neil taking the picture. It is a truly astounding shot, and was the result of an entirely serendipitous moment on Neil's part.

Later, pundits and others would wonder why most of the photographs on the moon were of me. It wasn't because I was the more photogenic of the two helmet-clad guys on the moon. Some even conjectured that it must have been a purposeful attempt on my part to shun Neil in the photos. That, of course, was ridiculous. We had our assigned tasks, and since Neil had the camera most of the time we were on the surface, it simply made sense that he would photograph our activities and the panoramas of the lunar landscape. And since I was the only other person there . . .

Ironically, the photography on the moon was one of those things that we had not laid out exactly prior to our launch. NASA's Public Affairs people didn't say, "Hey, you've got to take a lot of pictures of this or that." Everyone was interested in the science. So we did the science and the rest of it was sort of gee-whiz. We had not really planned a lot of the gee-whiz stuff that, in retrospect, proved quite important. But those pictures became the storyboard of our adventure that the public got to see and are now in history books.

The time went by all too rapidly while we were outside the LM, and before we knew it, Houston was giving us our three-minute EVA termination alert. We had to prepare to head back inside. When it came my turn to depart the surface, oddly enough, explorer that I am, I sensed no desire to lengthen our stay. On this groundbreaking first mission, we had planned to limit our EVA, and stick close to the lunar module, rather than explore the low hills on the horizon. Those hills would yield to future exploration, but our mission had been accomplished. With Houston in constant radio contact with us to keep us on our strict time schedule, we didn't worry about the potential hazards of venturing off too far and possibly encountering problems on the lunar surface. We were extremely conscious that we were setting precedents with everything we did, so we were extraordinarily careful to avoid any mishaps. We didn't want to trip and fall on our faces in front of the whole world.

According to plan, I was the first to climb up the ladder and reenter the *Eagle*. I was already on the ladder when Neil called out to me, "Hey, Buzz. Did you forget something?"

I realized that in our excitement, I had indeed forgotten something—something extremely important to Neil and to me. I reached into my pocket and pulled out the small pouch that I had carried with me in my spacesuit while on the moon. It contained a patch from the Apollo 1 mission, the mission in which our three friends had died, and whose sacrifice carried a special meaning for us. Ed White had encouraged me to become an astronaut, so to me it was only a fitting tribute that Ed had come along to the moon with me. It also contained two medals commemorating Soviet cosmonauts Vladimir Komarov, who had perished, and Yuri Gagarin, the first human in space. Also in the pouch was a tiny silicon disk etched with goodwill messages from seventy-three nations, including the Soviet Union, our space rival and nemesis during the Cold War. Then there was a small gold pin in the shape of the olive branch of peace. We had thought long and hard to come up with this universal symbol of peace to include on our mission patch depicting the American eagle landing on the moon. It lent a greater meaning to our mission. I took a long last look at the pouch and tossed it onto the moon's surface.

Neil brought over the rock boxes—we later discovered that we had collected an astounding 21.7 kilograms of lunar samples, about forty-seven and a half pounds—and we hoisted them up to the LM on our makeshift pulley system, and stored them in airtight containers. When Neil was safely inside, I closed the hatch to seal us from the harsh lunar environment.

Once inside, Neil and I helped each other to remove the heavy backpacks and hook up to the *Eagle*'s life-support systems. After depressurizing the *Eagle* one last time, we opened up the hatch again and threw out some trash and the backpacks to reduce our weight for liftoff. When the backpacks hit the ground, the people back at Mission Control could hear the impact through the seismometer. They actually said they could detect our prancing around while we were on the lunar surface. It was an exceptionally sensitive seismometer. The laser reflector we set up helps scientists to measure with nearly perfect accuracy the moon's distance and movement in relation to the Earth. The solar foil that we brought back with us has enabled laboratory analysis of the sun's electrically charged particles.

The science was brief, but it was very revealing, and of course the rocks were fascinating. Even though they were quickly collected, and were not documented with photographs because we were in such a hurry, they revealed that the moon was formed differently from how we had surmised beforehand. Following our mission, scientists concluded that a large object in the first billion years of the Earth's existence hit the planet, blasting pieces of the Earth away, and one such piece became the moon.

◗   ○   ◗

THE MAGNIFICENT DESOLATION of the moon was no longer a stranger to mankind. We came to experience firsthand the utter desolation of the orb's lifeless terrain. In contrast, the achievement realized by scientific enterprise and teamwork in designing and engineering the rockets that could send two men to land on the moon was magnificent. I could not help marveling that the very first footsteps we had taken, and the footprints we had left on the moon's surface, would remain undisturbed for millions of years to come.

3

HOMEWARD
BOUND

IT WAS 1:11 A.M. (EDT) ON JULY 21, BY THE TIME NEIL AND I got back inside the LM and sealed the hatch. We had started this leg of the trip just before 9:00 a.m. the previous day, and we were exhausted.

The entire time Neil and I were exploring the moon, the third member of our crew, command module pilot Mike Collins, was orbiting the moon all by himself. No human being had ever spent so much time orbiting the moon alone. Making matters worse, during each trip around the far side of the moon, Mike was out of sight and out of radio contact. He was completely isolated, unable to talk with Neil or me on the moon, and unable to talk with anyone on Earth. Mike later commented about his orbital solitude, "I knew I was alone in a way that no earthling has ever been before."

Besides getting us to and from the moon, Mike's job was to conduct scientific observations and to photograph the lunar landscape. With each orbit around the moon, Mike took more photos, thousands in fact, that would later be used to map mountains and craters and to identify landmarks for future explorers.

Although the world's attention focused on Neil and me as we bounded along on the moon, Mike was an indispensable team member. Clearly we could not have accomplished our mission without him. We were looking forward to making our rendezvous with him and *Colum-bia* later that same afternoon.

Back in the *Eagle*, Neil and I took time to eat—snacking on such tasty goodies as cocktail sausages and fruit punch, since we had no hot food on the LM—and to grab some much-needed rest. The LM had no space for cots or beds of any kind, and we had been so busy we really hadn't decided who was going to sleep where, so I put my dibs on the floor. Neil said he was going to sit on the ascent-engine cover and lean back, and after rigging up the waist tether for a hammock to hold up his legs, he felt he could sleep okay there.

The ascent engine cover was where we put the contingency sample of rocks that Neil picked up and put in a pouch in his pocket when he first climbed out, in case we had to make a hasty exit. When Neil and I got back in the LM, we watched carefully to see if the sample was affected by the oxygen in the cabin. Some "extravagant science" people had warned that lunar dust and rock might burst into flames if they were exposed to oxygen.

Certainly, both Neil and I did not believe that the rocks or dust would combust, and in fact they did not, but the night before the launch, I had met with my uncle Bob Moon, who had come to the Cape for the launch of the flight, and was then going on to Houston to stay with my family during the remainder of the mission. In the course of our conversation, I told Bob that we had attended an unusual briefing that day. "Some harebrained chemist is afraid that lunar rocks and dirt might be combustible once they are introduced to oxygen."

"Are you worried about that?" Bob asked.

"Naah, not at all." I told Bob that most NASA scientists scoffed at such nonsense, but we would take no chances, especially in light of the Apollo 1 accident. I explained what we planned to do with the rock samples we gathered from the moon's surface, which was basically to store them in vacuum-sealed, flameproof boxes. But we would take time to place the contingency sample on the ascent-engine cover while we were still in our pressurized suits. Then, as we turned on the oxygen in the cabin, if smoke started to come out of the rock sample, we could still open the hatch and toss it out. All of this was planned, just in case. If any problems ensued, we could dump the samples immediately.

On the plane back to Houston, the person sitting next to Bob struck up a conversation with him. Bob told him why he was on the trip, and, in the course of the flight, mentioned his conversation with me about the rocks. Turns out that Bob's seatmate was a reporter—although he never identified himself as such. A few days later, Bob was appalled to see a headline in a newspaper: ALDRIN FEARS LUNAR ROCKS. I didn't fear lunar rocks; I feared unscrupulous, inaccurate reporters.

● ○ ●

WITH NEIL TRYING to sleep leaning back on the ascent engine cover, I curled up on the bottom of the LM, where I noticed some of the moon dust on the floor. It had a gritty, charcoal-like texture to it, and a pungent metallic smell, something like gunpowder or the smell in the air after a firecracker has gone off. Neil described it as having a "wet ashes" smell.

In my fatigue, I was still thinking about the dust when I noticed something lying on the floor that really did not belong there. I looked closer, and my heart jolted a bit. There in the dust on the floor on the right side of the cabin, lay a circuit breaker switch that had broken off. I wondered what circuit breaker that was, so I looked up at the numerous rows of breakers on the instrument panel without any guard protectors, and gulped hard. The broken switch had snapped off from the engine-arm circuit breaker, the one vital breaker needed to send electrical power to the ascent engine that would lift Neil and me off the moon. During our powered descent, this same engine-arm circuit breaker had been in the closed position, pushed in to engage the descent engine for our landing, and once we touched down we pulled it back out, in the open position, to disengage the circuitry and disarm the engine. Somehow, one of us must have bumped it accidentally with our cumbersome backpacks as we moved around in the cramped space preparing to get out of the LM, or as we came back in. Regardless of how the circuit breaker switch had broken off, the circuit breaker had to be pushed back in again for the ascent engine to ignite to get us back home.

We reported it to Mission Control and then tried to sleep and forget about it—as if that were possible. But we knew Mission Control would help figure out a solution, and if we could not get that circuit breaker pushed in the next morning when we were ready to lift off, then we would have to do something else. For now, they wanted us to leave the circuit breaker out anyhow. So, while Neil and I tried to rest, the guys in Houston debated how we could work around that circuit, in case it had to be left open.

● ○ ●

TRYING TO SLEEP in the lunar lander was difficult. Not only was it cramped and uncomfortable, it was cold. We turned the heat full up inside the cabin, put on our helmets, and tried to get the water circulation system in our suits to warm us, but it was still awfully cold. After about three hours it became almost impossible to sleep. We could have raised the window shades and let the sunlight in to warm us, but with the sun so bright, that would have kept us from sleeping, too. So our rest was more like a fitful state of drowsing. I don't imagine, though, that anyone would have slept too well after walking around on the moon all evening, and then planning to lift off for the journey home in six or seven hours.

When we received our wake-up call from Houston, the question of how to handle the broken circuit breaker had still not been solved. After examining it more closely, I thought that if I could find something in the LM to push into the circuit, it might hold. But since it was electrical, I decided not to put my finger in, or use anything that had metal on the end. I had a felt-tipped pen in the shoulder pocket of my suit that might do the job. After moving the countdown procedure up by a couple of hours in case it didn't work, I inserted the pen into the small opening where the circuit breaker switch should have been, and pushed it in; sure enough, the circuit breaker held. We were going to get off the moon, after all. To this day I still have the broken circuit breaker switch and the felt-tipped pen I used to ignite our engines.

Astronaut Ron Evans had taken over as Capcom at Mission Control the morning we were preparing to lift off from the moon. He and I began the extensive rundown of checks before firing up our engine. Technically, once we were off the surface, we would no longer be known as Tranquillity Base, but *Eagle* once again, even though we were the same people on the same communication systems. But such was the NASA procedure.

Ron instructed us to make sure the rendezvous radar was turned off at the beginning of our ascent. I wasn't too happy about that, as I preferred having it on, just in case, but at the time I hadn't yet learned that it was the rendezvous radar that had overloaded our computers during our landing on the moon. I acquiesced to Mission Control and turned the radar off.

We performed an intricate series of star-sightings through our telescope, ascertaining our position vis-à-vis several different stars including Rigel, Navi, and Capella, to align our guidance platform prior to liftoff. By averaging our readings, we would know what kind of orbit we needed to rendezvous with Mike again.

The liftoff from the moon was intrinsically a tense time for all of us. The ascent stage simply had to work. The engines had to fire, propelling us upward, leaving the descent stage of the LM still sitting on the moon. We had no margin for error, no second chances, no rescue plans if the liftoff failed. There would be no way for Mike up in *Columbia* to retrieve us. We had no provision for another team to race from Earth to pick us up if the *Eagle* did not soar. Nor did we have food, water, or oxygen for more than a few hours.

As we completed all the liftoff procedures, Ron Evans gave me one last bit of instruction. "Roger, *Eagle*. Our guidance recommendation is PGNS, and you're cleared for takeoff."

Knowing the pressure everyone felt, I spontaneously injected a touch of humor into the situation. Maintaining a steady, serious tone to my voice, I responded, "Roger. Understand. We're number one on the runway."

Unfamiliar with my sardonic sense of humor, Evans paused for a few seconds as he processed my remark, and then simply replied, "Roger."

The computer continued to count down the seconds to liftoff. Standing side by side again, Neil and I looked at each other, took one more furtive glance at that impaired circuit breaker, threw the switches, and held our breath. The LM engine fired, belching a plume of flame and blasting lunar dust as we rose off the surface. The liftoff went as smoothly as could be. I wanted to cast a last look back at the surface, but our attentions were focused on navigating the spacecraft. The ascent of the *Eagle* was strikingly swift compared with the liftoff of the huge Saturn V rocket from Cape Canaveral. For the *Eagle*'s liftoff, we had no atmosphere resisting us, and only one-sixth gravity to overcome, so even though we had worked on this aspect of the flight in simulators, the *Eagle*'s speed in whisking us into space was almost surprising. Nothing we had ever practiced in simulators could compare with our swift swoop upward. Within seconds we were streaking high above the moon's surface.

Unfortunately, I neglected to turn the camera on just before our ascent, so we didn't get a good shot out the window as we left the ground. It would have been interesting to study the effects of our liftoff around the descent stage that remained on the moon. But I was more concerned with our actual liftoff than with getting good pictures. It was critical to get into orbit with the right speed. As the ascent engine sent us into orbit, we sort of wallowed around, momentarily struggling to correct the center of gravity with the four rod thrusters. It was a little unnerving.

In fact, we were somewhat concerned because we knew that shortly after liftoff the spacecraft was going to pitch forward about 45 degrees, so it could be more nearly horizontal as it gained more velocity and not so much altitude, a procedure necessary for us to rendezvous with Mike, who was guiding *Columbia* around the moon in an orbit sixty miles high.

Despite the surprises, I described our liftoff to Houston as, "Very smooth, a very quiet ride."

We lifted off the moon at 1:54 p.m. (EDT), and, within a couple of hours, we had completed the first of two orbits necessary to rendezvous with Mike. During our second orbit, the *Columbia* came into view. We had a little jolt at the moment of docking because Neil and I had arbitrarily altered the flight plans slightly in a spur of the moment decision opting for a more direct path to Mike. Nobody at Mission Control seemed to mind, although there were probably a couple of rendezvous experts sitting there staring at their computers fretting, "What are they doing? What are they *doing?*" But I was known as "Dr. Rendezvous" around NASA—sometimes respectfully so, and at times derisively—because of my passion for the subject and my rendezvous doctoral thesis at the Massachusetts Institute of Technology (MIT). I didn't really mind; in fact, usually after my fellow corps of astronauts hemmed and hawed, balking and complaining at my ideas, they more frequently than not embraced them and incorporated my ideas and calculations into their plans. I just took it as a backhanded compliment. Perhaps when the guys on the console noticed Neil and me changing the rendezvous details, they figured, "Well, Buzz knows what he's doing."

Overall, the rendezvous and docking with Mike were absolutely beautiful. We came up from below, evenly, steadily, as if we were riding on a monorail. Nothing disturbed our line of guidance. It was the kind of thing I had dreamed of while developing my theories and techniques at MIT on manned rendezvous. During the Gemini 12 mission, we had faced some challenges in our rendezvous and docking maneuvers with the Agena target vehicle, when our guidance radar went down. I pretty much had to calculate the coordinates in my head, with the help of my Pickett slide rule that I had brought along just in case. But it gave me a chance to test out the theories I had developed, and they worked!

We docked with Mike at 5:35 p.m. (EDT), nearly four hours after lifting off from the Sea of Tranquillity. The sound of those latches snapping shut as Mike secured the *Eagle* to the *Columbia* was one of the sweetest I'd ever heard. Neil and I vacuumed up as much moondust as we could, so we would be able to get into the command module without carrying too much of it in from the lunar module. No one knew the effects the dust might have on our skin, lungs, or blood, so Mission Control didn't want us to drag along any more of it than necessary.

Once we were certain it was safe to do so, Mike unsealed the access tunnel between the LM and the command module, and we opened the hatch. It was great to see Mike's smiling face at the other end of that tunnel!

We carefully transferred the rock boxes and the cameras' film magazines, and then Neil and I went back into the *Eagle* for a final look to make sure we'd gotten all that we needed to get out of it. We knew we were saying good-bye to anything we left inside the LM. Our home on the moon would not be making the trip back to Earth with us. Before leaving lunar orbit, we would cut the *Eagle* loose, this time letting it fly on its own around the moon for what we thought might be hundreds of years. In fact, it crashed on the moon shortly after its fuel and batteries ran out. But this was no time to be sentimental. We still had a long journey ahead of us.

We prepared to leave lunar orbit, firing an engine burn on the backside, while out of radio communication with Houston. I had barely slept in more than three days, and had been running on adrenaline for the last two days at least. Now, as I sat in the command module, I could feel my body winding down. I wanted to close my eyes and sleep all the way back to Earth, but we still had several critical moves to make before we could relax.

The first came up soon enough, when Mike guided us into the Trans-Earth Injection burn, the extra push that would consume five tons of propellant in less than two minutes, boost our speed by 2,000 miles per hour, and, most important of all, break us free of the moon's gravitational pull, sending us on our way back to Earth. Once again, there was no room for error; we had only one chance to get this right. If we failed, we'd share the fate of the LM, orbiting the moon until we ran out of fuel and batteries, and eventually crashing into the barren gray surface we had just left.

Mike eyed the guidance computer as he counted down, "Three, two, one . . ." barely breathing. The *Columbia*'s engines flared and ignited, just as we had hoped, right on the mark. Twenty minutes later we emerged from the back side of the moon for the last time. Once that maneuver was done, we could watch the moon getting smaller and smaller in our windows. I leaned back and closed my eyes. We were on our way home.

● ○ ●

THE THREE-DAY journey back to Earth's upper atmosphere was relatively uneventful. On the last night before splashdown, we took the opportunity to share some prepared remarks with the world via a live television broadcast. The words I chose to share remain deeply meaningful to me:

> We've come to the conclusion that this has been far more than three men on a voyage to the moon. More still than the efforts of a government and industry team. More, even, than the efforts of one nation. We feel that this stands as a symbol of the insatiable curiosity of all mankind to explore the unknown. Neil's statement the other day upon first setting foot on the surface of the moon, "This is a small step for a man, but a great leap for mankind," I believe sums up these feelings very nicely. We accepted the challenge of going to the moon. The acceptance of this challenge was inevitable. The relative ease with which we carried out our mission, I believe, is a tribute to the timeliness of that acceptance.
>
> Today, I feel we're fully capable of accepting expanded roles in the exploration of space. In retrospect, we have all been particularly pleased with the call signs that we very laboriously chose for our spacecraft, *Columbia* and *Eagle*. We've been particularly pleased with the emblem of our flight. Depicting the U.S. eagle, bringing the universal symbol of peace from the Earth, from the planet Earth to the moon, that symbol being the olive branch. It was our overall crew choice to deposit a replica of this symbol on the moon. Personally, in reflecting on the events of the past several days, a verse from Psalms comes to mind: "When I considered the

heavens, the work of Thy fingers, the moon and the stars which Thou hast ordained, what is man that Thou art mindful of him."

We were rapidly nearing the expansive oceanic beauty and the cloud-covered landmasses of the Earth, a welcome sight in contrast to the monochromatic moon we had just left. All too soon, we were getting ready for one last tense, action-packed portion of our mission. We had to reenter Earth's atmosphere, and we had to do it just right, without getting incinerated.

In many ways, this last part of our mission was as dangerous as the liftoff, the lunar landing, and the ascent from the moon. By this point, the service module that had been integral to *Columbia* had been discarded and with it our remaining fuel to maneuver our craft. Now we were operating with the command module only, and a minimal fuel reserve that limited our guidance control to minor "attitude" changes. The CM was the only part of our enormous spacecraft and rocket launch system that had stood so gallantly at Launch Pad 39-A and that was designed to return intact to Earth—we hoped. When the command module hit the Earth's atmosphere, we would be traveling at over 25,000 miles per hour, about ten times faster than a bullet shot from a rifle. Again it had to be right. If we hit at the wrong angle and came in too steep, the g forces would be too high, our heat shield would be ineffective, and the intense heat of reentry would be fatal. If we came in too shallow, we would skip out and be deflected by the atmosphere, shooting off into space, where our fuel and other consumables would run out long before we could return. If this occurred, NASA was on alert to discontinue the live TV feed to the public. Lots of things could have gone wrong upon our reentry. Thankfully, none of them did.

Eight minutes after first entering the atmosphere, the command module slowed down enough for the three large red-and-white-striped parachutes to open. If the chutes failed to open on time, the capsule would hit the ocean too hard. If we landed too far off course, we could possibly sink before the recovery ship reached us. The timing was highly critical.

With the precision that we aimed for throughout the Apollo program, the parachutes opened at exactly the right moment, and the splashdown worked as planned. As we floated down toward the ocean, we were all strapped into our seats, Mike on the left, Neil in the middle, and me in the right-hand seat, with our backs pressed against our couches, basically falling upside down. I reached over and braced my hand in position on top of the circuit breaker I needed to throw that would activate the switch on the other side of the spacecraft that Mike could pull to release the parachutes. This had to be done as quickly as possible upon impact so the chutes wouldn't drag us under the sea. Mike and I had to be careful not to activate the circuit too early, or we could release the parachutes prematurely, thus making our impact with the ocean more dangerous. Even with the braking power of the parachutes, we hit the water with such force that my hand was ripped away from the circuit breaker. Mike pulled the switch to release the parachutes, but nothing happened. The spacecraft plunged into the water, and for a long moment or two, we hung upside down below the surface. I scrambled to pull myself up and push the circuit breaker in, and Mike was able to throw his switch to jettison the parachutes. At about that time, heavy balloons inflated—similar to the way an automobile's airbags inflate upon impact—and turned the capsule upright.

Even with the inflated stabilizing rubber ring around the capsule, we were tossed around, bobbing in the sea for several minutes. But almost before we knew it, a helicopter came over and dropped a diver, then a life raft, and then more Navy divers to help us out of the scorched command module. They handed us three quarantine suits to change into inside the CM. The divers were protected as well, in their fully masked and sealed suits. One by one, Neil, Mike, and I were lifted from the raft into the hovering helicopter to transfer us to a waiting ship.

◗ ○ ◗

IN FULL QUARANTINE suits from head to toe, we were plucked out of the ocean and plopped onto the deck of the recovery aircraft carrier,

USS *Hornet,* where we found our first quarantine quarters, a modified aluminum trailer similar to an Airstream camper, parked on the deck of the ship.

The flight surgeon came into the trailer to give each of us a quick exam, and then my first act was to take a much-needed shower. We had been gone from Earth for eight days, so letting the hot water cascade over my body for what seemed like hours was a pleasure I relished. Since we had a little time to kill before President Nixon came down to the deck where our quarantine trailer was located, the flight surgeon had brought us a special treat—videos of newscasts from all over the world showing the crowds of people and their reactions as they watched us take those first steps on the moon. It was amazing to see their expressions of wonderment, their flag-waving cheers and celebrations. Across cultural barriers, there was something taking place of historic proportions. Reports already indicated that our moonwalk drew the largest television viewing audience in history, estimated at 500 million people, about 20 percent of the world's population at that time. It seemed like the entire world was having a party, and I couldn't resist turning to Neil and saying, "Hey, look. We missed the whole thing!"

Odd as it might seem, I have always wished that I could have shared that exhilarating experience with everyone else on Earth as they watched the electrifying moments leading up to our touchdown. We missed sharing in the reaction, the emotion embodied by the sight of broadcaster Walter Cronkite wiping away his tears.

◗　○　◗

AFTER WE SHOWERED, we were given a more thorough medical exam. Then Neil, Mike, and I, dressed in our freshly provided light blue flight suits, replete with our Apollo 11 insignias and special pins reading HORNET PLUS THREE, went to the window of the quarantine trailer.

The sight outside our window was a bit unnerving. A barrage of television lights nearly blinded us, about two hundred officers and dignitaries stood to the rear, and standing there amid all the hoopla was

President Richard M. Nixon. The President had a reputation for being serious and stoic, cold and calculating, but on this warm morning in the western Pacific Ocean, he seemed ebullient. He practically did a little dance when he first saw us in our window; we looked more like a circus spectacle than space explorers. Nevertheless, the President leaned in toward the microphone by the window to talk with us. Millions of people watched on live TV as President Nixon welcomed us back to Earth. The ceremony lasted about ten minutes with a lot of smiles, and a lot of lighthearted banter going back and forth. The President remarked how the world seemed bigger now, but that its population had never before felt as close together as they did watching the mission unfold. Following the brief ceremony, President Nixon flew off and we relaxed as the *Hornet* carried us back to Pearl Harbor in Hawaii.

From Pearl Harbor to Hickam Field we were transported along with a flight surgeon and staff in a trailer that was loaded on a flatbed truck. From there we were flown to Houston, quarantine unit and all. When we got to Houston, they backed up the trailer next to the building set aside for our prolonged quarantine at NASA's Manned Spacecraft Center (now known as Johnson Space Center), so they were able to transfer us from the trailer into the building without letting loose any germs. The building had sleeping quarters and a mess hall, and the people who were debriefing us were on the other side of a glass partition. If anyone came inside the quarantine unit, that person was not permitted to leave until we did. Someone had whimsically placed a sign over the door, PLEASE DON'T FEED THE ANIMALS.

We were in quarantine for twenty-one days after we came back from the moon. From the time we were picked up from the ocean until the time we entered the more permanent quarantine quarters in Houston, we wore biological garments to protect the rest of the world from any potential toxicity or strange new microbes we might have picked up from the lunar surface. Nobody I knew at NASA actually feared that we had been contaminated, but it was better to be safe than sorry. Beyond that, the mandatory quarantine served a much more functional purpose in keeping Mike, Neil, and me away from the public, and the public away from us, for a few weeks, till we had a chance to process all that we had experienced—to write our mission reports, as well as to debrief and help the Apollo 12 astronauts with any information we might have gained from our experience. Quarantine also provided us with time to pause and reflect on the events of the past week or so, trying to understand it all, and wondering how it would impact our future.

Craig Fisher, the medical doctor, brought in plenty of booze for us to celebrate, and I discovered that he kept the supply in the filing cabinet. When nobody was paying attention, I helped myself to a little extra of Craig's stash. His sleeping quarters were right next to mine, and one morning I was in my bedroom reading—since our time in quarantine was a period of catching up on the news, rest, relaxation, and isolation—and that morning I heard the doctor say, "Who's been drinking all the booze?"

I shifted uneasily. My need for a release to take the edge off the tremendous excitement we all felt in completing this mission had me drinking his stash. But that's how it was over the span of my military career, where we would go to Friday-night beer calls after our rigorous Air Force flight-training exercises, sorties, and missions. Drinking was our way of celebrating a successful mission. Apollo 11 was clearly the most momentous mission I had ever flown. I felt I deserved a little extra indulgence.

During the three weeks we stayed in quarantine, we had several executive debriefings. We attempted to convey all that we had experienced to NASA and to the astronauts who would follow us on the next lunar landings. The three of us sat on a panel behind the glass walls that separated us, and NASA personnel quizzed us about our experiences. The questions were surprisingly benign, mostly I suppose because the other astronauts had been at various key positions in the control room and throughout Mission Control, and had experienced each step of the flight along with us. Either that, or they felt we had little they could add to their already arduous training.

While in the quarantine units, we had numerous medical checkups to ascertain whether our journey had had any ill effects on us. There was some concern that even though we were all pretty healthy guys, exposure to radiation might cause a problem. We had little dosimeters that we wore while in quarantine, and when we left, the doctors said that the radiation to which we had been exposed was nothing to worry about. When we were finally released from the quarantine facility in Houston, it was determined that none of us had suffered any adverse effects from contact with the lunar dust or any other aspects of our journey. Physically, we were in top shape.

● ○ ●

THE MOST OBVIOUS, inevitable question still remains the hardest to answer: What was it like, being on the moon? What did it feel like, what were your thoughts and feelings as you walked on the moon? I've grappled with those questions for forty years, and still have not come up with an adequate answer. As military men, we were not expected or inclined to express our thoughts or feelings. In some respects, it was distinctly discouraged by NASA during the course of our missions. Consequently, on the moon, our heartbeats and brainwaves were measurable, and our activities on the moon verifiable. But there was no "emotion recorder" to measure my feelings or capture my emotional response.

Simply stated, I was exhilarated, but also guarded. Neil, Mike, and I knew that our every move and word were on display to the entire world, even though we were the only living creatures within a quarter of a million miles. With the camera on the moon's surface, Neil and I were visible to millions of people watching their TVs on Earth, and audible to millions more listening in on their radios. But we tried to force that awareness to the back of our minds. We had a job to do. I know I tried my best to focus my attention on the tasks at hand, and to make sure that I wasn't making mistakes. Yet it was impossible to ignore the fact that we were on a worldwide stage without precedent.

Many people have asked me since, "Weren't you afraid up there, afraid that maybe something would go wrong and you'd never get off the moon?" Sure, my heart was pounding the entire time we were on the surface, but thanks to our preparation, I had a fairly good idea of what to expect. We had rehearsed nearly every possible scenario, and we encountered few surprises on the lunar surface. Similar to the apprehension an athlete feels before the beginning of a big game, or that an actor or musician feels before the curtain goes up on stage, certainly I felt some anxiety, some concern about wanting to make our nation proud. But it was not fear. We were extremely confident in the outlook for the success of our mission.

I've often wondered why it is, to this day, that people feel compelled to tell me where they were the moment when we first landed on the moon. Of course I pause, and with a twinkle in my eye, I pull out my little black book and thank them, often adding, "Well, I'm trying to keep track of where everyone was!"

Over the last forty years I have had time to refine my insights with added perspective, and I have come to believe that the real value of Apollo 11 was not the experiments we set up or the rocks we brought back. It was in the shared experience in which people throughout the world who witnessed our landing participated. Nothing like that had ever happened before, no other single event had ever galvanized the world's attention to such a degree; people on every continent shared in our triumph as human beings, and bringing the world together in that way was one of the most tangible, meaningful, and valuable aspects of our accomplishment. In my lifetime I have not seen any other single event evoke such a response.

We won the race to the moon. We demonstrated America's potential to carry out a unique mission, and we made it before the end of the decade, with a few months to spare. The relative ease with which we carried out our mission was the direct result of our hundreds of hours of training and the indefatigable efforts of so many people working together. Other problems can be solved in similar ways, by taking the long view, and committing ourselves to accomplish the necessary tasks. To me, that is a big part of the shared experience, and one of the greatest lessons of realizing the Apollo dream.

4

AFTER the MOON, WHAT NEXT?

W HAT NOW?" I SAID ALOUD TO MYSELF AS I CHEWED ON THE
tip of the pipe I rarely smoked—the same pipe I had taken with
me on my Gemini 12 mission. *What's next?* I sat on a chaise
lounge out by our family swimming pool, supposedly relaxing on a
waning Saturday afternoon in the hot Houston August sunshine of
1969, my eyes scanning the low horizon above the flat land around me,
but mostly pondering the speeches I knew I would be making within a
few days. *What's left?* I wondered. *What's a person do when his or her
greatest dreams and challenges have been achieved?* I reached over to the
small table next to the chaise and reached for my drink, Scotch poured
generously over some ice cubes.

I sipped the whiskey and swished it around in my mouth, savoring
the taste. I let it slide slowly down my throat as I leaned my head back
and looked up at the sky. The sun was already beginning to decline on
the horizon. I felt much the same way. Little more than three weeks
before, I had been kicking up dust on the moon along with Neil Armstrong, the first two human beings ever to set foot on another planetary
body in space. The entire world had watched us, listened to us, felt the
tension as we nearly ran out of fuel attempting to land on the lunar surface. Now we were back, and I wondered what the next phase of my life
would be. Everything was different now, and would be forever. I didn't

know it at the time, but the rest of my life would be measured in terms of the phases of the moon, and every quinquennial and decadal anniversary of that dusty July walk.

What does a man do for an encore after walking on the moon?

I was only thirty-nine years of age, and I'd been to the top of my world. What else was left for me? What was I going to do with the rest of my life? During the three weeks in quarantine along with my fellow astronauts, Mike Collins and Neil Armstrong, I had tried to drive such thoughts out of my mind by staying focused on how we could help support the next moon landings planned by NASA. Why worry about the future? We had enough to do just getting our thoughts together and going through debriefing procedures with NASA and the astronauts who were yet to venture on their missions.

And what did I have to worry about anyhow? I *should* be on top of the world. I *was* at the top of my game. After all, I had just walked on the *moon*! For an Air Force fighter pilot and a rocket scientist from the Massachusetts Institute of Technology, that was the epitome of success. I took another gulp of Scotch, a much larger one than earlier. Hey, I should be feeling good! We'd done it; we had beaten the Russians to the moon, we had landed two men on the surface and had returned safely within the decade, just as President John F. Kennedy had challenged us to do. The entire world knew my name and more about me than I ever cared to have known. I was king of the hill!

Yet a nagging doubt about playing the role of a hero pervaded my mind. Blasting off and riding a fireball into space had been a task I was fully prepared to perform. Exploring the moon, ascending off its surface, and rendezvousing and docking with Mike, who was orbiting in the *Columbia* and waiting for Neil and me to rejoin him for the ride home—it all had gone much as planned. Oh sure, we had a few close calls, a few things that, looking back from the comfort of a lazy afternoon lounge around the pool, could have proven catastrophic. But they hadn't. We worked with the team on the ground and together we made history, what some were already referring to as the pinnacle of modern man's achievements.

In a few days my fellow astronauts and I would be off to New York, Chicago, and Los Angeles—President Nixon would join us in California for a black-tie event—and at each of the stops I'd be called upon to give a speech. As with most people, speaking in public didn't exactly fall into my comfort zone. Sure, I had some speaking ability, and felt confident enough to stand in front of a crowd, but already I was discovering that everyone wanted me to answer that inevitable question: "What was it like, being on the moon?" I struggled with an answer. I wanted to say something profound, something meaningful. But I was an engineer, not a poet; as much as I grappled with the quintessential questions of life, questions of origin, purpose, and meaning—where did we come from, where are we going, why are we even here—I found no adequate words to express what I had experienced. Yet I recognized that people wanted me to provide them with some cosmic interpretation gleaned from the lunar landing. While on the surface of the moon, I had taken in the pervasive gray-ash barrenness all around, with the Earth hanging off in space like a tiny blue-green orb, and had called it "magnificent desolation."

Now those words seemed to describe my own inner turmoil as I thought about the days ahead.

◐   ○   ◐

NASA RATHER EXPECTED a media circus from the moment we landed, and the three weeks in the quarantine unit did little to quench the public's thirst for information about our journey, or the uncontrollable intrusions of the press into our private lives. Neil, Mike, and I left the quarantine facilities on Sunday, August 10, 1969, around 9:00 p.m., pronounced fit to go by the doctors there. Excited to see our families, with whom we had hardly even talked in more than a month, the three of us said hasty good-byes and piled into three separate NASA staff cars for the drive home to Nassau Bay, a short distance from the space center complex. Our cars had barely pulled away from the gate when a television crew nudged in behind us. My driver roared away from headquarters with the TV crew following closely behind us, careening

wildly, trying to get a better camera angle. The race was on. It was no
better when I arrived home, where a bevy of reporters and photographers were waiting in the dark on my front lawn. I pressed through the
crowd to my waiting family inside the house. My wife, Joan, and our
three children—Mike, thirteen; Jan, twelve; and Andy, eleven—all
threw their arms around me and welcomed me home. Somehow, we all
knew our lives would never be the same again.

● ○ ●

OF COURSE, BEING first on the moon had its advantages. We were informed before leaving the Manned Spacecraft Center in Houston that
on Wednesday, August 13, 1969, the three Apollo 11 astronauts and
our families would be going to New York, Chicago, and Los Angeles
all in one day, to enjoy ticker tape parades and the accolades and appreciation of the American people. What an honor that was sure to be!

Joan and I had difficulty convincing our children of that distinguished honor as we tried to rouse them out of bed shortly after three
in the morning to board our flight from Houston to New York at 5:00
a.m. But what a day it was!

Our means of transportation for the day was one of the presidential
planes, *Air Force II*, whisking us first to New York, where we were met
by Mayor John Lindsay and his wife. The streets were lined with thousands of people as our motorcade made its way slowly up Wall Street to
Broadway. What seemed like an avalanche of confetti poured from the
windows and decks of the buildings as the enormous crowd embraced
us with an unbelievable outpouring of appreciation. For a while the
skies above us literally turned white with all the confetti and ticker tape
as we waved to the people in the streets. Hands reached out to touch
us, many people tried to shake our hands, but our security guards
warned us about trying to shake hands with those we passed by. We
could easily have been pulled right out of the car and mobbed by well-
wishers.

In front of us marched a troop of Boy Scouts, each one carrying an
American flag. As I saw those young people marching, and the re-

sponse of the crowd all around us, I was suddenly overwhelmed with a flood of patriotism unlike anything I had ever before experienced. Not at West Point, not in Korea as an American fighter pilot, not even when I first donned the spacesuit with the American flag on the left shoulder. But seeing those young Scouts and hearing the cheers of the people, not just for us, but for all of those who had worked so hard to get us to the moon and back, evoked a powerful response in me. I wanted to say to the American people, "Don't thank me; let me thank you!"

The parade lasted more than an hour, ending up at City Hall, where Neil, Mike, and I briefly addressed the crowd. The theme of my speech was one I would repeat many times and still believe to this day: that the footprints we left on the moon were not ours alone, but belonged to all humankind.

From New York's City Hall, we drove to the United Nations for a brief ceremony, and then it was on to Chicago, where we repeated a quite similar scene, the parade leading down Chicago's famous Michigan Avenue and State Street. The crowd in Chicago was even more demonstrative and ebullient than the New Yorkers had been! Once again, confetti and streamers poured down on us like snow, covering the streets as the city went wild. It was a sight and a feeling I will never forget. I don't think I'd ever smiled so much in my life!

The outpouring of adulation was especially heartwarming in light of the fact that our nation had experienced such tumultuous times in recent years. Few people were extolling the virtues of America on the news each evening. Racial tensions, body bags and other grotesque images of carnage in Vietnam, riots on college campuses, and antiwar demonstrations pummeled the national psyche. So when America discovered something to feel good about, our people cut loose in a big way, celebrating our achievement. It was as exhilarating as it was gratifying.

On to Los Angeles! The flight took three and a half hours, and I spent almost that entire time preparing another speech for the big night ahead. As in New York and Chicago, we were welcomed by the mayor, given the keys to the city, and treated like royalty. Making the Los Angeles trip even more exciting was the gala celebration that evening with President Nixon and about a thousand of his closest friends. My mother had passed away the year before, but in addition to Joan and our children, my father attended the Los Angeles event, as did my two sisters and other extended family members. As President Nixon presented Neil, Mike, and me with the Medal of Freedom, the highest honor given to civilians in our nation, all of my family members were beaming, especially my father.

Then on August 16, 1969, only six days after Neil, Mike, and I were released from quarantine, more than 300,000 people crowded downtown Houston for a parade welcoming us back home. It was a tremendously heartwarming experience to receive the applause and smiles from our hometown crowd. Later that evening, 45,000 people packed the Astrodome for an event hosted by Frank Sinatra to celebrate our accomplishment. All three of us were on stage with Frank as he sang "Fly Me to the Moon." I had been a fan of Frank Sinatra since junior high school, so for Frank to be honoring us was indeed something special.

Another marvelous celebration took place a few weeks later, when my hometown of Montclair, New Jersey, pulled out all the stops to honor me with a parade and banquet. It actually rained on my parade as Joan and I rode through town in a convertible, but the drizzle didn't dampen my spirits a bit. One of the highlights that I would cherish all my life took place when the longtime U.S. senator from New Jersey, Albert W. Hawkes, told the banquet crowd, "In all my years as a senator, in all the many votes and suggestions I have made, I shall remember that, to me, the most significant decision I made was to nominate a young man from Montclair, New Jersey, as a cadet at West Point. His accomplishments exceeded my wildest dreams."

◐ ○ ◑

IF MY HOMECOMING in Montclair was a dream come true, the next big event on our schedule was the nightmare every public speaker dreads. On Tuesday, September 16, 1969, we traveled to Washington, D.C., to speak at a joint session of Congress. It was simultaneously one of the greatest privileges and one of the most terrifying experiences of my life. By now I'd given dozens of speeches, and had stood in front of huge crowds of cheering well-wishers, so it wasn't stage fright that caused my apprehension, but the majesty of it all, standing in the U.S. House of Representatives as the Vice President and members of both the House and the Senate filed into the cavernous and stately room. Members of the President's cabinet, ambassadors, and high-ranking government officials from other countries were on hand as well. I fretted over that speech more than any of them. In putting that speech together, I drew from every source I could find, even political cartoons and caricatures.

It was a relatively short speech in which I wanted to recognize the tremendous commitment it took on the part of our government and the hundreds of thousands of people all across our country working together to get us to the moon, while laying out a vision for the future. I told the joint session of Congress, "This should give all of us hope and inspiration to overcome some of the more difficult problems here on Earth. The Apollo lesson is that national goals can be met where there is a strong enough will to do so." The audience responded with a rousing and gratifying ovation.

◑   ○   ◐

THE DAY PRIOR to appearing before Congress, the Washington, D.C., post office hosted Neil, Mike, and me for the unveiling of a special postage stamp commemorating the mission of *Apollo 11* and our landing on the moon. That sounded exciting enough, until the new stamp was revealed and, under a drawing of Neil stepping off the *Eagle* onto the lunar surface, the caption read, FIRST MAN ON THE MOON. I smiled rather weakly when I first saw the stamp, though it was a bittersweet honor. I didn't even dare to think what Mike must have thought, but it seemed to me that something referring to "first men" would have been more accurate and more appropriate. As it was, our being there felt like we were backup singers for Elvis.

I wasn't upset about the stamp; it just felt odd, especially when the post office asked Neil, Mike, and me to sign a large number of first-edition sheets of stamps that would then be sold. I thought, *Why would you want me to sign this if you didn't think it important to include Mike and me somehow?* But we dutifully signed a large stack of first-day issues, because, after all, that's what American heroes do.

If I was mildly disappointed by the post office's callous exclusion, my father was furious. He set about on a one-man crusade to get the stamp caption changed to "First Men on the Moon." He even spent some time picketing in front of the White House, but his efforts proved more a source of amusement for the media than an encouragement for including Mike and me in the honor. I just shrugged. What was done was done.

·◗ ◯ ◖

NEIL'S FAMOUS WORDS upon our landing set the theme for our worldwide goodwill tour to be known as "Operation Giant Step." We stopped first at Marquette University in Milwaukee, Wisconsin, a rather odd place to begin a world tour. It was the fall of 1969, and student protests were common on American campuses. Some young people were bitter and angry over the war in Vietnam; others had their own agendas. Nevertheless, I would never have imagined that as Mike, Neil, and I approached the auditorium, we'd be pelted by a barrage of eggs and tomatoes. Fortunately the students were lousy shots and none of us were hit, but I felt sad that these young people could be so disgruntled with America. Rather than being proud of us for going to the moon, they chided us for wasting so much money while wars and famine plagued parts of the Earth. This was a different America than the one to which my father and the heroes of World War II came home.

We were on the world tour for forty-five days. During that time we visited twenty-three countries, as well as the Vatican, and were received by twenty heads of state, including presidents, kings and queens, and prime ministers. To each we presented a replica of the plaque we left on the moon, which stated, WE CAME IN PEACE FOR ALL MANKIND. Everywhere we traveled, throngs of people swarmed the streets in an effort to see us. It was truly a heartwarming experience, but after a while we began to feel a bit like circus animals on display. We greeted several million people in twenty-seven cities directly, and many millions more through television, radio, and the press. And of course there were the obligatory speeches that Neil, Mike, and I had given so many times now that we could almost stand in for each other.

Nevertheless, the predominant feeling we had from people all around the world was one of warmth and friendliness, even in some of the countries that were not necessarily as pro–United States as we would have liked. The trip was inspiring and exhausting.

We returned to the United States in time to attend the launch of *Apollo 12* at Kennedy Space Center, a lunar landing mission carrying Alan Bean, Pete Conrad, and Dick Gordon on a journey quite similar to ours. NASA thought it wise to call us home in case there was something we could contribute should there be trouble during Apollo 12, but it was also a precaution against bad publicity. If something went wrong, they didn't want us halfway around the world, being asked pointed questions we would have no immediate way of answering. We really didn't mind returning home for a few days. It was wonderful to sleep in our own beds, to celebrate Thanksgiving at home, and of course to see our children, whom we hadn't seen now for several weeks.

It was also a thrill to watch the majestic Saturn V rocket thunder off the pad, carrying our friends and colleagues toward the moon, knowing more than they about the adventure they were about to experience.

President Nixon attended the launch, as well. We had recommended to the President that he watch this launch outdoors to better appreciate the impact of the sound and shock waves coming from the launch pad, rather than view it from inside Launch Control Center, where onlookers experience a mere rattling of the windows. But as it turned out, the liftoff of *Apollo 12* occurred during a thunderstorm, so the President was better off inside. Within the first minute, the rocket was struck by lightning, requiring the crew to quickly reboot their systems. Unimpaired, the flight continued safely from there, and the Apollo 12 mission could not have been a better follow-up as mankind's second moon landing.

All too soon, though, Neil, Mike, and I were heading to Canada, on the next leg of our own journey. I have to admit, going to the moon felt a lot easier than going around the world on the goodwill tour.

The world tour stretched from August 13 to November 5, with a few short breaks. In September we came back from the international portion of Operation Giant Step for a two-day "vacation." I walked into my office and was greeted by huge mounds of mail everywhere. I could barely find my desk! The letters and cards came from around the world, from well-wishers, students, space aficionados, and of course, a plethora of school, corporate, and civic groups offering speaking invitations. Secretaries in the NASA mail room opened the mail and, whenever possible, answered it, but most needed a direct response from me. This mail was sent on to me and stacked in my office awaiting my return. I started working on the stacks of mail, answering a few, before I realized this was a bottomless pit. As I answered one letter, the secretary brought in several hundred more. While I greatly appreciated the congratulatory wishes, and the sincere interest on the part of the public, I lamented that I couldn't do a better job of answering the many requests. I pictured a young boy, a future rocket scientist, writing a letter with well-thought-out questions about the Apollo 11 mission, and then sending off his letter, checking the mailbox each day, and awaiting a response that likely would never come. I sure didn't want to let that young man down, yet when I looked at the stacks of mail, I knew I couldn't possibly keep up, either.

The traveling and speechmaking slowed down a bit over the Christmas holiday, but then resumed in early January 1970. Now, however, Neil, Mike, and I were often split up, one of us speaking at an event in California while another went to Iowa, and another to Georgia. The three of us continued crisscrossing the country for months, with most of the events scheduled by NASA, and a few of our own thrown in wherever we could fit them. Throughout 1969 and 1970,

Neil, Mike, and I served as unofficial space ambassadors traveling the country on NASA's behalf.

After a while, I felt that NASA was taking advantage of our willingness to be cooperative. Certainly we were still employed by the space agency, and we were honored to represent America's astronauts, but we were not public-relations guys. All we really wanted to do was get back to work. Even before going to the moon, we understood that there would be a fascination on the part of the public when we returned, and we were willing to deal with that, up to an extent. We realized that we were now regarded as public property, and we did our best to maintain as much of a sense of pre–Apollo 11 normalcy in our lives as possible. But for nearly two years NASA paraded us out in front of one group after another, on display as it were, to do our routine promoting space exploration, and especially reminding anyone with any influence of how important congressional funding was to the program.

◗ ○ ◖

AFTER THE WORLD tour, on November 5, 1969, the three of us wrote a formal letter to President Nixon, kind of a final report. In describing the residual impact of our mission, we said, "The predominant impression is the warmth and friendliness shown us as representatives of the American space program. Although the world recognizes the Apollo 11 mission as an outstanding American achievement, people everywhere felt that they too had participated in the event. . . . We believe that the people we met are also persuaded that the application of science and technology combined with the will to do so can produce solutions to the problems of men everywhere." Along with the letter, we presented the President with a huge photo album chronicling the highlights from all of the countries we visited.

At the conclusion of the tour, we had a special dinner with President Nixon in the White House. He was quite interested in every aspect of our trip, and seemed genuinely concerned about our future plans. He said to Mike Collins, "I know you have been talking with Secretary Rogers about a position with the State Department."

"Yes, sir," Mike nodded. "I'm looking forward to that."

"And, Neil, what is it that you want to do?" the President asked.

"I'd like to stay with NASA for a while, and maybe work in the aeronautics department." It seemed odd to me that Neil wanted to divorce himself early on from space activities, and devote himself to aviation, but that was his heart and soul, so I didn't fault him for that. Neil was a true test pilot; he enjoyed flying airplanes, running them through a variety of maneuvers, whether they were space-related or not.

The President turned to me, and asked about my plans. At the time I didn't really know, but I was thinking of returning to the Air Force, and I could see myself as a role model for young airmen at the Academy, so the position of commandant of the Air Force Academy seemed appealing to me. I didn't feel comfortable in voicing that to President Nixon at the time, but I did put in a good word for my dad. I suggested to the President that my father would make an excellent ambassador to Sweden.

At the time, the United States was not on the best of terms with the notoriously neutral country. Olaf Palme was the prime minister, and was strongly opposed to our involvement in Vietnam. From the U.S. standpoint, our government was not pleased that Sweden had welcomed those regarded as draft dodgers and deserters. I knew there was an opening in our embassy in Sweden, because during our round-the-world trip, we had not visited Sweden. We visited England, of course, where Neil had his roots, and Italy, where Mike had been born in Genoa, but rather than going to the homeland of my heritage, we went to Norway instead. It was not an accidental change in our itinerary. It was a statement.

I slept in the Lincoln Bedroom in the White House that night, and the sense of history surrounding me inspired me to consider how I might best serve my country. Ever since my days at the Military Academy at West Point, where our motto was "Duty, Honor, Country," service to my country has been a predominant motivation in my life. During our quarantine, Neil, Mike, and I had talked often about the "what next" question, and we decided that it would be selfish of us to return to NASA and take positions back in the Apollo lunar flight rotation. The normal routine would have had us return to lunar training as a backup crew for a flight, possibly Apollo 14, then, two flights later, being the primary crew. Since Mike Collins had not actually set foot on the moon, he would no doubt have precedence for a mission that would get him back to the surface. Nevertheless, Neil, Mike, and I felt that the more noble gesture on our part would be to give other astronauts a chance to reach the moon. While we continued to work for NASA, we elected not to stay in the crew rotation cycle.

Besides, by that time, we had become in essence the public face of NASA. When anyone called the agency for a speaker, whether it was for a university symposium or a Little League baseball field dedication, we were always at the top of the list. No doubt, some people thought we could better serve America's space program by representing it to the world. Nice thought, but we were trained as pilots, not as public-relations people, and of the three Apollo 11 astronauts, none of us was prepared to be a person under constant fire from the media, someone whose every word—even if it was nonsensical—instantly showed up in newspapers, magazines, and other media around the world. Imagine the biggest rock star or Hollywood celebrity dealing with the media feeding frenzy that happens nowadays; now multiply that exponentially and you have some idea of what we three PR novices experienced for months following the landing on the moon. NASA of course expected a barrage of interview requests and public appearance requests, but they never anticipated the physical and emotional drain the instant fame would put on men who had spent most of their adult lives in a cockpit.

◖ ○ ◗

THE TRANSITION FROM "astronaut preparing to accomplish the next big thing" to "astronaut telling about the last big thing" did not come easily to me. For the previous eight years, from the time I had been studying rendezvous techniques at MIT, and working on my doctoral dissertation, which contained many of the ideas we incorporated in the Gemini and Apollo space programs, my life had revolved around astronautics—not just talking about it, but doing it, getting ready for it, and making something happen. Now, as much as I understood that in America "heroes have duties," talking about it was growing old quickly. Nevertheless, I was committed to doing my best, hoping to inspire other people through my experiences, especially the younger generation, who I hoped would take the exploration of space further than even I could imagine.

That's why, in early January 1970, I resumed traveling from one end of the country to the other, making public appearances and giving speeches on behalf of NASA. Following my appearance on NBC's flagship morning news program, the *Today Show,* host Hugh Downs and I discussed the negative response Neil, Mike, and I had received at Marquette University. Hugh shared my consternation over the disenchantment of America's high school and college-aged youth. A few weeks later, outbreaks of deadly violence at Kent State and Jackson State universities brought the issue into Americans' living rooms in graphic detail.

I wasn't sure what to do, but I felt compelled to find some way in which I could get involved—something that would offer a new challenge, as well as an opportunity to perhaps capitalize on some of the public's familiarity with my name. My mind started to cogitate on the possibilities.

In February 1970, my father's close friend, General Jimmy Doolittle, approached me about becoming a part of the board of directors of Mutual of Omaha, a once-venerable, well-known insurance company. The company perpetuated its clean-cut, wholesome image by hiring military heroes and other nationally known figures, although it was probably more popular for sponsoring an outdoorsman show, *Wild Kingdom,* on television each week, starring the legendary sportsman Marlin Perkins. Since retiring from the military, General Doolittle had been a member of Mutual's board. "I'll put in a good word for you," he assured me.

Sure enough, at their annual meeting in February, Mutual of Omaha elected me to their board of directors. Board chairman and chief executive officer of the company V. J. Skutt extolled my virtues. "Colonel Aldrin, the great astronaut and young man of good judgment and high principles, will help get our organization off to a flying start in new products and service for the decade ahead," he told the press.[1] Before long, Mr. Skutt would change his tune.

About the same time that I joined Mutual of Omaha, I also joined the board of Amvideo Corporation, a Massachusetts-based parent company of Annapolis CATV, Inc. Cable television was a fledgling industry at that time, with only a handful of stations operating around the country and even fewer with original programming. But I felt sure that the cable television industry held tremendous promise, so I looked at my involvement as an investment in my future.

NASA approved both of my corporate affiliations. The space program restricted astronauts' outside business interests, tenaciously guarding the image of the program, so NASA's imprimatur was important to me.

● ○ ●

I WAS BACK in Houston on April 11, 1970, for the launch of *Apollo 13*, carrying astronauts Jim Lovell, John "Jack" Swigert, and Fred Haise to the moon for what was supposed to be America's third landing on the lunar surface. The first two days of the mission went well, with the crew encountering and overcoming a few problems, but overall the trip was looking good. Some people around Mission Control were regarding it as the smoothest Apollo flight yet.

Then, shortly after 9:00 p.m. on April 13, 1970, about 200,000 miles from Earth, an oxygen tank exploded and the shrapnel punctured a second oxygen tank, causing that tank to fail as well, knocking out the *Apollo 13* command module's electricity, heat, lights, and water. With classic understatement, Jack Swigert poignantly reported the emergency: "Houston, we've had a problem here."

The astronauts soon discovered how serious the problem really was;

---

[1] "Insurance Firm Chooses Aldrin," *Montclair Times* (NJ), Thursday, February 26, 1970.

two of their three fuel cells, which were the spacecraft's prime source of electricity, were lost. One oxygen tank appeared to be completely empty, and the oxygen in the second tank was depleting rapidly. Then, when Jim Lovell looked out the CM's left window, he saw a truly frightening sight. "We are venting something out into space," he reported to Houston. "It's a gas of some sort." Houston confirmed it was oxygen escaping from the second, and last, oxygen tank.

With the planned landing on the moon aborted, Mission Control frantically worked toward a "successful failure," to bring the crew back home safely. It was no easy task, as they used the lunar module to power the command module back to Earth. Although the story has often been told, it is still a wonder of training, teamwork, and ingenuity that saved the lives of three brave astronauts.

As soon as the crisis developed, I received a flurry of phone calls. They had plenty of talented experts on hand at Mission Control, so they didn't need me hanging around, but somebody suggested that Neil Armstrong and I go over to Jim Lovell's mom's home to be with her. Maybe we could allay some of her fears.

Neil and I were glad to help, so we went to the home of seventy-three-year-old Blanche Lovell. She welcomed us warmly and invited us in. "It's so nice of you to come," she said. "Are you boys part of the space program, too?" We stayed with her and watched the proceedings on television for a while, until some other friends and family members came to stay with her.

Apollo 13 left a lasting impression on America's space program. Many people regarded bringing back Jim, Jack, and Fred alive as miraculous; from my perspective, it was a tremendous ending for a failed mission. That's what our teams at NASA and the backup crews were trained to do—to deal with almost any possible problem that might occur in space. The people who worked so feverishly to get our astronauts home were doing exactly what was expected of them, what they had trained for. Even in the face of the oxygen explosion and the aborted lunar landing, if the astronauts hadn't come back safely, then the NASA system would have failed.

The often-used phrase regarding America's space program has been: "Failure is not an option." We all understand the concept that the equipment and the people need to perform as planned, with no miscues. But if failure is not an option, then you need to stay on the ground. Everything about space travel is subject to failure, and if it is worth doing, it will involve taking calculated risks. We had risks in Apollo 11 as well, and that mission could easily have turned out similar to Apollo 13, but thankfully it didn't. Only the possible rewards of exploration make the risks tolerable.

❂　○　❂

THAT SAME YEAR, I engaged in explorations of a much more earthy nature. While attending an Air Force gathering with my father at the New York Athletic Club, my attention drifted toward an attractive, bright-eyed woman with long brown hair. She was attending the event with another West Point guy, but the attraction between us was immediately obvious to both of us. Her name was Marianne, and my relationship with her nearly wrecked my life. Things at home with Joan had not been going well for quite a while, and I was vulnerable in more ways than I wanted to admit.

Joan was from Ho-Ho-Kus, New Jersey, not far from my hometown, and we had met on a blind date set up by our parents before I went off to war in Korea. When I came home, we went out a few times before I was transferred to Las Vegas, and I proposed to her shortly thereafter. We married on December 29, 1954. Joan had a master's degree from Columbia University and a fascination with theater. Wherever we lived, she enjoyed participating in numerous local productions, providing a creative outlet for her talent. She had been a good military wife, adjusting to the many moves involved in my career. But we had long since grown apart, and we both knew it.

I knew that several astronauts had compromised their marriage vows. That was no excuse, but knowing that I was not the only astronaut to succumb to temptation made the rationalization to pursue Marianne much easier. I assuaged my conscience by reminding myself that we all had feet of clay, that a West Point cadet I knew could compromise the honor code and still be promoted to general, that a minister of the Gospel could preach against sin while indulging in it, and that a clean-cut, All-American astronaut could think of himself as above the rules while bending them to accommodate his own desires. I revisited my rationalizations each time I climbed aboard a T-38 aircraft in Houston and pointed it toward New York, ostensibly to keep up my flying time, but in reality to facilitate my relationship with Marianne.

● ○ ●

AT THE SAME time, I was committed to using my newfound fame for good, to try to increase communication between generations that regarded one another with mistrust at best, and often with downright disdain. With the specter of Kent State still hanging over our nation, in the spring of 1970 I set about organizing a "Conference on Youth Representation," a program in which young people could have ongoing opportunities to voice their opinions and articulate their views with adults. I secured commitments from a wide array of recognized leaders who were willing to meet with young people, and sent out invitations to leaders of college-aged young men and women around the country.

Hugh Downs was tremendously helpful, and hosted our first organizational meeting on the set of the *Today Show* at NBC's studios in Rockefeller Center in New York City. Some of the adult leaders who agreed to participate included the anthropologist Margaret Mead; Fran Tarkenton and Lance Rentzel, two popular NFL superstars; Sargent Shriver, an in-law of the Kennedy family; Congressman Robert Taft; and members of academia such as Kingman Brewster, president of Yale University.

I proposed that the advisory group and the young representatives could choose an issue and discuss it in an open forum. The idea was, "If you have a gripe with the government or some other aspect of society, let's sit down and talk about it. Then together, we can decide how we might better approach the problem and hopefully come up with some viable solutions." I hoped that through this interaction we could nullify some of the disenchantment younger men and women felt toward our country. Our goal was to provide an environment in which both students and adult leaders could have a dialogue about current issues that troubled them without fear of criticism, castigation, or condemnation. We wanted the youth group to address an issue during a broadcast on public TV, to be followed by further discussion at local levels, then a vote or sampling of public opinion, and a response during another segment on public TV. My plan was to make use of voting machines and other vote-counting methods that were unused between elections. Why not use that structure as a national polling device by which we could get a quicker, more accurate response to the questions and issues facing modern young adults? I thought existing high schools and colleges provided centralized locations where these issues could be addressed, and answers given by responsible leaders in society.

We planned our kickoff event for June 16, 1970, at the American Friends Service Committee Building in Washington, D.C. We contacted national student organizations, as well as such groups as the National Association for the Advancement of Colored People (NAACP) and members of the Young Republicans and the Young Democrats. Surprisingly, a mere eighteen young adults accepted my invitation to the initial Conference on Youth Representation in Washington, D.C., and I paid the lodging expenses for nearly half of them.

With Hugh Downs as moderator, I spent two days listening to young people pour out their complaints, attacking the adult participants, and telling them everything they felt was wrong about America, but at the end no one budged on their opinions or beliefs. In spite of this intransigence, I considered the conference a success, because at least the young people and adults were talking. I began making plans for another conference, and was disappointed when a number of our adult sponsors began to drop out; worse yet, the young people seemed uninterested in returning for a second conference.

Having three young people of my own to help keep me in touch with issues that burned in the hearts and minds of young America, I had hoped I might be able to act as a role model for this group, but it all fell apart when the young adult leaders wanted to have their own meetings without adult input. That seemed counterproductive to me, and the enthusiasm for my initial ideas dissipated, especially since I had held such high hopes for the conferences. It was a noble idea, but it ended in failure, and in some sense I assumed responsibility for the poor results.

Ironically, in recent years I have invoked similar approaches to initiating the ShareSpace Next Century of Flight Space Imperatives (NCFSI), a one-day space conference in D.C., after which I wanted to have a public opinion poll taken. While the conference was broadcast live by C-Span and concluded with success, the polling never did get that far. I have had similar ideas in connection with a Science/Space Studies/Math education outreach for youth that I have tried to initiate. And I envisioned a Lunar Renaissance series of panel discussions to be broadcast on public TV or networks such as Discovery, National Geographic, or even a ShareSpace Channel on YouTube, to raise awareness of the current challenges facing America's space program. I am still convinced these efforts to communicate a vision to the next generation are vital.

◗　○　◗

ON JULY 20, 1970, Neil Armstrong and I celebrated the first anniversary of our moon landing by getting together at the state capitol building in Jefferson City, Missouri. The *Apollo 11* capsule, the charred command module *Columbia*, was being exhibited along with an assortment of moon rocks in all fifty U.S. state capitals, and it happened to be scheduled in Jefferson City on the anniversary. It was the first time I had seen the *Columbia* since the crew of the *Hornet* had hauled it aboard the huge carrier following our splashdown. The spacecraft still looked mighty good to me, despite its charred and distressed metal. I remembered well how those markings got on that spacecraft, and I was deeply grateful for every one of them.

Neil and I addressed a crowd of about three thousand people. "We left some footprints on the moon," I said. "They were made ideally for all the people of this country, and all the people of the world." Following the celebration, Neil, NASA administrator Dr. Thomas O. Paine, and I flew to New York for a meeting at the United Nations.

We presented UN Secretary General U Thant with a four-ounce lunar rock sent by President Nixon as a "gift from all the people of the United States." The rock was to remain on exhibit at the UN in perpetuity. Neil, Tom, and I were surprised when the secretary general took this opportunity to chide the major powers, and in particular the United States. Referring to Neil's first words on the moon's surface, Thant said, "It is a cause for deepest regret and dismay that in the year since that act, man on Earth has not made even a small leap toward peace in those brutally war-torn areas of Indochina and the Middle East."

We looked at each other in amazement, shrugged, and left. What did Thant want from us? We did our part. We felt that the UN secretary general had simply used us to make a political statement stabbing the U.S. government.

That was one of the last events at which I'd see Neil for a number of years. He became more private and less interested in being on stage as an astronaut, or degrading his lofty status by lending his name to endorse commercial products. Neil did not enjoy being in public; he attempted to hold himself aloof, just as Charles Lindbergh did for many years. Lindbergh was known as Mr. Aviation, an American hero Neil emulated. Neil loved aviation; even his e-mail address in later years was, at one time, OWright2, for Orville Wright 2. But he wasn't really a space guy. He didn't really like to talk about the intricacies of space, though he was the most qualified test-pilot astronaut, truly Mr. Aviation. For the next forty years, about the only time Neil showed up in public as part of an event promoting space was at each of the five-year anniversaries of our July 1969 lunar landing. These events were hosted by the President of the United States at the White House. Apart from that, I simply didn't see Neil or Mike often, although Mike later took a job with the Smithsonian in Washington, D.C., and helped guide the development of the capacious Air and Space Museum. More recently, Mike joined me on a salmon-fishing trip to Alaska. I have reached out occasionally by phone about possible reunion dates to get all the

Apollo astronauts together, especially the twenty-four who have been to the moon and the twelve who walked on the surface, but as the years went by, my hopes for such reunions grew dimmer and dimmer.

◗ ○ ◗

INDEED, FOR MOST of my life, success has come relatively easily to me. Certainly I had worked hard, and I was fortunate to be in the right place at the right time. I was grateful to have had so many opportunities in which I had excelled and achieved at peak performance throughout my life. I had flown to the moon and gotten its dust on my feet. But what was there for me now? What new goal could I set? What could possibly top that accomplishment?

Sure, I had always come out smelling like a rose, but following the world tour, the bloom was off the rose in my life in almost every area. I was physically exhausted and emotionally drained. I sensed things going from bad to worse in my marriage. Guilt and despair began to envelop me. I felt a growing sense of meaninglessness in my work as an astronaut, knowing that I would never return to the moon, or even fly another mission anywhere. I had been relegated to little more than a public-relations ambassador. NASA planned to return to the moon a few more times and then develop a reusable space shuttle. That pretty much closed the door for me as far as getting back to business as usual in the NASA routine and taking an active role as an astronaut in America's space program. And as I would discover years later, as America's space program flourished or languished, so did I.

How could I have gone almost overnight from being on top of the world to feeling useless, worthless, and washed up? I wanted to resume my duties, but there were no duties to resume. There was no goal, no sense of calling, no project worth pouring myself into. Although I didn't realize it at the time, I had started drinking more. Life seemed to have lost its luster. On some days I couldn't even find a reason to get out of bed. So I didn't. Something was wrong; something within me was beginning to crack. I only hoped that I could figure it out before I broke down completely.

5

REALIGNMENT

NASA CONTINUED TO KEEP ME BUSY GIVING SPEECHES AND making other public appearances, and I always enjoyed challenging people to think beyond the stars, to reach for their own "moon" or "outer space," whatever that might imply for them. Yet for me personally, by the autumn of 1970, there was a growing frustration and anxiousness at the center of my being that I could not resolve. I had hoped to continue working at NASA on future space developments, but came to realize that I would never be able to go back to "business as usual" in light of my moonwalker status. Public interest in the space program was waning, the Apollo program was ending, and NASA would soon be retreating for a period before refocusing on space activities confined to orbiting the Earth. Simply put, I was without a career, and I was feeling the aftereffects of it all. As always, I was standing by, ready for liftoff, but I needed to realign my direction and find a new runway.

I even made an oblique mention of my concerns in a speech at a conference of aerospace doctors in St. Louis. I reminded them that a huge amount of time, money, and effort had been applied to determining the effects of space travel on the human body. All of the astronauts, and perhaps especially Neil, Mike, and me, were closely monitored medically after journeys into space. (To this day, forty years later, I still go back to NASA every year for a medical checkup.) Surprisingly, however, nobody from NASA and no medical or scientific study group has ever analyzed the emotional aftereffects of space travel, especially the effects of instant celebrity and the pressures of a public life on those who were pilots or scientists.

Becoming a public personality may sound like a laudable and rewarding goal to some people, and today I actually enjoy my public life for the most part. But at the time, the impact of Apollo 11 and the instant celebrity brought to us by the lunar landing took a toll on everyone in my immediate family. Besides my own frustrations and the increased tension between Joan and me, we could see the residual effects trickling down in the lives of all three of our children. Jan and Andy, although proud of their daddy, preferred their anonymity. Mike, our oldest, became obstinate and argumentative in his teens, displaying much more than the usual know-it-all attitude many teenagers adopt. Joan and I realized that he was crying out for love and attention, and with my being away so much, that created even more stress in our home. When Mike began developing chronic severe headaches, we sought medical help.

After examining Mike, the doctor quietly informed Joan that the attention Mike needed might be better received from a psychologist. Dr. Robert Prall began working with Mike and Joan, and at the doctor's suggestion, I started attending the weekly sessions as well. Within six months, Mike's issues—many of which stemmed from five years of age, when he had been separated from Joan and me for months, as we both were hospitalized with hepatitis—were fairly well resolved. But Joan and I continued to meet with Dr. Prall in an effort to grapple with some of our own problems. Eventually, Dr. Prall focused on me as the primary source of the problems. I was becoming increasingly moody and dismissive of other people, including Joan and the kids. A volcano was seething within me, below the surface of my life, the pressure building more with each passing week. The only relief I found was in another shot of Scotch—and then another.

When NASA asked me to consider an opportunity that would require my visiting Sweden, the land of my ancestors, I thought that perhaps turning it into a family vacation might help. We spent fourteen days in Sweden, and while there I received the Swedish Order of the Vasa, an honor presented to Swedish-Americans who had accomplished a great achievement. I guess going to the moon qualified. And in some ways this trip made up for the fact that we did not visit Sweden during the worldwide Apollo 11 goodwill tour.

Because it was a technology-oriented trip rather than a diplomatic one, I spent some time speaking at various engineering and aeronautical functions, but I tried to focus on my family more than on official groups. And to some extent we were successful. Our youngest son, Andy, and I went scuba diving down to a sunken ship in the harbor; Mike found a new pet, a borzoi puppy that we ended up shipping back to Houston; and Jan, Joan, and I enjoyed getting to know more about my relatives in Värmland, where my grandfather had been born.

While in Sweden, I had been scheduled by the U.S. State Department to meet with King Gustaf VI, but just prior to leaving, I received a notice that the king had to cancel. The suggested date for rescheduling was five days after we planned to leave the country. That was a bit of a disappointment, but not an inconvenience. Then we received word from the State Department that the meeting with the king was not optional. Our trip was extended by five days, and King Gustaf VI and I had a pleasant visit. But it bothered me that I was once again being moved around as little more than a pawn in a diplomatic chess game, with little regard for how it inconvenienced my family, our hosts, or me.

Moreover, the NASA protocol officer who had accompanied us to Sweden and was supposed to facilitate our trip proved inefficient and a constant source of irritation. It may have been unfair to do so, but I took his inattention and insolence as a reflection of NASA's attitude toward me. Had I not given them eight years of my life? Could they not find someone better than this fellow to help take care of my family and me on a foreign trip? I felt deserted. The more I thought about it, the more it bothered me.

Back home in Houston, as I reviewed our trip, I slowly slid into the doldrums. I found myself spending most of the day or evening staring at the television set. Joan and the children didn't know what to do for me, and I passed off my blues as fatigue from our trip. Nobody mentioned that the family had been just as tired as I had been, and they were functioning just fine.

During my periods of melancholy, I again pondered my future. What was I going to do? I was barely forty years of age; I couldn't continue this way. I pulled myself together and decided to go to Washington, D.C., to meet with the Air Force chief of staff to consider my possible return to the Air Force. Although I had several business interests, nothing challenged me enough to want to pour myself into a career, so resuming my status as a colonel in the Air Force seemed a viable option.

Meanwhile, NASA was moving ahead with preliminary plans for developing the space shuttle program that would follow the Apollo program. When NASA asked me to be part of a committee to assess the design of the shuttle, I willingly took on the task. Perhaps there still was a way to continue my activities at NASA, and work on concepts that would contribute to the future of manned space exploration. So I dived into the project. We were looking at the features of a fully reusable spacecraft system in which *both* the shuttle and the booster rockets that had separated after liftoff would fly back to Earth for a runway landing. These rocket boosters used liquid propellant, as we had on the Saturn V, in keeping with Wernher von Braun's premise that we should never launch human beings on boosters with solid propellant because of the associated hazards. But squabbles arose between NASA's flight centers as to whether the rocket boosters should be manned or unmanned. I probably surprised a lot of people by supporting the unmanned booster, and a number of the committee members agreed. After all our discussions, however, our plans were tabled. Ultimately, due to funding restrictions, NASA would opt for the cheap fix over the costly runway-landing reusable liquid boosters, and use solid propellant boosters for the shuttle that are then dropped in the ocean to be recovered and refurbished for further flights.

Ordinarily such debate wouldn't have affected me greatly; since my days at MIT, I was accustomed to the give-and-take of rocket science. But for some reason the futility of these discussions sent me back into a negative mindset again. Even today it is one of the few regrets I have from my time at NASA, since our space program would be much different if we had stuck to liquid rocket boosters, rather than adopting the solid rockets that have caused so many problems with the shuttle, including the first shuttle mishap, the *Challenger* explosion in 1986.

Fortunately for me, in October 1970, NASA gave me an assignment that I thought I might enjoy. Two Russian cosmonauts, Andrian Nikolayev and Vitaly Sevastyanov, were coming to the United States, and NASA wanted me to join them on their tour of American space centers. This was years before the Cold War had ended or the Berlin Wall had been torn down, so to have two cosmonauts poking around in U.S. space centers was not like taking them on a trip to Disneyland. Nevertheless, America has always operated its space program out in the open, with success or failure readily seen by the world. Thanks to our tremendous technological expertise, and a little luck, we have had far more successes than failures. The Soviets conducted their space program as clandestinely as possible, which always gave rise to questions about their intentions, whether they viewed space exploration as something to help mankind or merely as another weapons-delivery system in their already dangerous arsenal. Unquestionably, part of what motivated President Kennedy and succeeding presidents to pursue the "space race" was to make sure that the Soviet Union did not gain a military or technological advantage over us.

Yet, despite our suspicions, the American astronauts and the Soviet cosmonauts shared an explorer's mentality. We wanted to know what the other side knew. I felt great appreciation for what the Russians had accomplished, and we actually got along quite well, although we had to communicate through an interpreter. We invited the Soviets to view our entire operation, including our launch facilities at Cape Kennedy, but the Soviets refused, knowing that if they accepted a tour of our launch facilities, it would be almost obligatory to invite Americans to tour their launch center in Tyuratam, and the Soviets were not open to doing that.

We did tour the Marshall Space Flight Center in Huntsville, Alabama, as well as the Space Center in Houston, the Jet Propulsion Laboratory, and many American tourist sites. We consumed a great deal of vodka, and the trip was considered a huge step forward in space cooperation on both sides. Although when the Soviet cosmonauts were asked in a press conference before their departure why they hadn't visited the Kennedy Space Center, they replied with a straight face through an interpreter that they hadn't been invited to visit the Cape. So much for our new openness!

Nevertheless, with the acknowledged success in my favor, I returned to Washington, D.C., and met with Secretary of the Air Force Robert Seamans, and several top generals. Secretary Seamans was a friend of my father's from MIT, and I felt I had an ally in him for making my return to the Air Force more amenable.

Two jobs in the upper echelons of the Air Force held potential: one was the commandant of the Air Force Academy in Colorado. This position especially appealed to me since I felt that I could be a positive role model for the cadets at the Academy. Secretary Seamans seemed to indicate that he thought this position might be a good fit for me, too.

The second interesting possibility was that of commandant of the USAF Test Pilot School, to be renamed the Aerospace Research Pilot School at Edwards Air Force Base in California. When I'd first applied at NASA to become an astronaut, I was turned down because I had not attended a test pilot school, so the possibility of heading up such a facility was intriguing. Either of those positions would most likely lead to a promotion to brigadier general, and that piqued my interest as well. I indicated my desire to return to the Air Force and resume my career as an officer, although I asked that a move not be made until the end of our children's school year in June 1971. The Air Force brass was delighted.

When the Air Force extended its offer to me, however, the only position on the table was commandant of the USAF Test Pilot School at Edwards Air Force Base in California. The position at the Air Force Academy was not even an option. I learned later that the Academy's new commandant would be the son of the legendary Air Force general Hoyt Vandenberg. Although the job at Edwards would be challenging, and they were training pilots for the future shuttle flights, my spirits sank once again. I had allowed my heart to get set on the Air Force Academy, and Joan was already mentally packing and planning our move.

Nevertheless, on Tuesday morning, January 14, 1971, I was back in Washington, D.C., to announce officially that I was leaving NASA and the space program in June, and would be returning to the Air Force to serve as the commandant of the test pilot school at Edwards. I tried to put the best light on my new responsibilities, noting that heading up the school would be a new learning experience for me.

Although I could not have imagined it at the time, I was about to learn more than I ever wanted to know.

6

FLYING HIGH,
FLYING LOW

O N JULY 1, 1971, I OFFICIALLY COMMENCED MY ROLE AS commandant of the USAF Test Pilot School at Edwards Air Force Base. I was welcomed by the forty test pilot students in the program, who were excited and a bit awestruck to have a moonwalker Apollo astronaut as their new commandant—especially since the school was becoming known for supplying a pool of astronauts to the space program. In fact, the name of the school had been officially changed to the Aerospace Research Pilot School at Edwards Air Force Base, California, to reflect this goal. Two thirds of the one-year program was similar to the Navy's test pilot program, but the last third of the program was geared to astronaut training. A fierce competitiveness has always existed between the U.S. Navy and the U.S. Air Force. Although it may seem odd to someone unfamiliar with the history of American military, the Navy was flying planes before the Air Force even existed as a separate branch of the U.S. armed forces. In 1971 the Navy was still the U.S. leader when it came to aircraft, but the Air Force wanted to be in charge of America's fledgling space program, so a space mission simulator had been installed in the school, one of the first of its kind, offering simulations of an entire space mission, including rendezvous and docking in space.

Later that month, at the crack of dawn on July 26, my family and I watched the launch of *Apollo 15* on a portable TV while on the beach in Carpenteria, California. I was familiar with every step of the launch and watched carefully, but I felt no remorse for not being a part of it. A mere two years earlier it had been me sitting atop a rocket, ready to travel to the moon, but I was now content to be sitting on the beach— or at least I thought I was.

As the commandant of the test pilot school, I was the chief administrator, but I knew the test pilot instructors in the program would probably be teaching me a lot, not having been a test pilot myself. None of the students seemed to mind my lack of test-pilot experience; quite the contrary, they seemed honored to know me. They were a good group of students, and I enjoyed getting to know and encourage them, along with interacting with the instructors and occasionally flying myself. At the time, we were having the students fly advanced supersonic F-104 Starfighter aircraft and the modified NF-104 aerospace trainer rocket-powered jets that could soar to over 100,000 feet, in effect becoming spacecraft in thin air. The exercises tested each student's ability to fly with extraordinary precision under unusual conditions, including zero gravity, high-angle maneuvers, and steep landing approaches, and required the pilots to report on the performance of the plane in those conditions.

As much as the students appreciated my presence out in the field to observe their test flights, and as much as they were fascinated by my moonwalking experiences, they were equally, if not more, intrigued by my early years as a fighter pilot. While a number of them had joined the military to become fighter pilots, few of them had actually seen combat action at war. I had.

I graduated from West Point, number three in my class in June 1951. Thanks to my high academic rating, I had several choices for pursuing my military career. The Air Force was most attractive to me because I had wanted to fly from the time I took my first flight with my father when I was only two years old.

From West Point I went straight to flight training school at Bartow Air Force Base in Florida, and then to Brian Air Force Base in Texas, where I earned my wings. The Air Force needed pilots of all sorts, but my goal was to become a jet fighter pilot. The competition was intense, and after eighteen months of concentrated training, I qualified as an F-86 Sabre jet pilot.

The Korean War—or the Korean Conflict, as it is often referred to today, although it was definitely a war to those who fought in it— had been raging for a full year, ever since Communist North Korea, equipped by the Soviet Union, invaded Democratic South Korea, backed by the United States. Before long the Chinese also entered the fighting, and it looked as though things could escalate further at any time.

Not surprisingly, with Korea still a powder keg, I put in for combat duty, but by the time I arrived there in December 1952, the ground war had slowed and cease-fire negotiations were underway. The battle in the air was still furious, but because their defenses were disintegrating, the North Koreans, Chinese, and Soviets had moved their air bases as far north as possible, north of the Yalu River, the dividing line between Korea and China. American commanders ordered their pilots not to cross the Yalu into China, even if engaged in aerial combat. But the standing orders were often ignored, as U.S. fighter jets gave chase to Soviet-built MiG-15s, their elusive and dangerous adversaries.

I was assigned to the 16th Fighter Squadron of the 51st Interceptor Wing at Suwon Air Base, located about twenty miles south of Seoul. By then, American pilots regularly flew all the way north to the Yalu, where they could often catch the enemy at lower altitudes, or better yet, still on the ground at their air bases. We affectionately but respect-fully referred to that area as "MiG Alley."

I flew a total of sixty-six combat missions over the war zone while I was stationed in Korea. Many days, I was simply patrolling the air, hunting for MiGs that might be heading south toward our troops, often seeing little more than the mountainous terrain below and the blue sky above. It was never a joy ride, though. I was constantly on alert. Occasionally, I'd spot white exhaust contrails high overhead, or the glint of the sun reflecting off a wing below, and I knew that I was not alone in the sky. MiGs were nearby, lurking, looking for their opportunity to blow me to bits.

The Soviet-built MiG-15 was a formidable foe, and had a definite advantage over our American-built fighter jets. In a dogfight, the planes were closely matched because of our technical superiority, but the MiG could fly more than 2,000 feet higher than our F-86 Sabres, which had a maximum altitude of 49,000 feet. They could also fly faster, since their planes were stripped down for combat and carried a smaller fuel load than ours. The MiG was a wicked fighting machine, too, fortified with a 37-millimeter cannon that could send an F-86 screaming to the ground with one strike; it also housed two 23-millimeter automatic guns that could make Swiss cheese out of a plane in a single burst of fire. Because of the MiG's deadly firepower, the one thing a U.S. pilot avoided at all costs was letting a MiG get on his tail.

I shot down two MiGs while in Korea, my first kill coming on May 14, 1953. The guys at Edwards loved to hear me tell about it, always wanting me to embellish the story, but I never did, because it was a rather inglorious engagement. I was flying just south of the Yalu when I spotted an enemy fighter jet flying straight and level, probably oblivious to my existence. I trained my guns on him and fired. The MiG spun hard and headed for the ground, the pilot quickly ejecting from the cockpit. The camera on my gun recorded the entire incident, clearly showing the plane being destroyed and the pilot's desperate ejection. Photo frames from that film sequence appeared in the next issue of *Life* magazine. When my father found out that I was the one who had brought down the MiG, he could not have been more proud.

My second battle with a MiG nearly took me out of this world—literally. On June 7, 1953, I was scheduled for a mission with three other pilots attached to the 16th "Blue Tail" Squadron (the tails on our planes had a checkerboard design with a blue stripe), but as we taxied to the runway, my number four wingman aborted, leaving three of us in the formation. Just ahead of us, taking off from the runway, were four Sabre Jets from the 39th "Yellow Tail" Squadron in a Tiger flight formation commanded by Marine Captain Jack Bolt. But their number four pilot also aborted, so I radioed my Wing Commander to take leave and join up with the Yellow Tails. I took to the air in formation with the Tigers, but they were flying the new F-model Sabres with a 20-knot airspeed advantage, with more power and a bigger wing than my F-86 E-model. Try as I might, I was having a hard time keeping up with them.

When Bolt's team dove toward a broad valley farther to the north, I followed them all the way, trailing at a distance. I soon found myself flying north of the Yalu, alone. With my airspeed indicator pegged, and the F-86 approaching Mach 1, the speed of sound—a prohibited speed for my Sabre—I streaked below 15,000 feet. My aircraft began to roll and became more difficult to control as I pushed it to the limit, following the Tigers into heavier air. I grasped the control stick as hard as I could, holding on for dear life, trying to maintain my airplane's stability. Finally, the heavier air slowed me down enough that I could regain control of the aircraft, but I was still flying mighty fast.

Ahead of me, Bolt and Company leveled out at about 5,000 feet, as they streaked right across an enemy airfield, blasting away. Some MiGs immediately rose to do battle, while others were racing along the runway taxi ramps, preparing to take off.

"Tiger Three," I called, "I'm behind you."

Just then, from seemingly out of nowhere, a fighter jet angled across my sight from right to left, climbing toward the Tigers. The plane was not one of ours. I tried to remain calm, knowing that if he kept going, he'd fly right into my gunsight. But if I didn't get him, he'd be on the Tigers' tail. Not good.

I pulled back on my controls, trying to slow down before he saw me, but I was too late. The MiG pilot spotted me and had banked hard in my direction; he was coming after me. I quickly realized as I saw him turn that as fast as I was moving, I was going to fly right past him, and then the faster, lighter MiG would be sweeping around behind me, precisely where I didn't want him to be. My only hope of avoiding being hit was a high-G right turn that would send me cutting across him as he banked to the left. It was a dangerous move that pilots called a "scissors," in which two opposing aircraft keep crossing back and forth, each trying to turn more sharply than the other, hoping to get the advantage.

The MiG and I ripped through one set of scissors turns and banked so steeply on our sides that our wing tips nearly pointed straight down toward the ground. In my peripheral vision, I saw the enemy runway flash by, then trees and green fields below. But I had no time for sight-seeing. The MiG pilot had rolled off to avoid a high ridge below us. This was my chance; it might be my only chance, since I was flying so close to the enemy base. Enemy anti-aircraft fire filled the air around us.

I tried to fire, but the aiming dot on my gunsight jammed, probably due to the violent twists and turns I'd been putting the plane through. With my left wing tip still pointing toward the Earth, I used my plane's nose as a sight and pressed hard on my trigger, firing a short burst from my .50 caliber machine guns. I saw something spark on the MiG. I rolled off my wing back to a position parallel to the ground, and slammed the throttle of the F-86 wide open so I could shoot across the ridge behind him. I saw the MiG in front of me, in a steep right turn. One of us was going down. I fired while he was still climbing and saw the tracers sparking across his wing. *Don't let him go!* Smoke billowed from his wing. The MiG rolled out of the turn and dove. As he did, I fired two more rapid bursts of ammunition. The enemy plane's nose came up as my shots struck and his plane looked as though it was momentarily suspended in the air as he stalled out.

I saw the canopy over his head pop open and the flash of his ejection flare. The pilot sailed out of the plane and was gone. Whether his chute had time to open, I'll never know. I did see the now pilotless MiG slow in the air, heel, and then plunge toward the Earth.

I would have loved to have stuck around a while to determine the damages I had inflicted, but I was about twenty miles north of the Yalu, close to the enemy base, and there were more Russian and Chinese planes in the skies, with still more rising off the runway. I was low on fuel too. I turned south and climbed, picking up "the Manchurian Express," a jet stream that helped whisk me down the Korean peninsula toward home.

As I landed my aircraft, I knew I now had a conundrum. I was so thrilled that I had downed a MiG, but if my commanders discovered that I'd been above the Yalu when I brought it down, it would not be an officially recognized kill. My buddies knew, though, slapping me on the back and cheering me on. It was time for a drink. No, actually it was time for several drinks, and I enjoyed every one.

When my gun camera film was examined, it was clear that I had destroyed the MiG but it was unclear which side of the Yalu River I had been on when I brought it down. The Air Force presented me with an Oak Leaf Cluster as well as the Distinguished Flying Cross I had received for dropping the first MiG.

After Korea, I was assigned to Nellis Air Force Base in Nevada as a gunnery instructor. During that time, I married Joan in 1954, and she accompanied me on my three-year assignment in Bitburg, Germany, in 1955, where our first son, Mike, was born. I flew F-100 Super Sabres while there, and we trained regularly on how we could deliver nuclear weapons inside the Iron Curtain, the Soviet-controlled bloc of communist nations. I had a number of tension-packed, harrowing experiences there, too, but nothing thrilled the guys at the test pilot school as much as those life or death days in Korea.

I enjoyed sharing with the test pilots some of the lessons I learned during that time, most notably, a healthy respect for Russian built aircraft—a grudging admiration that I still maintain today. While it was commonplace for many Americans to deride the Soviets' technology as grossly inferior to our own, I did not find that to be accurate. While their airplanes weren't as fancy or elaborate as ours, they certainly got the job done. The same could be said of their spacecraft. Every time we have underestimated the Russians, they have surprised us.

Although the Korean War will never receive as much space in the history books as World War I or II, besides keeping the communists from overrunning South Korea, it served American interests in a manner that often goes unnoticed. Namely, most of America's early astronauts were veterans of the Korean War, and the experience of aerial combat left indelible impressions on all of us. Gus Grissom flew one hundred combat missions in Korea; Wally Schirra flew ninety; Jim McDivitt flew 145 missions, some in F-80s and some in the Sabres similar to what I flew. John Glenn was a Marine pilot attached to our Air Force wing, and he shot down three MiGs. *Apollo 11* commander Neil Armstrong served in Korea, too, as a Navy pilot aboard the aircraft carrier *Essex*. Neil flew seventy-eight combat missions and once had to eject when his wing caught a cable stretched over a bridge as a protective device. Fortunately, he was able to make it back to American-controlled territory before his plane went down.

For me, the experience as a fighter pilot was great training for my future role as an astronaut. Making quick decisions, many of which were life or death, as well as seeing the best way to rendezvous with friendly aircraft and to avoid the enemy, all played into my future studies at MIT, and my later contributions at NASA. For all of us, flying combat missions in Korea required concentration and skill far beyond anything we could have experienced otherwise. We had to face our fears and overcome them; we had to remain calm in the face of dangerous, high-altitude, high-speed situations. Our experience in Korea also immersed us in the competitive U.S.–Soviet conflict that would permeate the space race during the next several decades.

I returned home a hero—especially according to my father—with a renewed sense of patriotism and with confidence that I could do anything I put my mind to. So when the Air Force offered to pay for my graduate studies at MIT, I jumped at the opportunity. My mettle had been tested and found solid. My Air Force training and experiences would color everything I did for the rest of my life. Now that I had resumed my Air Force career as commandant of the test pilot school, it seemed I had come full circle, and my students never tired of hearing my fighter pilot combat stories.

◑　○　◑

EARLY IN MY tenure at Edwards, I learned that a trip to Europe for 1971 had been approved, and that I would be leading a group of our upper-class test pilot students, as well as instructors, to visit test flight schools in England and test centers in France, Italy, and Germany, to study how they ran their schools in comparison with ours. While we were gone, I left our school in the capable hands of my deputy officer, Ted Twinting. An accomplished test pilot himself, and well up to the job of keeping the program running without a hitch, Ted really set the tone for the place, whether I was there or not, and he did an excellent job. I had no qualms about leaving him in charge.

My only reticence about the trip was dealing with the media swarm that was sure to surround us. Although I had grown accustomed to being inundated by questions, blinded by camera flashes, and besieged with autograph seekers, my personality still did not gravitate naturally to such clamor. During the world tour, Neil, Mike, and I at least had some help in fending off the more aggressive members of the media. On this trip I'd be handling the press largely on my own.

We began our trip in Rome, where we had a vigorous schedule of briefings and testing aircraft, as well as a full social card. At the test center, they had a G-91 single-seat Italian fighter, and our hosts offered to allow me to fly it. "Since you've been to the moon, we want to give you the honor of flying our new airplane," the commandant said.

I'd never trained on such a plane, and there was no time to learn. Since it was a single-seater, I'd be on my own, with no instructor or copilot. Several of my instructors and students looked at me as though to say, "Are you really sure you want to do that?" I talked to the operations officer, and he gave me a quick rundown on how to start the plane and how the controls worked. It seemed similar to the T-38 airplane that we flew from Houston, so I said, "Sure, I'd love to take it for a ride." The rest of our group went back to town, but I stayed over and studied the plane's manual a bit, then took it up for a whirl. Flying a plane like that without hours of instruction would never happen in the U.S. Air Force, so it was quite a treat to fly the G-91 with just an overview. The plane had a quickness that inspired me, so I pulled some precision maneuvers—and did so with glee.

Later that afternoon, I called the sultry Italian actress Gina Lollobrigida, and told her I was in town. I had met Gina during the world tour following Apollo 11, and she sounded delighted to hear from me. "Come on by," she said, "I'll be here this afternoon." A staff driver and I began searching for her villa on Via Appia. We were about to give up when we saw several television vans parked in front of the entrance to a villa. Sure enough, the paparazzi told us that we were at the right house. I had changed out of my uniform before leaving the air base, and was wearing casual clothes, so I didn't think anyone would recognize me.

"Drive up as close to the entrance as possible, and wait for me here," I told the driver. As soon as I got out of the military staff car, one of the media people saw me and said, "Hey, I know you." I kept walking and didn't respond. "I know you!" the guy said again, following after me, his face beaming with the excitement of presumed recognition. "You're Neil Armstrong!"

I smiled to myself and kept on walking.

Gina greeted me warmly and we spent a marvelous few hours getting reacquainted. I would have preferred to stay right there, but the U.S. embassy attaché had informed us that our hosts had planned an escorted tour of Roman night life. Our hosts meant well, but they hadn't anticipated the press of paparazzi following us everywhere, blocking our path, trying to get pictures and statements from me. It had been only two years since I walked on the moon, so the interest level was still high, especially for photographers who specialized in capturing celebrity photos.

The next night during our visit, Italian general Giorgio Santucci invited me to join him for the premiere opening of the Number One Club in Rome. It was a celebrity-laden event, and Giorgio and I arrived early, before most of the stars showed up. In an attempt to remain inconspicuous, we sat down at a table off to the side of the room. The paparazzi proved particularly relentless. They were far more than annoying; they were downright obnoxious. Before long, a photographer recognized me, then another; soon we were surrounded by paparazzi. Giorgio looked at me and said, "I'm sorry, Buzz, but I think it is time to leave."

We got up and headed toward the door, when a photographer jumped in front of me, purposely blocking the way. I pushed him aside and he tumbled backward onto the floor. Giorgio and I elbowed our way out of the building; I was careful not to spill my Scotch on the rocks that I carried along with me. Outside, the paparazzi continued to swarm around us until we finally made our way down the street to the car. Giorgio jumped in the driver's side and I hopped in the passenger's side, and he revved the engine. One overly zealous reporter planted himself in front of our car, refusing to budge while snapping photos of me through the windshield. In exasperation, I raised my hand and gave him the finger. As soon as I saw the flash go off, I knew that I had made a gigantic mistake. When we got back to the hotel, my first call was to the attaché at the embassy to see if he could quash the picture. He must have been successful, because the photo never showed up in the States.

Our reception in France was much more subdued, though I had to watch out for the Swedish flight attendants my students managed to meet up with. In Germany, a large crowd and a slew of reporters and television cameras greeted us upon our arrival. I answered a few questions, but made it clear that I was visiting with a group of students and would not be granting interviews. This was supposed to be a quiet, educational trip; the last thing I needed back home was my name in the papers.

Overall, the trip was fascinating and we developed a tremendous rapport with our fellow pilots. One major difference was that the Europeans quickly clamored around any and every new plane that landed on their airstrips, hoping for a chance to inspect the plane and possibly even fly it. By contrast, our American test pilots were extremely restricted as to what planes they were allowed to fly.

While in Europe, we were exposed to more than twenty-five new aircraft, and each of our pilots flew seven or more European planes. My group of students and instructors arrived back at Edwards tired but enthusiastic. From an educational standpoint, we all regarded the trip as a tremendous success. We were excited to make our report to our immediate superiors, General Bob White and his staff, who would in turn pass on our recommendations to the top brass in Washington. Basically, our report suggested that we could improve our military pilot training program by doing something similar to what the British did, allowing our test pilots to train on a wide variety of aircraft. Unfortunately, our report advocating a greater variety of training planes came at a time when the Air Force was about to announce a draconian cutback in the number of planes test pilots could fly. It was a self-defeating measure. We were, after all, training *test pilots* at our school. We weren't teaching them how to *fly* planes; we were teaching them how to *test* planes. How could a good test pilot feel confident to test new types of aircraft, not to mention future spacecraft, if he or she was permitted to fly only a few types of planes over and over again?

It was ludicrous. But the Air Force was insistent on reducing the variety of planes on which pilots trained, thereby making crashes less likely.

When our report suggested using a broader variety of planes, General White's staff balked. They thought it might draw unwanted attention to the test pilot crashes at Edwards and urged the general to nix the report. I countered with the case of the British, who tested a variety of planes and did more hazardous spins during their training exercises, yet their safety record was similar to our own. General White and his staff didn't see it that way, and the report was filed away in obscurity.

The disappointment that the Air Force was not even going to submit the report of what we had learned in Europe sapped our students' and instructors' morale, and sent me into a personal tailspin. If my own commanding officer did not see merit in my ideas and suggestions, why waste our time and the taxpayers' money playing silly airplane games? What good was I doing here, anyhow?

Throughout September, after returning to Edwards from Europe, I struggled with my role as commandant. When I went to my office, I looked at the stack of paperwork on my desk and it seemed overwhelming. I could fly fighter jets and I could walk on the moon, but none of my training had prepared me to run a test pilot school. What was I really accomplishing if I couldn't change anything for the better as commandant of these test pilots? I felt no purpose, and I was having difficulty performing my regular duties. I was distracted, discouraged, and disappointed. I was sinking into despair, and I did not see any hope or reason to try. Maybe I needed a fresh challenge, and the test pilot school was *not* the answer.

Gradually, I could sense myself slipping into a blue funk, but I felt powerless to thwart the downward slide. At home, I became a recluse. I hardly talked to Joan or the kids. I did nothing but sit in front of the television set, watching the news aimlessly for hours on end. I couldn't sleep, so I stayed up late each night, which only exacerbated my edginess the following day. Some days I'd go in to the office, only to leave early, bringing home a pile of work that I would then let sit untouched on the counter. Emotionally, I felt like a mass of tangled wires inside, and physically there was an inexplicable pain in my shoulder and neck that seemed to be intensifying with each day.

I considered going for help, but I didn't know where to go or what to ask for. The Air Force provided medical care, so they might be able to help my neck and back problems, but if I sought treatment for my mental and emotional traumas, a report would surely make its way into my official permanent records, thwarting any hopes I might have for future promotions. The public's perception regarding rehabilitation programs in the early 1970s was quite different from what it is today. Now, when a high-profile celebrity seeks help to overcome an addiction or depression, we pat that person on the back. In the early 1970s, certainly in the military, to let it be known that you were seeking professional help for mental illness or alcoholism or drug addiction was a death knell to your career and certain to ostracize you socially. No, I decided, I'd suffer through on my own, hoping things would get better, and that I could weather this colossal midlife crisis. But, in truth, I had little confidence that anything would improve.

Finally I went to see the base flight surgeon, Dr. Dick Slarve, a colonel who specialized in working with pilots. As a flight surgeon he wielded the power to ground any pilot, including me, whom he felt was not medically ready to fly. Dick had accompanied our group on the trip to Europe, and we had gotten to know each other. I liked him and, more important, I trusted him. I felt sure that I could talk to him about my inner turmoil as well as the physical pains I was experiencing. By this time I knew that I desperately needed help, even if my malady went on my permanent records, and I expressed that to Dick. Since coming to Edwards, I told him, I had begun to experience two problems: reoccurring episodes of the blues, and a very real physical manifestation of pain in my neck and shoulder. I thought perhaps that I needed a back operation because of the numbness I was feeling in my back and some of the sensations I felt in my arm, and to some extent in my leg as well. I knew that Mike Collins had undergone a back operation that had also alleviated a leg problem, and he had returned successfully to the astronaut corps. Maybe, if there was a physical malady, the doctors could fix it, and I could get back to work. I asked Dick about the possibility of going to the Air Force hospital in San Antonio to be checked out for my shoulder and neck problem—and perhaps any other problems.

We talked for a while, and he suggested that we call Dr. Carlos Perry at Brooks Medical Center in San Antonio. Dr. Perry was an Air Force doctor, but he could be discreet; he could oversee exams of my physical condition, and decide what was the best course for dealing with my mental distress. We set an appointment with Dr. Perry for October 26, 1971, in San Antonio.

A few days before that date, my West Point class of '51 was gathering in New York for its twentieth class reunion. I had little desire to see old classmates, but it seemed like a good time for Joan and me to go home for a visit, and perhaps have the opportunity to inform our families that I planned to seek professional help. We didn't want them learning about my going to Brooks secondhand. We visited Joan's dad and stepmother in Ho-Ho-Kus, New Jersey, where I had a chance to have a good heart-to-heart talk with Mike Archer, Joan's father. Mike and I had always gotten along well, even though he could probably guess from Joan's disposition that things were not great for us at home. Nevertheless, Mike and I sat up one night talking about my concerns. I told him about my neck and shoulder pain, and about the lack of any sense of accomplishment I was experiencing at Edwards. Mike tried to offer advice and suggestions, but I could tell he was baffled. He couldn't understand why a guy like me, who had been so goal-oriented all his life, simply could not find another nut to crack. Surely there were other things in the Air Force for me to accomplish.

The next morning I refused to get out of bed and drive to West Point. "I don't feel like going," I told Joan. "Spend the day with your family and I'll stay right here."

Joan wouldn't hear of it. She enlisted her father's help, and between the two of them, they cajoled me into making the trip. We arrived late, having stopped along the way several times ostensibly to view the multicolored fall foliage, but mostly for me to breathe and clear my head. By the time we got to West Point, the homecoming football game had already started, so Joan and I slipped into our seats inconspicuously. After the game, Joan encouraged me to attend my class reception, and it turned out to be an enjoyable evening.

The following day, Joan returned to her family's home in New Jersey and I went into New York City for a directors' meeting of the cable television company on whose board I sat. The new chairman of the board had asked that directors not involved with the company should resign, and I was only too happy to comply. I was convinced the company was simply using my Apollo 11 fame in an effort to stave off an inevitable financial collapse. I left the meeting and returned to the hotel where I had checked in, but didn't stay for long.

I hadn't seen Marianne in months, so I wasted no time in heading for her apartment. She greeted me passionately at first, but before long our conversation took an unexpected twist. "Buzz, I'm thinking of getting married again," she said almost casually, and then informed me that a rival had actually proposed to her. Whether Marianne's statement was sincere or merely meant to prod me to action, I'll never know. Regardless, her words sent a surge of panic through my system, and I began offering her everything but the moon. "I'll change, I'll get some help, I'll divorce Joan—anything, Marianne, but please don't do anything rash. Give me a chance to get things in order, just wait for me."

If I was making only half-promises, Marianne was offering even less. "I might wait a bit, but not for long, Buzz. Make up your mind."

● ○ ●

I LEFT NEW YORK and headed back to New Jersey to meet Joan, her dad, and my father. Trying to explain my mental and emotional troughs to Joan's dad was tough enough; hoping that my father might understand was an exercise in futility. I could have made his arguments for him: "Depression? What's depression? There's no such thing. People didn't get depressed in my day, especially soldiers; they just got up and got going and toughed it out. Why, look at me. Do you think life has been easy for me? No. And what about you? You have a reputation to uphold. You are not only a pilot, you're an MIT scientist, an astronaut who walked on the moon!"

Dad became especially agitated when Joan and I told him about the appointment in San Antonio, and he encouraged me to cancel it. "Son, don't you know what that could do to your career? That could ruin you!"

I didn't even have time to respond before Joan jumped in adamantly. "I don't care whether going for help has an adverse effect on Buzz's career or not. I just want Buzz to feel good and get well."

For a few long moments we all sat silently, then, one by one, we drifted off to bed. The decision had been made.

The next morning Joan and I flew from Newark to San Antonio to keep the appointment with Dr. Perry. We unloaded on the doctor, telling him everything we could in our efforts to explain the changes we both recognized since I had returned from the moon. The nights of restless thoughts tormenting me with questions. The mornings I woke up with no answers. What was I going to accomplish that day? What was my assigned mission? If it wasn't something extraordinary, why even get out of bed?

Dr. Perry didn't seem to think there was anything wrong with me physically, so he focused more on the issues of emotional and mental stress. Then he surprised me by turning to Joan, probing into her thoughts and feelings about our marriage. Joan answered the doctor's questions so straightforwardly, I turned to look at her, and when I did, I noticed the tears trickling down her cheeks. For the first time it hit me just how much of a toll my emotional struggles had taken on Joan. "For some time now, I have been considering a divorce," she admitted to the doctor and me at the same time, "for the sake of the children." Dr. Perry didn't seem nearly as surprised as I was. Joan continued, "But I don't want to even think about a divorce right now. I want Buzz to get well. We can decide what to do about our marriage later, but right now I just want my husband well."

I didn't say a word to Joan or to the doctor the entire time Joan spoke. I simply sat there, staring at my hands. Dr. Perry quickly concluded our session and promised that he would be in touch with us within a week or so. I urged him to get me in sooner if possible.

Joan and I spoke very little as we returned to Edwards, but we had a glimmer of hope that something good might come from our attempt to get help. Two days later I went to see Dr. Slarve again, insisting that I needed help immediately, not a few days from now as Dr. Perry had promised. Dick informed me that he had been in contact with Dr. Don Flinn, the Air Force psychiatrist who just a few years earlier had examined me and declared me mentally and emotionally fit to be an astronaut. Dr. Flinn was no longer working directly with NASA, but was nearby on the staff of UCLA's neuropsychiatric institute. Dick let me know that Dr. Flinn wanted to see me. I hadn't seen Flinn in eight years, but I figured I had nothing to lose. More than anyone, he probably had some insight into what goes on inside an astronaut's head. Maybe he could help.

Dick called Flinn back and set up an appointment for that same afternoon. Dick had no sooner hung up the phone when the analytical part of me kicked into gear. Wait a minute! Flinn was the doctor who had certified me as competent to be an astronaut; it might not look too good on his record for me to be anything less than one of the supermen NASA projected us to be.

But my meeting with Dr. Flinn proved uneventful and of little consequence, other than speeding up the process of getting me back to see Dr. Perry in San Antonio. He talked with me for less than an hour, then walked me to the staff driver and instructed him to stay with me until I boarded my plane.

It was late when I got off the plane in Texas, but Dr. Perry was waiting for me at the airport. The doctor took me directly to Wilford Hall, the hospital adjoining Brooks Air Force Base. Ostensibly I was there to be examined for the pain in my shoulder and neck, so I was given a private room on the second floor in the section with patients who had suffered neck injuries. Two floors up was the psychiatric ward, where I might just happen to stop by.

The nurse gave me a sleeping pill, which I gladly accepted. I awakened the following morning, half expecting to find myself in a straitjacket in some sort of mental hospital, but I quickly discovered that Wilford Hall looked and functioned much like any other military hospital. Nurses bustled in and out of rooms, doctors passed while staring at their clipboards, and recovering patients waved to each other as they hobbled up and down the sun-drenched halls.

That morning the doctors gave me a complete physical examination, and took extensive X-rays of my neck and shoulder areas. The neck scans proved inconclusive; the doctors couldn't find anything wrong. Years later I underwent several neck operations, so maybe the doctors at Brooks missed something. Could the problem in my neck have been caused by the g forces I had endured as an astronaut? Nobody could tell, and nobody at NASA was concerned enough to find out.

That first afternoon the doctors put me through a series of mental aptitude and psychological tests. Ironically, they were the same types of exams I had taken when Dr. Flinn was testing me to ascertain my readiness to be an astronaut nearly a decade earlier.

The doctors at Brooks quickly ascertained that my problems more likely stemmed from mental and emotional stress than from any physical ailment. I stayed in my private room on the second floor for my neck treatments, but several times a day I slipped upstairs to the psychiatric ward. The real reason for my visit was kept a secret, although no doubt more people were aware of it than I realized at the time.

On Saturday morning I met Colonel John Sparks, chief of psychiatry at Wilford Hall, and the primary doctor handling my case. Sparks was an easygoing, friendly sort of man, and seemed more like a drinking buddy than a "talk and pills" psychiatrist. He informed me that my psychological tests had yielded almost the same results as when I had first applied to be an astronaut. Whatever was causing my mental trauma, it was not a change in mental acuity. Sparks said that they wanted to run me through some more tests. He and I would not begin working together in earnest until Monday.

I took that as a good sign. At least the doctors weren't wringing their hands and saying, "We've got to get Aldrin fixed, *now!*"

That first weekend at Brooks, I grew restless at the prospect of a weekend of inactivity at the hospital, so I asked the nurse for a weekend pass. The nurse looked up my chart, and since I had not yet been diagnosed with any illness and had not been admitted as a psychiatric patient, she filled out a form and handed me a pass, signed by Dr. Sparks that allowed me to leave. A few days earlier I'd been so dazed and distressed I probably could not have found Wilford Hall, and now they were letting me out on my own recognizance!

I didn't really have any place in particular to go, but since I was in Texas, I decided to call my friend and former neighbor in Houston, Merv Hughs. Merv invited me over to visit, so I hopped on a plane from San Antonio. Late Saturday night, liberally lubricated by Scotch, I confided to Merv the real reason why I was in Texas. Merv looked at me quizzically and seemed somewhat surprised. I enjoyed the weekend with Merv, and visited with other friends as well, including Dean Woodruff, the minister of the church my family and I had attended while I worked in the space program. I let Dean in on my clandestine hospital stay, and he, too, seemed nonplussed. "Depression? You're the last guy I'd ever figure to be depressed," Dean chortled. By midday Sunday, I returned to Wilford Hall and, for no apparent reason, once again found myself strangely in a down mood. Maybe being around "space stuff" had energized me, but then I had to walk away from it and head back to Wilford Hall. I was relieved to be away from Edwards, but I was frustrated that I had no future that I regarded worth pursuing.

Back at Wilford Hall, I had given no indication that I might also be concerned about alcoholism, and nobody suggested at the time that I had such a problem. In fact, I kept a bottle of Scotch with me in my duffel bag. Occasionally the colonel came around to visit, and almost instinctively I hid the bottle when I saw him.

Monday morning I began working with Dr. Sparks, attempting to verbalize what I was feeling. For those who know me now, it might be hard to imagine Buzz Aldrin as speechless, but expressing those deep, innermost thoughts, fears, and feelings did not come easily to me. Dr. Sparks sat at his desk, asking questions, making notes, and listening intently. I sat opposite him in a large, comfortable, padded green chair, rather than on the stereotypical psychiatrist's couch. For the first few days we met in the mornings and afternoons, then, after two weeks, we had sessions only in the mornings. Early on, the doctors fed me a steady diet of antidepressants, and combined with the Scotch I managed to have brought in to me by a cooperative nurse, my tongue loosened.

Dr. Sparks and I reviewed every aspect of my life, from early childhood to the present. We talked a lot about my father, his influence in my life, and his lofty expectations of me. Over the years my dad had developed a reputation as being an overbearing tyrant in my life. That simply was not the case, and I attempted to explain as much to Dr. Sparks. My dad was a military man, and yes, he did have high expectations for me. Moreover, he was not good at giving praise and encouragement. But he did not rule me with an iron fist. For instance, he had wanted me to attend the Naval Academy; instead I'd attended West Point. My father had wanted me to fly bombers stateside as part of our national air defense; I had opted for a tour of duty as a fighter pilot in

Korea. Nor was my father intent on my becoming an astronaut, but I chose my own way once again. My father's opinion of what I ought to be doing with my life was not always in sync with my own, but I believe he was nonetheless supportive. Like many parents, my father may have tried to live vicariously through me, hoping to see his own dreams fulfilled through his son, but to this day I am convinced he wanted only the best for me. He never quite understood that what I needed most was his smile of approval. Even years later, when I legally changed my name from Edwin Eugene Aldrin Jr. to Buzz Aldrin, it was not an affront to my father. It was more a matter of convenience, since I'd been known as "Buzz" from childhood.

Over the days and weeks that Dr. Sparks and I talked, we probed my deepest fears, fears so strong that I had never mentioned them to anyone. I told him about my maternal grandfather, a military chaplain, who, after a long period of melancholy, chose to end his life by putting a gun to his mouth. I told him about my mother, Marion Moon Aldrin, who in the last years of her life had been morose and unhappy most of the time, except when her grandchildren visited during family gatherings. My mother once took too many sleeping pills, and my father had to rush her to the hospital. We all pretended that her overdosing was accidental, but I think we knew that wasn't the case. In May 1968, Mother's second attempt at an overdose proved fatal. Even then, my family and I preferred living in denial and never openly spoke of how she had died. We asked the coroner to list her cause of death as cardiac arrest, and the coroner graciously complied. Part of what I revealed to the doctor was information passed on to me from my oldest sister, who told me that our mother had great difficulty dealing with the fame that came along with my successful 1966 Gemini 12 space mission. When I returned to my hometown for a celebration, the enormous attention heaped on my family made my mother extremely uncomfortable. To conceal her feelings, she wore dark glasses in public, including at our Gemini 12 "welcome home" event, held during the evening. My sister confided that our mother did not think she could handle the acclaim that was sure to accompany a son who had landed on the moon. She took her life instead, and I carried that extra burden of responsibility in my heart and mind.

Coming to grips with the truth about my mother's death brought me to the crux of my concern: My grandfather had committed suicide; my mother had committed suicide. Several close relatives in our family had ended their own lives. I looked at Dr. Sparks imploringly. "Am I next?"

Dr. Sparks couldn't say. "Do you think you are suicidal now?" he asked.

"No, I don't think so."

"How can you tell?"

"I couldn't possibly kill myself because I couldn't possibly make up my mind how to do it!"

Dr. Sparks and I both laughed. We became friends that day, and the doctor promised to delve into my concerns about inherited suicidal tendencies or other predispositions toward suicidal behavior.

● ○ ●

I SPENT NEARLY four weeks at Wilford Hall. Meanwhile, back at Edwards, General White covered for me, and Ted Twinting kept the program flying right on schedule. Few people, if any, thought it unusual that I was away from the base for so long. They assumed that I was on some important business, and I was.

The doctors at Wilford Hall used a combination of psychiatric therapy, relaxation techniques, and strong medication to get me back on an even keel. It seemed more and more obvious to all of us that my life prior to Apollo 11 had been highly structured and goal-oriented, from growing up in a military family to attending West Point, to becoming a fighter pilot, to earning my doctorate at MIT, to joining the astronaut program. I'd always had recognizable goals, and for the most part I had attained them. Although I had not grown up with the dream of going to the moon, when that became a goal of mine (and of America's) in the mid-sixties, I did it. Afterwards no other objective compared. Now, I was struggling to find a reason big enough to get me going again.

I contemplated leaving the Air Force and writing my autobiography. Other people who were not nearly as well known to the public as I was had written their stories, and there was still a fascination with our trip to the moon. Surely somebody would want to publish that story. Maybe writing the book might prove to be cathartic, freeing me from the past. More than anything, I wanted to begin life all over again— even if that meant leaving NASA, the Air Force, and my marriage.

●　○　●

ONE MORNING I walked into Dr. Sparks's office and told him that I had come to some conclusions. I wanted to start afresh; I planned to leave the Air Force, leave Joan, and marry Marianne. Dr. Sparks listened thoughtfully and then responded calmly, "I think you are making a mistake."

The doctor's advice notwithstanding, I called Marianne that night and told her of my decisions. I expected Marianne to be thrilled; instead, she was noncommittal; then, after a while, she admitted that she was close to marrying the man who had been pursuing her. Once again I practically begged her to wait, and she reluctantly agreed.

As Thanksgiving approached, I felt a strong desire to go home. Dr. Sparks was quick to remind me that just days ago, I'd been determined to divorce Joan. Nevertheless, he granted a ten-day pass, after which I was to return to the hospital for a complete analysis of how things had gone. "In the meantime," Dr. Sparks stressed, "if anything goes wrong, I want you to return immediately." I informed him that I planned to spend some time with my family and contact my father. I conveniently didn't mention Marianne.

My family welcomed me home enthusiastically, albeit somewhat awkwardly. Jan and Andy especially didn't seem to know how to take me. Was it safe to be loud around me? Was it okay to play the radio or turn on the television? Did I want to be around them? They didn't know, and I did little to reassure them. Our oldest son, Mike, seemed more aloof than usual, and Joan later told me that when she could bear the burden no longer by herself, she had acquiesced and informed

Mike of the real reason for my hospitalization. Mike had stood by her valiantly during the weeks I had been gone, and he seemed somewhat reluctant to give up his position as Joan's protector now that I was home.

Joan herself knew little of my progress. Her only contact with me had been by telephone, and my reports to her had vacillated with my moods. She tried desperately to maintain a sense of normalcy as we celebrated a traditional Thanksgiving, complete with a robust turkey dinner. Afterwards, I suggested to Joan that she and I go to Acapulco during the week after Christmas, without the kids, just the two of us. Joan no doubt thought that I intended to enjoy some time together to begin rebuilding our marriage. In fact, I planned to ask her for a divorce.

Feeling good about my renewal, I even went in to my office and began weeding through the piles of work and mail that had accumulated over the last month. I was encouraged that I did not feel overwhelmed by it all. I felt confident that when I returned, I could step right into the role of leading the test pilot school until my retirement, for which I was eligible as of June 1972, having completed twenty-one years of service in the Air Force. I hadn't really thought much about life after retirement, but now it seemed that was all I was thinking about. The process of treatment for my mental state forced me to reevaluate how I wanted to live my life.

I stayed with Joan and the kids for five days before heading to New Jersey to visit my father. Dad and I talked for two days, and although we didn't always see eye to eye, at least we were communicating. When I told him that I intended to retire from the Air Force, he disagreed adamantly, suggesting that I stay in the service until I became a general. I said no way.

"Well, what are you going to do when you retire?" he asked. "You have three children to put through college, you know. How are you going to make a living?"

"I'm going into business for myself," I heard myself saying, although I had no idea how I was going to bring those words to fruition. "Surely I have some knowledge and experience that will be valuable to somebody, maybe an aerospace company. I have some other ideas in mind—and I might even write a book."

My father remained unimpressed.

The following day, my sisters arrived, Madeline from Philadelphia and Fay Ann from Cincinnati. I took a deep breath, and in a rush I informed them that I was leaving the Air Force, divorcing Joan, and planning to remarry as soon as possible. My father and sisters stared at me in sadness and disbelief. Then, almost as if the dam of emotions had suddenly burst, they began imploring me to wait. "Be certain, Buzz, that you are healthy before you make such difficult decisions." But I did not intend to be deterred, and the more my loved ones insisted I wait, the louder and more indignant I grew. I retired to my room that night, convinced that I was finally in control of my own destiny.

My sisters and father, however, were so upset that when I awakened in the morning, my sisters had already departed, and my father had, too, leaving behind a note telling me to have a good time and be careful in New York. Basically he was saying, "Have a nice life."

As fast as I could pack my belongings, I was on my way to New York to see Marianne. Or so I thought. When I arrived at her apartment, Marianne refused to see me. Her other suitor had asked for her hand in marriage, and they were already planning a February wedding. I headed back to San Antonio, my spirit crushed.

At the end of another week, Dr. Sparks somewhat reluctantly agreed that I could return to Edwards and go back to work. I had been at Wilford Hall a total of four weeks, plus my ten-day leave. My prognosis, however, was not certain. "You may never have another depression," Dr. Sparks said. "Then again, you might, and you may need some form of treatment. There's no way to be sure what will happen. All I can tell you is to avoid any buildup of conflict in your life as much as possible."

From my perspective, I was convinced that I was well, that I had beaten the downward spiral of depression. Little did I realize that its relative—the decimating demon of alcoholism—was lurking in the shadows.

7

DUTY and
DILEMMA

I RETURNED TO MY RESPONSIBILITIES AT THE EDWARDS USAF Test Pilot School with new vigor and was happy to discover that many people did not even realize that I had been gone so long. That was in large part due to the outstanding management skills of Ted Twinting, my deputy officer. I had communicated with Ted by phone almost daily once I got into my medical routines at the hospital, and Ted kept the school right on schedule.

General Bob White, my commanding officer, welcomed me back somewhat uneasily. Known for being possessive of the lion's share of attention, Bob was a handsome, dapper officer, a renowned test pilot in his own right, who had earned his astronaut wings flying the X-15 on suborbital flights, as Chuck Yeager and Neil Armstrong had done. He was a highly decorated officer and deserved the respect of his men. I had gotten off to a less than stellar start with Bob through no fault of my own or his.

Prior to my actual taking command of the test pilot school, I was welcomed to Lancaster, California, the community adjacent to Edwards, at a dinner hosted by the local chamber of commerce. Unwittingly, someone seated General White and his wife at a lower table, and Joan and me at a higher table. The subtle implication was that Buzz Aldrin was more important than General Bob White. Such breaches of protocol just aren't done in military circles, and more than a few people thought that perhaps the general might not have appreciated my being at Edwards as much as he let on. Not because he didn't like me; in fact, Bob and I got along quite well. But my arrival created an imbalance in leadership since my celebrity was seen by some to supersede the general's well-established position in the esteem of his troops.

John Blaha, a student in the test pilot school when I arrived, and who later became an instructor, recalled:

> When Buzz arrived, everybody at that base turned their head and eyes away from Bob White and toward Buzz Aldrin. Buzz became the focal point, and the general was almost ignored. What I saw as a young captain was that the general moved to a less important position in the minds of the students at the center. It wasn't fair to Buzz or to General White, but it was probably unavoidable.

Nevertheless, at the banquet in Lancaster, General White presented me with an Air Force Legion of Merit award. The award was given for "exceptionally meritorious conduct" during my nearly eight years as an astronaut with NASA while assigned to the Air Force's first Special Activities Squadron at NASA's Manned Spacecraft Center in Houston. General White told the crowd, "Colonel Aldrin's leadership, diligence, and perseverance in mission planning and orbital rendezvous were contributions of major importance in the success of the Gemini and Apollo space programs."

I appreciated the general's kind accolades then, and I appreciated his willingness to help me get reacclimated at Edwards when I returned from four weeks in the hospital. Apart from my closest staff, thanks to General White and Ted Twinting, most of the instructional staff knew only that I had been away somewhere, but they were unaware why.

Going back home was tougher. Joan did her best to make everything seem normal, but our conversations were stilted. We didn't look each other in the eyes often. Our children slowly accepted that Dad had returned, and, after a few days of walking on eggshells, soon slipped back into their typical adolescent brother and sister banter.

I knew that Joan had been contemplating divorce; she had said so plainly during one of our initial conversations with Dr. Perry. I was conscious of my own ambivalence as well, and I had no clue how to ameliorate my troubled, convoluted emotions. As a sort of peace offering, I bought Joan an elegant blond mink coat. I wanted to placate some of the pain I had caused her in the past, as well as the pain I would no doubt inflict on her in the near future if I ended our marriage. The day after Christmas, Joan and I flew to Acapulco, where we were joined by Joan's stepbrother and his wife. The first few days of the trip were relaxing, but on December 29, Joan's and my seventeenth wedding anniversary, we all went to dinner together. As Joan raised her glass in a toast, she said, "Here's to seventeen, Buzz." Then, as the three of us lifted our glasses, Joan asked the question on everybody's mind: "Will we see eighteen?"

Joan's straightforward question took me by surprise. I looked at my raised glass, but said nothing. After a few awkward moments, I slowly put my glass back down on the table.

Joan burst into tears, and I'm not sure that I didn't join her, along with the in-laws. She hastily got up and left the table. My stunned in-laws sat in silence as I finished my drink and went to our room. By the time I got there, it was obvious that Joan had not stopped weeping. "I've known something was wrong, Buzz," she said softly. "I've known for a long time."

I wanted to express to Joan that it wasn't her fault, that I had been struggling to escape the quicksand that had been pulling me down for the past few years, and that even now I had no firm grasp on the present. Change in the future seemed to offer the only hope to me. "I can't go on like this," I said. We talked rather bluntly for the next several hours, and we both shed tears. Joan was a good woman and the mother of my children. She had been thrown into a world where neither of us knew how to function, but she had tried to make the best of it. I certainly didn't want to hurt her, but I told her honestly that I didn't see us growing old together, either. She seemed resigned that we would divorce and begin life anew, apart from each other. We were adults; we could handle this.

When I awakened the next morning, Joan was already sitting out on the balcony in the bright morning sun, having a cup of coffee. I went out and joined her, and she made no move to go inside. We sat silently for a while before Joan looked at me and asked, "Where will you go, now that you are going to begin again, alone?"

I dropped the bombshell. "I hope to marry Marianne, even though she is engaged to someone else."

Joan bristled. Then she lit into me. Who did I think I was, anyhow? Had I simply said I wanted a divorce, she probably could have handled that. These past years hadn't been easy for her, either. But to think that I was dumping her for another woman? Oh no! She wasn't going to roll over and play dead while I did that.

It would not be an amicable divorce. We went home together, walking around the same house but living on two different planets. Joan had asked that we not say anything to our children until we had a plan, but kids are smart; they know when Mom and Dad aren't doing well. Our kids easily picked up the tension between us.

Meanwhile, I tried to get in touch with Marianne, to no avail. She refused to answer any of my calls. When I finally reached a mutual friend, I was told that Marianne was getting married the following day. I was flabbergasted.

When I told Joan, she didn't gloat; it was just more sadness on top of sadness. Ironically, being jilted by Marianne somehow caused both Joan and me to reconsider our plans. Joan was a strong woman, and she handled things in her own way. We had nothing to lose and everything to gain by staying together. I was thinking more and more about retirement, so we decided to postpone any final decision on our marriage until after that.

In mid-January I flew to Washington, D.C., for a press conference to announce my retirement from the Air Force. The day before my announcement, while at the Pentagon, I bumped into General George Brown, my boss's boss, and thus mine as well. The general and I exchanged pleasantries, and then he floored me. "Colonel, did you know that your guys lost a plane at the test pilot school this morning?"

The look on my face told him that I had not yet heard. "And the pilot?"

"I don't know for sure, but I think he bailed out."

I breathed a sigh of relief.

"The plane was an A-7, Colonel," Brown said curtly, as he continued down the hall. I knew what that meant. It was one of our guys flying the subsonic A-7 jet. I called Ted Twinting as soon as I could find a phone. When Ted told me the name of the pilot who had lost the plane, I gulped hard. He was a student pilot who had a physical problem that made the safety of his flying questionable in my mind. Both Ted and I had expressed misgivings about his ability to fly, but his medical reports showed that he could handle it. While doing a lateral test, he had allowed the plane's altitude to get too low, and he'd lost it. Fortunately, he escaped with only cuts and bruises, but the plane was demolished.

On Friday, January 14, 1972, I arrived at the Pentagon to make my retirement announcement. Dan Henkin, the officer in charge of the proceedings, caught my arm before we went out for the press conference. "Buzz, the general suggests that you don't say anything about what you are going to be doing during your remaining months in the Air Force."

That should have been a hint. I had intentionally planned my retirement announcement before promotions were announced, so that if I were not promoted to general, it would not seem as though my leaving was sour grapes. And if I was promoted, then it wouldn't look as though I was an ingrate, just waiting for a pay raise before retiring at that level rather than as a colonel. But the more personal aspect of my announcement had to do with our children. Joan and I did not want to disrupt their lives in the middle of the school year, so while I had planned to announce my retirement now, I wouldn't stop working until about six months later, much as we had done when I left NASA.

With no time to mull over the ramifications of the general's request, I simply made a brief statement to the press, and obeyed orders—or, in this case, suggestions. Immediately following the press conference, I headed back to California and went back to work.

Upon my return to Edwards, General Bob White implied to me that I might want to consider relinquishing command of the school during my remaining time before retirement. He didn't overtly state that he thought I could soon be removed from my command, but that was the message I understood. I asserted that it was to all our benefit for me to stay on and finish some of the projects on which Ted and I had been working.

"I understand, Buzz," General White replied. "But we need to be prepared for all the possibilities."

The possibilities took care of themselves the following day, when, only four days after the A-7 crash at Edwards, another disaster struck. A T-33 advanced jet trainer carrying two pilots crashed just seconds after the pilots bailed out. The pilots walked away with only surface cuts and bruises. Bob White met me at the hospital with a knowing look. We both recognized that the handwriting was on the wall.

Indeed, when the Air Force investigators finished looking into the accidents, they deduced that the A-7 jet pilot had bailed out because he couldn't recover from a spin due to a mechanical problem that the plane's maintenance staff missed. The T-33 had been doing spins and spin recovery when the problem occurred. In both cases there weren't enough supervisory personnel observing the spin tests of the aircraft. That laid the blame for the destruction of two expensive planes, and nearly the loss of three pilots' lives, squarely on my shoulders.

Not surprisingly, when the new list of brigadier generals came out, my name was not on it. The lists had ostensibly been prepared in December, before the two crashes. In truth, my chances for promotion ended when I asked for psychiatric help, but I still had hoped that my overall career might be considered. I had spent more than twenty years in service to my country. Even after returning from the hospital in San Antonio, I felt that my performance as commandant and my relationship with staff members had been extremely good.

In February 1972, four-star general George Brown came to visit Edwards. His visit wasn't just a friendly stopover. The Air Force had sent down an edict stating that the school would no longer be known as the Aerospace Research Pilot School, since we would no longer be considered the primary training facility for potential U.S. astronauts. With the Apollo program winding down, the Air Force had decided to re-emphasize the traditional aspects of test pilot training, rather than astronaut instruction. Astronaut training was the one thing I knew about, and it provided a quasi-rationale for my being the commandant. Now that was gone, too.

General White called all of my young instructors to my office for a briefing so that General Brown from Washington, D.C., could explain the change to them. I stood along with the young officers listening to the general's presentation, struggling to keep my jaw from dropping. The astronaut program had been in existence for ten years before I arrived at Edwards, but General Brown made it sound as though I were the one who had instituted it. I hadn't created the program; I'd inherited it. Nevertheless, General Brown laid the responsibility for the dismantling of the program on my shoulders.

I accepted that, but the general's attitude surprised me when he then took me to task personally. "Well, let me get this straight, Colonel Aldrin. Why do you call this place the Aerospace Research Pilot School? Don't you think a better name would be the Air Force Test Pilot School?"

I replied that we did have the test pilot curriculum, but we also had a "zoom curriculum" to test NF-104 jets specially fitted with six-thousand-pound thrust rocket motors to familiarize students with some of the techniques required in space flight. The modified 104 jet could zoom well above 100,000 feet, providing the pilot with ninety seconds of weightlessness. "We're trying to run a top-notch test pilot school and astronaut training facility here, sir," I offered.

General Brown cut me off short. "Colonel Aldrin, that's the problem. Why do you have that course here? We aren't training astronauts for NASA. Let NASA train their own astronauts; your job is to train test pilots for the Air Force. So change the name of this school immediately to the U.S. Air Force Test Pilot School and get rid of those 104s and your 'zoom' curriculum." The general's attitude was almost as if he were saying, "Oh, you came from NASA and you think you're hot stuff around here because you were an astronaut? Well, I don't."

The instructor pilots at the school stood silent, appalled and embarrassed for me. To castigate me like that in front of my young staff was extremely unwise and exhibited poor leadership on the part of the general, and it was futile to argue with him.

A short time later, General Bob White and I met together to discuss my future. The Air Force offered me a project to fill my remaining months, but it required me to move to Los Angeles. I made a counteroffer. I could legitimately retire on March 1 rather than wait until June, if the Air Force would allow my family to keep our home until the children could finish school. General White thought that could be worked out, and it was. My retirement benefited both of us: General White could get back to being the commanding general at Edwards, and I could get back to being a functioning human being.

On March 1, 1972, General Jimmy Doolittle came to Edwards for my brief but formal retirement ceremony. I appreciated Dad's friend being there, and his continued support. General White was also there, as were Ted Twinting and all of my instructors and their students, who filled the large airplane hangar and stood in formation in one last show of support.

I have often wondered why the Air Force chose me to head up the test pilot school. They could easily have said, "Buzz, we don't have anything for you right now, but let's talk in six months to a year."

My friend Alan Bean helped put it in perspective for me. An

eighteen-year veteran with the space program, Alan flew to the moon as lunar module pilot on the Apollo 12 mission. Years later, when asked about the decision to appoint me as commandant of the test pilot school, Alan concurred with the Air Force:

> I thought it was a good decision. I thought Buzz was the perfect person for that position. He had airplane experience as a fighter pilot, having shot down some enemy planes. He had experience in space; few other candidates had that. He was certainly an icon, a hero to every student who came through that school. Unfortunately, when some other astronauts left NASA, they took positions for which they were not qualified. But I thought Buzz was perfectly qualified for the commandant's job. He could continue flying while being a positive role model.[2]

Alan's comments are heartwarming, but at the time I probably wouldn't have agreed with them. I was only forty-two years of age when I retired from the Air Force on March 1, 1972, even earlier than had been announced. I had been the commandant of the test pilot school a mere nine months, and it had been one of the most stressful periods of my life.

◗ ○ ◖

During my last few weeks in the service, I had already begun thinking about life after the Air Force and toying with ideas of what to do. I had previously engaged in talks with the Bulova watch company, about a specially designed watch I had in mind. Bulova used some of my ideas, so I felt we might be able to do something together in the future. I dabbled with digital watches, convinced then that many of the communication devices of the future, including telephone, camera, calculator, and other functions, would operate off a person's watch. This was in 1972, long before the Internet, cell phones, or text-messaging

---

[2] Author interview with Alan Bean, November 17, 2008.

services existed, but I felt certain that such technology would be the wave of the future.

Another, more immediate opportunity rolled my way. I did a rather tacky commercial for Dynamark Lawn Tractor's rotary lawn mower. The tag line went something like, "Dynamark Lawn Tractor. Astronaut Buzz Aldrin drives it around—it's out of this world." I had gone from walking on the moon to selling lawn mowers.

The Volkswagen automobile company hired me to do a sixty-second television commercial extolling the virtues of the VW's new digital computerized vehicle diagnostic system. The system was pretty amazing, and the work was relatively easy, just learning a few lines and delivering them with authority and credibility. We negotiated the deal while I was still at Edwards, and did the actual taping after my official retirement date of March 1.

For that, VW agreed to pay me a whopping $300,000. I thought, *Hey, retirement living might not be so bad, after all.*

I also continued to think about the idea of writing a book about my experiences. When I mentioned this to the attorneys at Loeb & Loeb, who were helping me handle a number of my new business deals, they introduced me to Wayne Warga, a former *Life* magazine editor who was now living in Los Angeles and working as an entertainment writer for the *Los Angeles Times*. Wayne suggested that we might be wise to test the waters by writing an op-ed piece for the newspaper, and then see how the public responded. I didn't want to write a book merely about going to the moon, but about the challenges I faced when I returned to Earth.

8

HUMAN SIDE
of HERO

BEING HOSPITALIZED FOR FOUR WEEKS TO RECEIVE TREAT-
ment and therapy for depression was not the type of thing you
publicly disclosed to the world on a whim. Seeking help had effec-
tively ended my career in the Air Force. Would sharing it openly in the
press jeopardize further opportunities as I sought a new direction in my
life? But if I was going to do it, then I wanted to be honest about it. I
wanted to have a chance of helping someone else. Such revelations
would be in marked contrast to the picture-perfect layouts in the 1969
Life magazine where the three of us who reached the moon on the first
landing were glamorized in our professional and family lives. If the
public responded positively to the idea that an American astronaut "superhero" could be vulnerable to the pitfalls of depression, and brave
enough to seek help, then maybe Wayne and I could use that leverage
to approach a publisher about a book deal.

On February 27, just a couple of days before I said good-bye to
my friends in the Air Force, Wayne's article appeared in the Sunday
edition of the *Los Angeles Times*. The article was titled, "Troubled
Odyssey—'Buzz' Aldrin's Saga: Tough Role for Hero."

Wayne began the article by quoting the psychologist Carl Jung:
"Space flights are merely an escape, a fleeing away from oneself, because

it is easier to go to Mars or to the moon than it is to penetrate one's own being."

I could bear witness to that. Dealing with the pressure of several times the force of gravity pushing on my chest at liftoff, and keeping cool under the stress of landing on the moon with only a few gasps of fuel remaining in the tank was relatively easy compared to overcoming the enormous pressures and stresses that were unraveling my life. To beat depression I had to look deep within myself, and while much of what I saw there was laudable, the dark areas were equally as forbidding.

Wayne's article was picked up in syndication and appeared in various forms in newspapers throughout the United States and abroad. The response was immediate and overwhelming. For the most part, the public cared deeply that I had not fared well following my return from the moon.

The *Los Angeles Times* article received such a stirring response from the public that Wayne and I decided to move forward on writing the book that revealed my experiences with depression, because I wanted to stand up and be counted as someone who fought the illness and had won. At that time I did not yet realize that the battles would keep coming, taking various forms, and occurring when I least expected them, and that the victories had to be won on a daily basis, with hard work and perseverance, rather than with a once-and-for-all "Get Out of Jail Free" pass.

Wayne's story spawned numerous follow-up articles; the public seemed to want to know every gritty detail. Again, most of the newspapers ran the story as a positive statement about mental health. For instance, a headline in the March 4 edition of the *Standard-Times* (New Bedford, MS) read, YOU'RE A-OK, BUZZ, and quoted my rationale for coming out publicly about my experiences: "Maybe I can give some person somewhere the courage to face his problems by saying something about mine," I had said. The article closed in a complimentary fashion:

No one could doubt the courage of the second man to set foot on the moon. But if other evidence was needed, then Buzz Aldrin stands all the taller for his revelations.[3]

The *Toledo Blade* took Wayne's basic story and spun it more negatively, the headline reading, ALL IS NOT SERENE IN US SPACE PROGRAM. SECOND MAN ON MOON REVEALS STRESS, ANXIETIES CAUSED NERVOUS BREAKDOWN.[4]

In an excellent story run the week after the original article appeared, Wayne's follow-up article included a tease about the book. "[Aldrin's] story, part of it, was told in Sunday's *Times*; he will tell more in a book he is writing."[5]

Once again, the response to Wayne's work was quite positive; clearly there was a market for a book. We signed the contracts with Random House to write the book while I was still living at Edwards Air Force Base. Wayne Warga and I would work together on the manuscript over the coming year.

● ○ ◐

BY THE TIME the kids had finished school in June 1972, Joan and I had packed up our belongings at Edwards Air Force Base and were ready to go. Moving is always an adventure—not necessarily a desirable one, but an adventure nonetheless. On June 3 we moved from sparse Air Force housing to our own home, a rambling ranch house in a "horse" community in Hidden Hills, California, on the west side of the San Fernando Valley, outside Los Angeles. A buddy of mine with whom I had flown in the 22nd Squadron while stationed in Germany during the summer of 1956 happened to be a realtor in Ventura County, and helped me with the purchase of this home, formerly

---

[3] *Standard Times* (New Bedford, MS), March 4, 1972.
[4] Wayne Warga, "All Is Not Serene in US Space Program. Second Man on Moon Reveals Stress, Anxieties Caused Nervous Breakdown," *The Toledo Blade*, March 5, 1972.
[5] Wayne Warga, "The Making of a Hero," *Los Angeles Times*, February 29, 1972.

owned by the L.A. Dodgers' All-Star pitcher Don Drysdale. The house was replete with a white picket fence and a swimming pool, set on two acres of land dotted with orange trees. Our neighbor across the street was the actor and entertainer John Davidson. Despite the difficulties that had brought us here, this was a dream come true!

We had animals of every kind at our house, thanks to Mike, our family's most broad-ranging animal lover. But since the community had been built with equestrians in mind, and our daughter Jan owned an Appaloosa horse, we installed a riding ring in front of the house. Behind stood a barn with two stalls, one for the horse and another for the chickens to roost in while they laid their eggs. We also had sheep, goats, and "rolling" pigeons, known for their amazing willful spins and dips while flying.

The pastoral tranquillity of Hidden Hills was a welcome change for me, especially since, during my last few months at Edwards, I was having occasional relapses into depressive behavior. After the Volkswagen commercial aired, I had received a letter castigating me for endorsing the German automaker, and accusing me of being un-American. Ordinarily I would have cast off such worthless drivel as the ruminations of somebody with too much time on his or her hands. But in my unsteady frame of mind, the letter had a devastating effect that fed into the familiar blue funk.

The reprieve I was feeling after our move to Hidden Hills was short lived, however, as I began to fall back into depression. At first I succumbed to my old ways and retreated to my bedroom, but Joan kept prodding me to get help. I called Dr. Sparks in San Antonio, and he suggested that I get in touch with Dr. Flinn, who had seen me briefly prior to the four weeks I spent at Wilford Hall in San Antonio. Back in the early 1960s, Dr. Flinn had certified me at Brooks Air Force Base, where the candidates for the NASA astronaut program went for their physicals, and had given me a passing grade, tantamount to a clean bill of mental health, with no reservations. Now, in the mid-seventies, he was the head of the Neuropsychiatric Institute at UCLA and I was his patient. On June 23, 1972, I called Dr. Flinn and set up an appointment for that same day.

The doctor helped me sort through all that had happened in recent months, and my recurring apprehension about the future. It was quite understandable, Dr. Flinn explained, that I should experience these feelings, since, for a former astronaut—not to mention one who had walked on the moon—it was totally unreasonable to think that I could have gone back to the Air Force and simply served in obscurity. Moreover, the two accidents that were laid at my feet due to "supervisory error" would have been difficult for any commander. When I was made to feel useless and expendable as a result, that exacerbated existing insecurities about leading the test pilot school in the first place.

Dr. Flinn's explanation made sense to me, but then he sealed it with a clincher. The real problem, he helped me to realize, was that I didn't feel that I was *allowed* to have such emotions. As a man, a strong man, a let's-get-it-done-and-here's-how-to-do-it man, I was not entitled to fail; when I could not control the situation, feelings of inadequacy and frustration flooded over me. Dr. Flinn helped me to recognize the futility of such feelings, and although it was nice to be regarded as a superman, it was an impossible image to live up to—and I was tired of trying. If someone wanted to go to the moon or even Mars, I could figure out a way to do that, and my competitive spirit would give it 100 percent. But to live up to the image of perfection foisted upon me by others and perpetuated by my own expectations was something I no longer was willing or able to do.

After that appointment, I met with Dr. Flinn periodically until the spring of 1975. During our July 1, 1972, session, we talked about my often misunderstood competitive nature. In his own handwritten physician's notes, Dr. Flinn recorded this statement: "Others consider him bright, but not smooth or friendly. Competitive. & others may see him as selfish."[6]

---

[6] From Dr. Don Flinn's contemporaneous physician's records. Used by permission.

In subsequent appointments we talked about my apprehension concerning the future, as well as some of the events that still dogged me from the past. When Dr. Flinn asked me about how it felt to be chided as "the *second* man to walk on the moon," his question opened a Pandora's box.

Believe it or not, I told him, I hadn't particularly wanted to be the first man to step on the moon. While we were training for the mission, I went home one night after work and told Joan, "I wish I wasn't going on the first landing. I'd rather be on the second or third mission to the moon because we'd get to do a lot more scientific experiments and other interesting things, and wouldn't have to be slaves to the media, after being the first ones to walk on the moon."

Yet I recognized that in all likelihood that great responsibility would fall on my shoulders. In all the previous Gemini and Apollo missions, the spacewalks—EVAs, as they were known to us—were taken by the junior officer, while the commander remained inside the space capsule. And as of February 1969, that was our plan as well. The *Chicago Daily News* reported as early as February 26, 1969, that I had "been named to be the first human being ever to step onto the moon."[7] The article went on to explain how the decision was made:

> The choice for one of the most momentous events in mankind's . . . history falls to the brainy 39-year-old Air Force colonel by virtue of his role as lunar module commander. . . . The disclosure of Aldrin as the choice comes as a surprise to many who had speculated that the top commander [Neil Armstrong] would be entitled to pull rank and take his place in the history books as the first man to set foot on a satellite of the earth. But a space agency official said the decision is not Armstrong's to make. The flight plan controls the mission and it calls for the lunar module pilot to make the initial egress."[8]

---

[7] Arthur J. Snider, "First Man on Moon Selected," *Chicago Daily News,* syndicated in the *Corpus Christi Times,* evening edition, February 26, 1969, p. 1.
[8] Ibid.

"It's not based on individual desire," Neil had explained, "but on how the job can be best accomplished on the lunar surface." The article concluded, "Now, six weeks later, the decision has been firmed up. It could be changed, but is not likely to be."[9]

I recognized that we were setting a precedent, so I asked Al Bean, the copilot scheduled for the next mission, "What do you think about this?" Alan recognized, as I did, that historical significance might trump NASA protocol in this case. I posed the question to a few other fellow astronauts, and their response was much the same.

Word soon got around that I was trying to lobby support for my being the first to set foot on the moon's surface, that I was soliciting the other astronauts' support in my quest to be the first man on the moon. That wasn't the case. I was simply behaving like a competitive Air Force fighter pilot would. In truth, I didn't really want to be the first person to step on the moon. I knew the media would never let that person alone. I suspected that such intense media coverage after my Gemini flight was a major factor in my mother's suicide. Why would I place myself in a position for even more attention than I was already sure to get, simply by being part of the mission? Also, something inside me said that for such a seminal event, it would be wrong for the commander to sit in the lunar module and watch while a junior copilot made history.

Rumors continued to swirl, and the media quoted unidentified NASA insiders saying that the first history-making step was still up for grabs. Thinking it best to clear the air, I went to Neil. "You know I don't care one way or another, but we need to settle this matter before it gets blown out of proportion and so we can get on with our training."

Normally a straight shooter, Neil seemed hesitant and aloof. Finally he looked away from my eyes and said, "Buzz, I realize the historical significance of all this, and I just don't want to rule anything out right now."

About ten days later, Deke Slayton came by and said, matter-of-

---

[9] Arthur J. Snider, "First Man on Moon Selected," *Chicago Daily News,* syndicated in the *Corpus Christi Times,* evening edition, February 26, 1969, p. 1.

factly, "Neil will be the first one out of the LM." Ostensibly the decision to have Neil go out first was made for practical, logical reasons. After a number of simulated practice exits, it was determined that it was easier for the man on the left, closest to the hatch, to go out first. That was Neil. When we tried to do it otherwise in practice, it required that we change places, and that I move to the left. When wearing pressurized suits and helmets with the large life-support backpacks, it was not impossible for me to exit the cramped lunar module first, but it was difficult if not downright dangerous, since we would run more risk of bumping into sensitive equipment inside the LM or banging the sensitive equipment in our backpacks. When Deke Slayton asked Neil his opinion on the matter, Neil said that from a technical standpoint it was preferable for the left crewman to egress first. That pretty much settled it.

◑　○　◐

TO ANSWER DR. FLINN'S question, certainly it was difficult and sometimes awkward to be known as "the second man on the moon," especially when, according to usual NASA protocol, I would normally have been first. Even more so, when one considers that I was a mere twenty minutes behind Neil. But although I was an intense competitor, I wanted to be a team player, too. I certainly was not jealous of Neil. Dr. Flinn helped me to sort through many of my thoughts about the ramifications of my being the second man on the moon.

He also helped me work through everything from my unfulfilled desires to become an Air Force general to my competitiveness with Apollo 8 commander Frank Borman. Frank and I had been rivals since our days at West Point together. He graduated one class ahead of me, and we both became jet pilots. In the Air Force, I'd edged Frank out for a couple of honors, and I don't think he ever forgot it.

On Apollo 8, Frank was the commander and I was the lunar module pilot in the backup crew. The mission was a bold move to help us step up the clock and get us closer to landing on the moon. Apollo 8 marked the first time that human beings had broken away completely from Earth's gravitational pull to fly around the moon. I could honestly say that any competition I felt with Frank fell away like the giant shards of frost breaking off the Saturn V rocket as it lifted Frank and his crew—Jim Lovell and Bill Anders—on their way toward the moon. Frank's mission was one of the most observed in history, the first mission to orbit the moon, as well as one of the most colorful, with the controversial and inspired Christmas Eve reading of Genesis, and the Christmas Day declaration by Jim Lovell, once they knew they were on their way home, "Houston, please be informed, there is a Santa Claus."

It wasn't until fifteen years later that I would discover by accident that I was not NASA's first choice for the Apollo 11 mission. I stumbled into this revelation when I was hired as a technical consultant for a movie produced by Mary Tyler Moore's company, MTM. While reading the script, I noticed that after *Apollo 8* came back from circling the moon, Frank Borman was offered the commandership of the first lunar landing.

"Where did you guys get this?" I asked the writers.

"Out of Frank Borman's book," they replied confidently.

I checked out Frank's book, *Countdown*, and sure enough, he writes that in effect it was his decision not to be on the first lunar landing. I approached Jim Lovell, with whom I had flown on *Gemini 12*, and who had also been on *Apollo 8* along with Bill Anders. "Jim, is there anything to this?"

"Yes, they offered the first landing mission to Frank Borman and he turned it down," Jim confided, "without asking the other two crew members, Bill and me."

Why would Frank not want to be on the first lunar landing mission? I don't know; maybe he recognized that the public pressure on that first group would be unprecedented, or perhaps, like me, he was more interested in the subsequent missions on which more advanced scientific exploration would take place. Regardless, to me that illustrated the sort of gamesmanship that went on at NASA during those early years of the Apollo program. It seemed that everyone was vying for position.

Dr. Flinn understood the NASA system as well as any doctor on earth, and he helped me understand the reasons for my anxiety while I was there and especially afterward. He also helped me grapple with the uncertainties I was feeling about the book project I was working on with Wayne Warga.

●   ○   ●

OUR HOME IN Hidden Hills, for as much as I enjoyed it, was both a blessing and a curse. It was a fantastic playground for our family, yet I worried how we were going to pay for it. The pressure to keep life functioning normally for my family members weighed heavily on me.

Following my retirement, I kept busy by working around the house, being Mr. Handyman, while constantly looking for new opportunities to do something significant with my life that would also encourage others to do the same. And I was spending hundreds of hours in interviews with Wayne from the spring of 1972 well into 1973, rehashing my past, especially on the events since the *Apollo 11* splashdown. Wayne chugged cups of coffee, and I matched him with Scotch on the rocks.

Although we mentioned my being inebriated in several stories in the book, it never occurred to me that I might have a drinking problem. Almost everyone I knew drank alcohol in some measure, astronauts included. The only astronauts who didn't drink while I was a part of NASA were Alan Bean and Bill Anders. For me, drinking was not a problem; it was simply something I did to relax. At least that's what I told myself.

When my father found out that I was writing a book, he was nearly apoplectic—especially when he learned that I wanted to tell the real story, about how not all astronauts were Boy Scouts or altar boys. Not everything was always well and good at NASA. But what concerned him most was my intention to reveal more information about how and why I had sought out psychiatric help for my own problems. Soldiers didn't do that—especially Aldrin soldiers. But I had, and I was glad that I had done so. Thanks to the doctors with whom I had worked at Wilford Hall, I at least recognized the signs of a depressive period coming on me, and could take some steps to fend it off.

Part of my father's concern related to how the good people at Mutual of Omaha might view me now that the news was public that I had sought help. Dad wrote letters to me frequently during this period, and in each letter he asked in a poignant, pleading tone, "Son, are you still on the board at Mutual?" His fears were not unfounded.

With each letter, Dad expressed increasing concern. On July 24 he wrote, "Are you on the Mutual of Omaha Board? Did you have to get off for a period? What about the response by the USAF?"

By October 27 my father was no longer camouflaging his concerns. In that letter he asked straightforwardly, "Will your book handicap your activity, like Mutual of Omaha?"

Despite my father's concerns and objections, in the fall of 1973 my first book, *Return to Earth*, was published by Random House. We launched the book tour with an appearance on *The Merv Griffin Show*, one of the popular talk shows of the time, and then a press conference at the Good Housekeeping Institute—of all places. In light of the exposure of my extramarital affair in the book, *Good Housekeeping* was putting its seal of approval and goodie-two-shoes-image on the line. But the book ended on a positive note with Joan and me back together, so perhaps that made it more tolerable to the wholesome organization that had then, and still has today, one of the highest ratings of consumer confidence.

I had worked for more than a year on the book, describing my adjustment to life on Earth after having attained the goal of reaching the moon. Joan had forgiven me for my infidelity, and still hoped that "the old Buzz" would return once I was "well." She even went along with me on the tour to help promote the book. Before long we received overtures about a possible deal in the works to do a television movie, so although Joan and I still weren't functioning well as a married couple, we were at least together. Indeed, we could have been fine, but for my recurring bouts of depression that led to drinking too much alcohol, which led to further depression. It was a downward spiral.

I wasn't obnoxious when I drank; I did, however, feel less inhibited. Drinking relaxed me, imparting an almost euphoric sense of wellness. I didn't realize that I was not impressing other people that way at all. I drank mostly at home, but occasionally I would go out to a bar and sit there drinking and talking with people until it was time to close and I had to go home. When I drank at night, I often woke up the next day with a hangover, and I soon discovered that the best cure for that horrible morning-after feeling was another drink. That is addiction.

Looking back, I see that Joan was a good woman who had to put up with a lot. It is devastating enough for any woman to learn that her husband has been having an affair and wants to marry the "other woman." When a husband is supposed to be a hero and a role model, and he reveals his infidelity in a book, how does a woman cope with that? We had been married for eighteen years when I started working on the book. Joan was uneasy about telling the entire story from the beginning, but when she read the details about Marianne, it was even more difficult for her. She really didn't want me to write it—she had grown accustomed, since the moon landing, to fighting for every bit of privacy we could maintain in our lives. Fortunately, Wayne Warga handled the information so tactfully and tastefully that Joan found it more palatable.

When we went out on the book tour, however, the painful reality hit even harder, as reporters and talk-show hosts asked probing questions. In some ways it forced Joan to sort out her feelings and to verbalize how she felt. In an interview with the *Los Angeles Times*, Joan admitted that when she learned about my unfaithfulness, her first reaction was to go off and have an affair herself. "But I didn't know how," she said. "Even when confronted with the opportunity, I didn't know what to do."

Joan almost made my infidelity sound as though it was her fault—

which of course it wasn't. "As for his casual affairs, I had played ostrich. He was gone a lot and I was always involved in amateur theater and I didn't think about it. I just didn't know. I may have suspected, and I guess maybe my philosophy was, 'Is he any different from any other man who travels and received adulation?' I had married an engineer and here he was a hero."[10]

Joan mustered great courage in facing those interviews; she was convinced our marriage could still be saved. "My big immediate goal is cementing the relationship between Buzz and me. . . . We now have a far more open and honest relationship than ever before. In a way, when things blew up, it was a tremendous relief. I think we're going to make it. I really do. And I couldn't say that for a long time. I didn't know if I could overcome the bitterness, but I think now that we have a good chance."[11]

But reality poked holes in the bubble of Joan's idealism. Our relationship was being compromised by alcohol, compounded by my blue funks, and neither of us was yet aware of it.

After the book tour, I still didn't know what I was going to do with the rest of my life. I had to find some way to make a living.

Many Americans assumed that all of the astronauts received huge sums of money for their services, or came out of the program as rich men and women. Not so. While a few astronauts parlayed their fame into wonderfully lucrative careers, most of us walked away with little more money than we had at the beginning. In addition to my regular Air Force salary, which was my source of income while an astronaut, I received $16,000 during the first year as part of a prearranged NASA contract with *Life* magazine, to publish exclusively all of the astronauts' stories. The royalties were split evenly with all the astronauts, so, the more people in the program, the less money each of us received. The second year I got a check for $6,000, the following year, $3,060, and

---

[10] Jean Douglas Murphy, "Life With a Space Superhero Who Cracked Up," *Los Angeles Times.*

[11] Ibid., p. 12A.

less than that the year I walked on the moon. Now, retired from the Air Force, I wondered, *How am I going to earn a living?* I didn't know. The Volkswagen commercial had provided the money we needed to get into our home, but those kinds of deals don't come along every day. I served on the board of a small firm dealing with supervisory electronics, but that income was not sufficient to take care of my family, either. More than money, what I needed was a cause, a calling, a new challenge.

What I really wanted was a new role in space exploration, but nothing significant arose, at least as far as I could see. When I was working with Wayne Warga on my first book, I had plenty of time to realize just how integrally my life was interconnected with space, since so little activity was going on in space exploration during that time. We launched Skylab in 1973; we sent people to it in '73 and '74. Then, in 1975, we cooperated with the Russians in Apollo Soyuz. Much to my chagrin, space exploration was dead; I felt somewhat lifeless, too.

Disingenuous reporters described me as suffering from mental illness. Today that would not even raise an eyebrow, but in 1973–74, those words held the power to ground any career, no matter how high-flying it had been.

In retrospect, being so forthcoming in *Return to Earth* may have worked against me. Shortly after the book appeared in print, Mutual of Omaha's chairman of the board, V. J. Skutt, asked me to resign, saying I was no longer a good figurehead for the company. Although I intended for my story to encourage people dealing with similar conditions to seek help, it also branded me as a philanderer and as a person who was mentally ill, in a constant battle with depression. Neither label was accurate, but I felt that despite the misconceptions, it was worth putting everything out on the table so people could deal with it and so I could move on with my life. Most of the public response to the book was wonderfully positive, although some people had difficulty accepting that an American astronaut and hero could be vulnerable to depression.

Although my honest and straightforward disclosure in the book proved damaging to me in some ways, it provided hope and inspiration to many other people—especially men, who, in the mid-seventies, were not accustomed to admitting that they struggled with depression. Everywhere I went, men thanked me for bringing the issue to the forefront. "I've never been able to admit that I needed it before," some guys told me, "but thanks to your example, I'm seeking help."

To me, that made the revelations in the book worthwhile, even though my father was appalled.

Nevertheless, after the original op-ed came out in the *Los Angeles Times* in 1972 about my hospitalization for depression, I was asked to serve on the board of directors of the National Association for Mental Health (NAMH). I was delighted to participate if my celebrity could help shed light on the subject. NASA probably did not see it that way, but I didn't mind.

Then, after *Return to Earth* came out and made such a splash, I was invited to serve as the 1974 national chairman for a one-year term, thanks to a suggestion by Bill Perry, NAMH's communication director. Bill had read my book, and wanted to know if I was serious when I closed the story by saying that I wanted to stand up and be counted as a person who has had to deal with depression and mental health issues. Bill worked with me to set up a series of appearances as the NAMH chairman to speak to mental health groups across the country, and the first one was to take place in Detroit. We became good friends, and we traveled together frequently for NAMH. My role was to attract a crowd to mental health events, and part of Bill's job was to promote the events and arrange media interviews for me while we were in town.

Bill was impressed by my high energy, but he had no idea how serious my own depression and drinking were until he spent seven days at our home in Hidden Hills. He had come out to accompany me in making some planned public appearances on behalf of NAMH, but while Bill was visiting, I fell into a funk in which I didn't get out of bed for four straight days.

When I did get up that week, I drank a fifth of Scotch or Jack Daniel's each day, and during that time somehow we misplaced four cars. I'd park a car, then we'd go off and do something, and I couldn't remember where I had parked. We temporarily lost my little red Saab sports car, a Ford Ranchero that my daughter Jan used to pick up hay for her horse, and even a pop-top Volkswagen camper! Eventually we found the vehicles, but it did cause Bill real concern. He recognized that I drank far more than most people, but could still function, seemingly with my faculties relatively unimpaired.

Bill was with me in Minneapolis when we got together with Princess Margaret of Great Britain. After an evening function, we were in a bar around midnight having a drink with Dave Zigenhaugen, the executive director of the Mental Health Association in Minneapolis. "It's nice to have two celebrities in town," Dave said.

With several drinks already in me, I looked at Dave impishly and said, "Two? Who's the other one?"

"Princess Margaret."

"Oh, I know her," I said. "I met her on the world tour after the *Apollo 11* moon landing. I'd like to see her."

"Well, she's leaving in a day or two, so I doubt that would be possible," Dave said.

"Of course, it's possible," I replied. I had an idea. Somewhere around midnight, I started calling the Minnesota governor's mansion, trying to get someone who could set up a meeting with Princess Margaret. The next morning I was doing a television interview at 8:00 a.m., and while I was on the set, Bill received a telephone call from the governor's office, informing us that the Princess would see me. We met with Princess Margaret and Lord Snowden at 11:00 a.m. that morning, and it became a big story in Minneapolis. Bill was duly impressed.

Bill knew that I could perform in front of a crowd. "It's like you're a refrigerator, and when you open the door the light comes on," he said. "You're always ready to go!" Bill usually wrote some general remarks for me to include in my talks, carefully guiding me away from any technical areas of mental health, since I was not an expert. All I really knew was derived from my own personal experience, so I talked freely about my depression, how I went from being on top of the world and landing on the moon, to plunging into an abyss after I returned to Earth.

Bill and I were a good team—until I started missing scheduled events. The first time I failed to show up at an NAMH event, Bill did his best to cover for me. More than eight thousand people had gathered in Indianapolis for an NAMH annual meeting, when I called Bill on Sunday afternoon to inform him that I wasn't feeling well, and that I couldn't make it. I wasn't lying to him; I wasn't feeling well, but my condition was not a physical sickness so much as mental and emotional.

"Don't worry about it, Buzz. I'll figure out something," Bill said. He frantically called Percy Knauth, a former Time-Life reporter from Magic Bay, Connecticut, and asked him to pinch hit for me. Percy consented and did a fantastic job, but Bill's hosts were not happy that I was not with him when he got off the plane in Indiana.

After that first no-show, it became easier for me to back out of meetings when I got down on myself. With increasing frequency I gave in to the depression. I'd contact Bill and inform him that I would not be making it to a scheduled event. Once, I had already arrived at the hotel, and I still called Bill and told him that I could not do the event. Bill never got angry, but I could tell that he was extremely disappointed in me, and embarrassed for me. Percy Knauth was a good speaker, and he got quite a workout filling in at events for me.

On the other hand, when I was on, I enjoyed being with Bill and his fellow mental health workers, and found many of them to be intellectually stimulating. For instance, one night after an event in Chicago, Bill Rice, a vice president with NAMH, and I sat up all night long talking through the theory of relativity! Rice was a bright mathematician from Salt Lake City, and we talked the night away, as I downed one drink after another.

On another occasion we were in Florida, where we met Richard Bach, author of the huge bestseller *Jonathan Livingston Seagull.* Bach was a pilot, so we sat up trading airplane stories, playing a game of "Can you top this?"

"Have you ever flown a Tiger Moth?" Richard asked.

"No, but I'd like to."

"Well, I have one."

The next day we went out to the private airport where Bach kept his planes. He gave me a quick overview of the Tiger Moth, and said, "Take it up and see how it flies." I climbed in the cockpit, and Bach took the copilot's seat. He flew with me for the first lap around the area, then let me take the controls. I put the plane through its paces, and when I landed the Tiger Moth, I looked at Bach with a grin and said, "What else ya got?"

Perhaps one of the worst disappointments to Bill was the time I scrubbed a scheduled speech at the District of Columbia Mental Health Association, and decided to remain home in Los Angeles because my depression had struck again. It was obviously never good to miss an engagement, but especially one in the Washington, D.C., area, where we could get some much-needed attention from Congress. But maybe that's what caused my consternation, that I felt I couldn't close the sale.

Bill made the excuses for me, telling the media that I was receiving medication and undergoing therapy. "He's on the down side of a depression cycle," Bill said, putting it mildly. Bill told the press that I had spoken in Minneapolis the previous week and I had been fine. "I think the thing Buzz wants to get out is that you can't hide a mental illness. He tells his own story and how he's coming out of it. I think he overestimated how far along he was."

One night Joan and I were attending an event in Antelope Valley honoring General Jimmy Doolittle. I enjoyed the evening and drank more than usual. Driving home in our sporty, red, two-passenger Saab Sonett, I got mixed up and was going the wrong way on some of the backstreets of Palmdale. I was angry with myself for having gotten lost, so for some totally illogical reason I decided to floor it, as though driving faster would get us out of the predicament more quickly. I headed south down an unfamiliar road, when we suddenly came to a "T" intersection and were supposed to stop, but some tree branches shrouded the stop sign and, driving as fast as I was, I didn't see the sign until it was too late. We went through the intersection, hit a ditch, and went airborne, landing upright but with a horrible crash. Joan's head slammed into the dashboard, and my body whipped forward and back violently, as well. Fortunately we were wearing seatbelts—a habit not practiced then as generally as it is now. Joan escaped with some bumps and two black eyes, and I survived with just some bruises, but the car was severely damaged.

Joan and I crawled out of the crumpled car and surveyed the damage. Because the car couldn't be driven and we were out in the middle of nowhere, we started walking toward town. Before long, a motorist came along and offered us a ride. The police did not go out to the accident scene for several hours, so I was never checked for intoxication levels, but no doubt my judgment was impaired by the alcohol. It was a condition that would unfortunately get much worse before it got better.

9

A CONTROLLED
ALCOHOLIC

IN EARLY 1974, A HOLLYWOOD TELEVISION AND MOVIE PRO-
ducer, Rupert Hitzig, came to our home in Hidden Hills to offer a
formal proposal for the television movie based on *Return to Earth*.
Rupert had written the Broadway musical hit *Pippin*, had produced an
installment of ABC's *Saturday Night Live with Howard Cosell*, and was
in partnership with the well-known comedian Alan King.

A friendly fellow, Rupert was fascinated by our home's "moon"
décor, including a life-sized photo of the "visor shot," as the famous
picture of me on the moon was now known. Much to my delight, Rupert was especially intrigued by our "Moon Room," which featured a
well-stocked bar. I had found a new drinking buddy.

"Come on, let's get a drink," I said, motioning for Rupert to sit
down at the bar. It was only twelve-thirty in the afternoon. We talked
and drank, talked and drank. Rupert loved drinking as much as I did,
and we downed one gin and tonic after another. Rupert and I talked
much about our fathers—his was a doctor in New York, who sounded
almost as opinionated and overbearing as my father. We both chuckled
over my dad's outrage when the U.S. Post Office issued the stamp with
Neil Armstrong's image and the caption "First Man on the Moon,"
though of course I had been taken aback as well. Rupert laughed uproariously when I told him that besides lobbying the post office inces-

santly, my father went so far as to picket in front of the White House, with a huge placard bearing the message, "My Son Was First, Too." By the time Rupert and I actually got around to signing the contracts, we were sloshed.

We arranged a follow-up meeting a few weeks later, at the Beverly Hills Polo Lounge at five o'clock. I arrived at the Lounge before 1:00 p.m. By the time Rupert showed up shortly before five, along with his friend John Roach, I was thoroughly intoxicated. Rupert tried to talk business with me, but my interest wavered, as did my conversation. At one point Rupert leaned toward me and spoke quietly but firmly, "Buzz, don't you understand what a hero you are? Don't you realize that every person in this room knows who you are and what you did on July 20, 1969?"

"Nobody remembers where they were on July 20, 1969," I groused.

"I'll prove it to you," Rupert said. A young man who looked as though he could have been in a heavy-metal rock band was passing by our table, and Rupert reached out and grabbed his arm. "Excuse me," Rupert said. "Where were you on July 20, 1969?"

The rocker looked at me, then back at Rupert as though he'd lost his marbles. "How should I know?" he answered, shaking off Rupert's grip and continuing on his way. That was the last thing I needed to hear. I ordered another drink.

Despite my attitude, Rupert was determined to see *Return to Earth* made as a movie, and we agreed to press on to build the production team and sell the project to a television network as a made-for-TV feature-length movie. At least I think that's what we agreed to, because that's what Rupert did. He said that he had high hopes of getting a first-rate actor, Cliff Robertson, involved in the project, as well as an attractive female to play Marianne. Rupert had my attention.

"What do I need to do?" I asked.

"Nothing right now. I'll be back in touch as soon as we have all the pieces of the puzzle put together." Rupert went his way while I had one more drink for the road, or maybe it was two or three.

● ○ ●

FOR REASONS INEXPLICABLE to me at the time, life just kept tumbling down around me. I would talk with aerospace companies about future projects, and they seemed quite enthusiastic, but when nothing materialized, my spirits would sink again. I had formed my own company a few years earlier, Research and Engineering Consultants, but that was going nowhere, too. At about the time my book came out, I was consulting with North American Rockwell on the development of the space shuttle, and they liked my ideas, but that door had closed as well. It seemed that everywhere I turned—my marriage, my career, my expectations as an American hero—life was unraveling all around me. With no mission or goal on which to focus, those words I'd uttered on the moon—"magnificent desolation"—mocked me as a poignant description of my life on Earth.

Increasingly, I saw divorce as an escape to a new life. My roller-coaster ride wasn't doing Joan and the kids any good, and divorce seemed a viable option. When I discussed it with my father, at first he was opposed to my divorcing Joan, but not because he felt we had such a happy home. The book had been bad enough, but at least we had pulled our marriage back together by the last page. To divorce now, after that ugly blot on my name, could be the death knell. He was more concerned about appearances, worried that an all-American astronaut should not be seen as anything but a successful, happily married family man. Of course, Dad had not been able to overcome the unhappiness my mother had suffered, so I wasn't surprised by his stance.

My father was especially upset that I confessed to having periods of depression. As a retired Air Force colonel who had gone on to earn his doctorate at MIT, and had become a successful aviation executive, he no doubt thought that my admissions were trivial matters that should be kept private. One would think that we had received enough wake-up calls in our family. After all, my mother lived many of her days struggling with the effects of depression, and eventually ended her life rather than face another day. I can't imagine that my father's obsession with my being the All-American boy surpassed his desire for me to be well.

But he was reluctant to admit that my problems were internal, psychological, rather than something I acquired, something imposed upon me as a result of going to the moon. Even after Wayne's articles and my book came out, he preferred to blame my difficulties on external influences. In one interview in which a reporter suggested that possibility, Dad concurred. "We have to have an open mind," he said. "Who is all-seeing to know what effect the moon might have on people? It has to be explored more. If the moon can affect tides, why couldn't it influence someone's judgment? We may be afraid of the answers, and Buzz deserves credit to come out and face that situation." My father even suggested that perhaps other astronauts had been adversely affected, too, and just weren't telling. "Maybe more guys are hiding things and won't admit them," he said.

●　○　●

I communicated with few friends during this time, at least not on any meaningful basis or about anything other than potential space projects. I can't recall ever sharing my pain with another male friend or confiding in anyone that I was struggling to hold life together. Nor was I in touch with any of my fellow astronauts during this period; we had all gravitated away to new phases of our lives. There was little esprit de corps among the third group of astronauts, and certainly very little other than superficial interaction away from the workplace. While some of them, I later learned, had heard that I was having problems, I never heard from any of them, and frankly didn't expect anything to the contrary.

More and more, I turned to alcohol to ease my mind and see me through the rough times. Because I could handle my drinking—or so I thought—and could consume a lot of alcohol without becoming uncontrollably inebriated, I refused to see it as a problem. I had been relatively open about my battle with depression, but I was not so forthcoming about my drinking problems. As far as I could see, there was nothing wrong. It was a time when almost everyone I knew was drinking heavily, so why not me?

When I was not drinking, my thoughts tended to lead me to a deeper sense of self-evaluation and introspection. What am I doing? What is my role in life now? I realized that I was experiencing the "melancholy of things done." I had done all that I had ever set out to do.

Worse still, when I left NASA and the Air Force, I had no more structure in my life. For the first time in more than forty years I had no one to tell me what to do, no one sending me on a mission, giving me challenging work assignments to be completed. Ironically, rather than feeling an exuberant sense of freedom, an elation that I was now free to explore on my own, I felt isolated, alone, and uncertain. Indeed, as a fighter pilot in Korea, making life-or-death decisions in a fraction of a second, and then as an astronaut who had to evaluate data instantly, I consistently made good decisions. Now, as I contemplated asking Joan for a divorce, I found that I could not make even the simplest decisions. I moved from drinking to depression to heavier drinking to deeper depression. I recognized the pattern, but I continually sabotaged my own efforts to do anything about it.

By Christmas 1974, I had mustered enough will to divorce Joan. We had planned to take our three children to Acapulco for the holiday season, and this was where I would lay out my intentions to her. I actually thought that divorce might be a relief to Joan. After all, she had witnessed so much of my withdrawal into myself since returning from the moon, she even said at times that she didn't feel I was the same person she had married. She told me that she would never walk away quietly and grant me the divorce, that she would fight for all she could get financially in divorce proceedings. I think she felt that if she could slow me down with financial concerns, she might be able to delay the divorce long enough to save our marriage. But I didn't care about money; I never really did, and still don't today. To me, money is a commodity that a person must have to function, not a goal in itself.

While Joan and I bounced from vitriolic conversations to silent, sullen, peaceful coexistence in the beachside hotel room, my sister Fay

Ann called to say that while visiting with her family for Christmas in San Francisco, Dad had suffered a heart attack. He was in the hospital. "It doesn't look good, Buzz," she said. I racked my brain trying to decide what to do. Should I head for California, or remain in Mexico? I was already up to my neck in stress from trying to deal with my relationship with Joan, and I figured that Dad was either going to recover or he was going to die before I could get there. Fay Ann was staying with him in the hospital, so I remained in Acapulco with Joan and the kids. The extra days did nothing to improve our relationship, and on December 28, before I left Acapulco, Dad died from complications stemming from the heart attack; he was seventy-eight years of age.

Because of his military service, Dad was buried in Arlington National Cemetery. Joan and our children did not attend the funeral, partially because of the costs involved in travel from California to Washington, D.C., but more because I chose to go alone. I stood stoically—as expected—while the uniformed soldiers carried my father's casket across the frozen grass. My face remained equally as frozen as the casket was placed in position, the flag presented to my oldest sister, and the lonely sound of a trumpet playing "Taps" echoed across the rows of white tombstones. I didn't flinch or shed a tear during the ceremony, but later that night I drowned my sorrows with alcohol.

◑ ○ ◐

AFTER THE FUNERAL, I returned to L.A., and initiated the divorce from Joan. We parted with no additional malice or rancor; we were both too mentally exhausted to fight over anything. Our marriage ended not so much with a loud blow-out as with a slow dwindling away of the energy required to maintain it. I moved into the Oakwood Apartments in Woodland Hills, a nearby section of Los Angeles, so I could stay in contact with our kids, and Joan and I remained friends over the years.

Meanwhile, my drinking was becoming more of a public issue. At one point, Perry Winston, a friend and fellow pilot, wrote a letter to me, frankly chiding me that as a national hero I needed to be more responsible about my drinking. Ironically, Perry worked for a liquor company, and the numbers on his plane were 100 PW, which could have been 100 Perry Winston, or 100 Proof Whiskey. Perry's letter irritated me. *Why is this guy on my case,* I pouted. *Doesn't he recognize that I know what I'm doing?* But then even a worse thought occurred to me: *Maybe he is right.*

Perry was one of the few people not in a recovery group ever to confront me about my drinking. Unfortunately, while landing his plane at Orange County, he hit some lights during his final approach and crashed. Perry did not survive, and I lost a true friend.

● ○ ●

DURING THE DIVORCE process, I lived alone and tended to get extremely down on myself. My friend Jack Daniel's, however, never failed to lift my spirits, albeit falsely. During this time, on my "up" days I was active, traveling, and working; I shared some of my latest homemade energy conservation inventions (along with a mock-up of Apollo) at the Inventors Expo II at the Los Angeles Convention Center, appeared at mental health and charity events, and even granted a few interviews. And I had the beginnings of an idea for a science-fiction story about space travel between star systems that I was calling "Encounter with Tiber." In what became almost a regular pattern, though, when I felt the paralyzing gloom coming on, I'd begin to drink heavily. At first the alcohol soothed the depression, making it at least somewhat bearable. But the situation progressed into depressive-alcoholic binges in which I would withdraw like a hermit into my apartment.

When I ventured out into the real world, I traipsed from doctor to doctor, trying to find help, thinking that I was fighting depression and not accepting the fact that alcoholism could be just as much of an illness for which I needed help. The best thing one psychologist had to offer me was information about where I could go to purchase a good-looking hairpiece. He suggested that I seek out the services of the same guy who had prepared a hairpiece for one of the stars on the television show *Bonanza.* I thought, *Why am I listening to this sick guy?* I left his office, went around the corner, and at the first liquor store I found, I bought a bottle of Scotch. I couldn't even wait until I got home. I swilled several swigs before pulling out of the parking lot.

I returned to UCLA to see Dr. Flinn, whom I had been seeing off and on over the last couple of years. Dr. Flinn referred me to the Veterans Administration hospital, where I could be admitted for a few days to dry out. While I was hospitalized there, Dr. Flinn came to visit me and suggested that I attend some of their Alcoholics Anonymous recovery meetings, held downstairs for the patients at the hospital.

I went to a meeting—in body, but not in spirit. As I looked around the room, I couldn't see myself with this group. There were master sergeants and airmen and others, but nobody with whom I could identify, or so I thought. I was convinced I had no future with these people. I felt that I was too smart for this program; surely their simplistic answers and open admission of alcoholism could not help someone like me.

Some people get mean, violent, loud, or rude when they drink. I did not respond to alcohol in that manner. I wasn't pugnacious, but I was less inhibited and felt more upbeat when I drank. I was charming in a sloppy sort of way; in my estimation, I was enlightened. To other people, I was smashed. But rather than admit I was running out of options as my drinking habits intensified, I chose to find new friends in different bars. That's where I met Beverly Van Ziles.

Beverly was an interior decorator, with the kind of personality who enjoyed taking care of others; she was willing to manage the details of my life, so I was glad to let her. I moved from Oakwood Apartments in the Valley, to Federal Avenue in L.A., to be closer to Beverly's apartment on Barry Avenue, one street over.

By 1975 I was drinking more heavily and more frequently. I'd stop drinking for a few days, and sometimes went as long as two weeks without a drink, but then I'd become frustrated over my inability to persuade anyone to use my scientific knowledge or ideas, and the gloom set in like an incessant London fog. The worse I felt, the more I tried to relieve my frustration through a bottle of Scotch, withdrawing into myself. I shut myself off from friends and family members, un-plugging the telephone and often staying in my apartment for days at a time, the shades drawn, the doors and windows secured. Slumped in a chair, or in bed, a bottle in my hand, I stared aimlessly at the news channels on television.

When my food ran out and I got hungry enough, I would throw on some clothes, get in the car, and drive down to the nearest Kentucky Fried Chicken to bring home several buckets of barbecued chicken, but not before stopping at the corner liquor store to restock my supply of the hard stuff. When I got back to my apartment, I retreated to my bedroom, feeling satisfied that I could hide away for another couple of weeks.

Beverly pleaded with me to stop drinking, to pour the booze down the drain, and to straighten up my apartment. When I ignored her, she did the dirty work for me, dumping the booze and cleaning the untidy mess in which I was wallowing. I appreciated her attempts to help me, but her words and actions only plunged me deeper into despair.

Finally, in early August, she threatened to break off our relation-ship, confiding to me that she felt defeated. I persuaded her to give me one more chance. Beverly brought me to her apartment so she could look after me, and that night I killed off one last bottle of Scotch. The next morning, August 7, 1975, I checked in—ironically—to Bev-erly Manor, a civilian hospital in Orange County, where Dr. Flinn had made arrangements. The hospital had formerly been a nursing home, but was now well known as a premier alcoholism rehabilitation center. I stayed there for twenty-eight days under the care of the hospital's medical director, Dr. Max Schneider.

As Cindy Simpson, the admissions receptionist, sought to fill out the paperwork, it was obvious that she didn't recognize me. When she asked for my mother's maiden name, I couldn't resist. "Take a guess," I said.

"I have no idea," the woman replied.

"I'll give you a hint," I toyed with her. "Her maiden name begins with an *m* and ends with *n*."

I grew up in Montclair, New Jersey, with my parents and two sisters, Madeline and Fay Ann. *Aldrin Collection*

When I was a center on the Montclair High School football team I gave this photo to my mother, with the inscription: "To the best Mother in the world with all my love, Buzz," 1947. *Aldrin Collection*

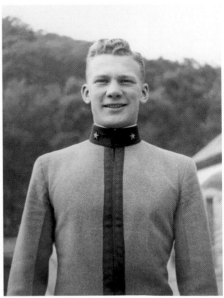

I was an eager plebe as I started my education at the Military Academy at West Point. I already knew I wanted to join the Air Force, 1948. *Aldrin Collection*

Learning to fly jets in advanced flight training at Bryan Air Force Base in Texas, 1952. *United States Air Force*

At K-13 air base in Suwon, Korea, in front of the flight operations building reporting on one of my sixty-six missions there, 1953. *Aldrin Collection*

Relaxing with my fellow fighter pilots in Bitburg, Germany, where I was on duty for three years, 1958. *Aldrin Collection*

Soon to be stationed in Korea, I explained to my father how I could intercept enemy aircraft as a fighter pilot, 1952. *Aldrin Collection*

As a colonel in the Air Force with my doctorate in astronautics from MIT, I was selected by NASA for the astronaut program in 1963. *NASA*

At the rear of *Gemini* spacecraft, training with the maneuvering unit for my first mission and spacewalk, 1966. *NASA*

I thought underwater training was the best preparation for space-walking and gladly became the first astronaut to do so, 1966. *NASA*

Ready to go into earth orbit on *Gemini 12* with Jim Lovell for five days, 1966. *NASA*

Back inside our *Gemini* spacecraft after a record five-and-a-half-hour spacewalk, 1966. *NASA*

Returning from a training mission, I am greeted by my first wife, Joan, and our three children, Mike, Jan, and Andy.
Aldrin Collection

Neil, Mike, and I are on a ship during a training mission to practice spacecraft recovery, 1969. *NASA*

As Lunar Module Pilot, I prepared the *Eagle* lunar module for separation from *Columbia* to commence our powered descent to the surface of the moon, 1969. *NASA*

I felt very fortunate to become part of the first moon landing on *Apollo 11* with Mike Collins (left) and Neil Armstrong. *NASA*

Neil, Mike, and I in front of the *Saturn V* on the day it was rolled out to the launch pad for our mission, 1969. *Michel Tiziou/Jacques Tiziou News Service*

My life had led me to the right place at the right time, and my passion for space has continued all my life, 1969. *NASA*

Enjoying the immense view of earth on my *Gemini* space-walk. Secured by a tether to the spacecraft, I had no sense of our actual speed—17,500 miles per hour—but I could feel the curve of the earth as we orbited every ninety minutes, 1966. *NASA*

Descending the *Eagle* ladder to join Neil and take my first step onto the lunar surface, 1969. *NASA*

Neil took this photo of me—known as the "visor shot"—and people often ask what makes it so special. I have three words: location, location, location!
NASA

My boot print on the moon's surface. It will remain intact for thousands of years.
NASA

We began our world tour with ticker-tape parades in major cities in the United States, beginning with New York City, on August 13, 1969. *NASA*

At New York's City Hall, where we were received by Mayor John Lindsay, following the ticker-tape parade. *NASA*

With Gina Lollobrigida in Rome on the world tour, 1969. Lois and I are good friends with her today. *Aldrin Collection*

My family attended the Nixon state dinner in Los Angeles. From left to right: me, my brother-in-law Chuck Crowell, my sister Maddi, President Nixon, my aunt Madeline, my sister Fay Ann, and my father. *Aldrin Collection*

Nineteen years after the world tour, I married the love of my life, Lois Driggs, on Valentine's Day 1988, at the bank headquarters of her family's company in Phoenix, Arizona. *Aldrin Collection*

On one of my trips to Sweden, I explained the Hasselblad camera we used on the moon to King Carl Gustaf and Queen Silvia of Sweden, and Queen Elizabeth and Prince Philip of England, 1983. *Aldrin Collection*

Every five years the *Apollo 11* crew reunites at the White House to celebrate America's great accomplishment of landing on the moon. In 1979 with President Jimmy Carter. *Official White House Photograph*

Neil, Mike, and I at the Smithsonian National Air and Space Museum, following our visit with President Carter for a ceremony on the steps of the White House. This 1979 reunion for our tenth anniversary was especially meaningful to me. *NASA*

The fifteenth *Apollo 11* anniversary with President Ronald Reagan in 1984. *Official White House Photograph*

The twentieth anniversary of *Apollo 11* with President George H. W. Bush in 1989. *Official White House Photograph*

The twenty-fifth anniversary of *Apollo 11* with President Bill Clinton in 1994. During President Clinton's term, we also visited with him in the Oval Office for the thirtieth anniversary. *Official White House Photograph*

The thirty-fifth anniversary of *Apollo 11* with President George W. Bush in 2004. *Official White House Photograph*

Congratulating Tom Hanks on his Emmy Award in 1998 for the miniseries *From the Earth to the Moon.* He has been a great friend and supporter to all astronauts. *Aldrin Collection*

My good friend and film director Jim Cameron and I share a love of adventure in the oceans and in space.
Jules Verne Adventures

Sir Richard Branson is definitely a fellow explorer. Here we are in the Mojave Desert for a test flight of Burt Rutan and Paul Allen's *SpaceShipOne*—the prototype for Richard's space tourism company, Virgin Galactic, 2004.
Aldrin Collection

I joined Hugh Downs on this Russian nuclear icebreaker to explore the North Pole. *Aldrin Collection*

I never tire of feeling the freedom of weightlessness. I have gone on six zero-gravity flights since 2004 to help share the experience with people interested in space tourism. This flight coincided with the launch of my brand, Rocket Hero. *Zero Gravity Corporation/Space Adventures*

In October 2008, my family gathered for a party at our home to help celebrate my thirtieth year of sobriety. From left to right: my grandson Jeffrey, Jan, Jan's fiancé Bruce, my son Andy's wife Maureen, Andy, and my stepchildren, Lisa, Brynn, and Bryant. My son Mike sent his Aloha greetings from Hawaii. *Aldrin Collection*

As we celebrate every Valentine's Day, Lois and I are grateful for the partnership we have enjoyed for more than twenty-one years. We intend to continue our great life for perhaps another twenty! *Aldrin Collection*

"I'm really sorry, sir; I honestly don't know."

"It's *Moon!*" I said. "I've been there, you know." The receptionist dutifully wrote the name into the space, no doubt wanting to complete the forms as hurriedly as possible. She probably never fully realized that my mother's maiden name was Marion Moon.

I was assigned to a room with a roommate. We used only first names; the hospital attempted to maintain some level of anonymity among its clients. In the early 1970s, it was not as socially acceptable for celebrities to seek treatment for alcoholism, so the hospital tried to handle matters as discreetly as possible. In some ways I appreciated that, but there was something else in me that wanted people to know me, to recognize me as one of the first men to walk on the moon. Few did, or if they did, they didn't let on, and it bugged me.

I had been treated for depression in several hospitals, but going to Beverly Manor was my first token admission that my problems stemmed from alcoholism as well. In truth, had it not been for Dr. Flinn and my girlfriend Beverly, I might not have acquiesced. I wasn't convinced I needed to be there, but the doctors, nurses, and staff at the treatment center recognized immediately that my pride and strong ego worked against me as far as getting well was concerned.

I was especially miserable during the first few days—the detoxification period. Dr. Schneider informed us that to ease the discomfort of coming off alcohol, most of the new patients at Beverly Manor started out on some sort of drug—benzodiazodine, lithium, phenobarbitol, or something similar—taken in decreasing amounts over three to seven days. I sat with my arms folded across my chest, moody and sullen and a reluctant participant in the multitudinous meetings, group sessions, lectures about addiction, one-on-one counseling, and other cognitive therapy, designed to help a person recognize his or her feelings, and learn how to deal with them without alcohol and drugs. These sessions were not always comfortable; many of the patients—like me—had great difficulty admitting the damage that alcohol had done to their families, careers, or cognitive abilities. I was a resistant patient, avoiding any real confrontation with myself, for as long as I could. I especially disliked the chores that the hospital expected me to do, as they did of all of the patients. My peers chided me, and eventually I did a better job of keeping my room neat and taking my turn in community tasks. But it was the loving, compassionate concern of the hospital's staff that ultimately wore me down. They created an atmosphere in which I could safely admit my innermost vulnerabilities.

Finally, I was able to say the words and mean them: "Hi, I'm Buzz, and I'm an alcoholic." At Beverly Manor I learned more about the dynamics of alcoholism, and was encouraged to begin a "twelve-step" type of recovery plan. The thrust of the program cut through all of the excuses for alcoholism and the predispositions toward alcoholism. The doctors, nurses, and staff were wonderfully supportive, and I felt that I was making progress again. My lead counselor was Barbara Phillips, a real drama queen with a great sense of humor and a contagious laugh; Barbara was a recovering alcoholic herself.

Linda Lederer, the occupational therapist who worked directly with me at Beverly Manor, was tremendously patient with me, and wonderfully encouraging, but she could also be firm when necessary. When I had several cases of my books sent in to the hospital and was signing them for my fellow patients, Linda balked. "Buzz, you can't do that. We're trying to maintain your anonymity here, not to promote your book!" Linda also recognized the issue of pride as a major part of my denial. She wanted me to drop the façade that everything was okay with me. "You don't have to be anybody special here, Buzz. Just be you. That's special enough."

Linda directed group sessions on assertive communication, time management, therapeutic exercise, teambuilding sessions, and even crafts workshops. Beverly Manor offered crafts of all sorts, everything from knitting to macramé, ceramics, needlepoint, and leather work. The idea was to have a hobby, but the activities also fostered camaraderie. I chose to make a pair of leather moccasins, but I had trouble with the instructions. I could land a spacecraft on the moon, but I had difficulty deciding which loop of rawhide to stitch through various parts of the leather. I eventually completed the moccasins and wore them for the remainder of my stay at the hospital.

On one of my better days, while still at Beverly Manor, I received word that I had a visitor. The actor Cliff Robertson had stopped by to talk with me about the script for the television movie based on my book, *Return to Earth*. The movie was being produced by Alan King, a man better known as a comedian, but who also had a desire to present dramatic works. He would be assisted by his partner, Rupert Hitzig, who had worked out the deal with me originally when I was still married to Joan and living at Hidden Hills.

Cliff Robertson was to play me in the movie, so he wanted to get to know me. I enjoyed talking with Cliff and discovered that he was an airplane enthusiast himself, and a pilot with more than 1,500 hours in the cockpit. He owned several vintage airplanes, including a British Spitfire and a German ME-108 trainer, and he flew them all. We quickly struck up a lasting friendship, and when I was released from Beverly Manor, he took me flying in one of his biplanes.

Cliff had been doing mostly feature films, but he seemed fascinated with my story. "I realize that this is an important story," he told me, "and one that might do some good." Cliff had a close relative who had battled alcoholism, so although the story touched only briefly on alcohol, Cliff understood that my depression had to be closely linked to my drinking. We talked further about the idea that with all of NASA's technology, one element still could not be totally programmed—the astronaut. "I want people to see you as a real human being," Cliff said. The movie was scheduled to air on the ABC network on May 14, 1976.

When I left Beverly Manor, to help control my depression and my craving for alcohol, the doctors admonished me about possibly de-structive behaviors. Dr. Schneider explained that it could take five years or more to get the effects of alcohol fully out of the human system. Even going to a hospital and being put under anesthesia could send my body into a tailspin. Most addiction experts believed that ninety days was the minimum time necessary to make headway against the disease. I had been sober for only twenty-eight days.

They also prescribed a lithium compound drug intended to help control my mood shifts. Drug treatments rarely seemed to help me deal with depression. Maybe they'd have been more effective if I hadn't chased them with Scotch.

In early October I was in New York, where I had lunch with movie producers Rupert Hitzig and Alan King. I realized that Rupert was the creative force behind the company producing *Return to Earth*, and Alan was the businessman. We ate in the Rainbow Room, at 30 Rockefeller Plaza, sixty-five stories over Manhattan. "We thought you'd feel more at home eating one thousand feet above sea level," Alan quipped.

I was still flying high back in California when I received a letter from Universal Studios, rejecting the movie treatment for my new science fiction story, "Encounter with Tiber." The rejection brought me back to earth with a resounding thud. When I told Beverly about it, she may have sensed I was close to the edge. She encouraged me to come home with her.

Four months after we met, I moved in with Beverly at her Barry Avenue apartment. Whether moving in with her was a knee-jerk response to my divorce from Joan or to the disappointment over the "Tiber" rejection, I can't say for sure. But it was definitely a rebound relationship. She was a strong woman, with a controlling nature, and she quickly took possession of a lot of the details of my life that I no longer cared to deal with, or had chosen to ignore. And she liked to drink.

Beverly and I were married on New Year's Eve 1975, at a Mexican resort in Cabo San Lucas. It was a tumultuous marriage from the start, although we had some good times, too. We traveled quite a bit, especially throughout 1976.

I was still working periodically with the National Association of Mental Health, and production had started on the TV movie of *Return to Earth*. The tie-in was a natural. I had visited the set only once, as had my former wife, Joan, but I had read the script and was looking forward to seeing the debut of director Jud Taylor's movie rendition of my story. In addition to Cliff Robertson, the movie starred Shirley Knight as Joan, and Stefanie Powers as Marianne.

On March 25, 1976, I spoke in Long Beach at a meeting of the Mental Health Association of Los Angeles County aboard the docked ocean liner *Queen Mary*. As in most of my talks for NAMH, I encouraged the audience to change their image of people seeking help for depression and other forms of mental illness.

"Superb accomplishments don't make people superhuman," I told them, "and America's placement of astronauts on a pedestal was probably to be expected, but was unrealistic. We're not all that superhuman." I also admitted to the audience that I had been hospitalized for alcoholism. "I've decided not to cover things up this time," I said, noting that for too long I had tried to keep matters quiet when I first suffered depression.

People shun help for mental illness for three reasons, I told the crowd. First, they may be afraid they'll get locked up. Second, they think it will cost them every penny they have for treatment. Third, they think job opportunities will be denied them and that their neighbors will laugh at them. Unfortunately, all of those things still happen today, but they were more likely to happen if a person admitted to depression and alcoholism in the mid-seventies. This was one of my first public admissions regarding my problems with alcohol. The relatively small crowd was not surprised; most of the people attending the meeting were well aware of the link between alcohol and depression. About six weeks later, however, the response would be quite different.

● ○ ●

ON MAY 8, 1976, I attended the "Operation Understanding" banquet at the Shoreham Americana Hotel in Washington, D.C., sponsored by the National Council on Alcoholism (NCA). I had achieved less than a year of sobriety at this point, and several people cautioned me against going public about my alcoholism. No doubt they were not only worried about the repercussions such public exposure might have in my life; they were also concerned that I had not been living sober long enough. They were right.

But this was the first time that a large group of celebrities planned to declare themselves publicly as "controlled alcoholics" in a campaign to encourage others afflicted with alcoholism to seek help for their drinking problems, and I wanted to be a part of it.

It was an amazing evening. The excitement in the air was almost palpable as twelve hundred people sat around banquet tables in the Shoreham ballroom. Although familiar big-band music played in the background, everyone sensed that this would be unlike any other event they had ever attended. Something special was about to happen.

When the house lights dimmed, a two-tiered dais was illuminated on the platform at the front of the huge hall. For the next twenty-five minutes, CBS television network vice president Thomas J. Swafford and entertainer Johnny Grant introduced a most unusual assortment of dignitaries. The fifty-two people included Arkansas congressman Wilbur D. Mills; entertainer Dick Van Dyke; Garry Moore, best known as the host of the popular *What's My Line?* television show; Robert Young, known to millions as television's *Marcus Welby, M.D.;* Sylvester J. Tinker, the chief of the Osage Indian Nation; as well as an airline captain, several sports stars, Broadway and recording stars, a surgeon, various Hollywood movie and television stars, a member of Great Britain's House of Lords, prominent leaders from the spheres of business, religion, labor, journalism, the armed forces, and, of course, me. Each person on the dais was greeted with tremendous applause.

When the last person was introduced, Thomas Swafford announced, "Ladies and gentlemen, we are recovered alcoholics."

The room exploded with even more thunderous applause as the audience rose to its feet in one motion. This was the first time in history that such a large group of public figures had identified themselves as alcoholics. Of course, prior to that event, rumors had swirled for years about certain individuals in the room, but now here we were, admitting to the world that we needed help to win the battle of the bottle. In his remarks, NCA's president, John MacIver, said, "I am more than a little awed. It is given to very few of us to be present at one of those moments when you know history is being made. This event will do more to reduce alcoholism's stigma than anything ever attempted. This is a historic occasion. It should dispel once and for all that alcoholism does not happen to nice people."

The intense emotion we felt in the room all evening long reached a peak when recovering alcoholics in the audience were invited to join those on the platform. Hundreds of men and women rose, as those of us on the platform gave them a standing ovation.

Afterwards, in an impromptu news conference, I told the media how I had begun drinking more heavily during my bouts of depression. "Some people may look down their noses at an astronaut who admits he has suffered from depression or alcoholism," I said, "but there are benefits and good feelings derived from standing up and being counted." I talked briefly about how astronauts were often thought of as "supermen" by the public, and that NASA did its best to support that image. "No career field is immune from alcoholism," I emphasized, much to the chagrin of some of my former colleagues in the military and in the space program.

Operation Understanding was a signature event. More than thirty years later, Robert J. Lindsey, president of the National Council on Alcoholism and Drug Dependence, recalled it as a milestone in American history. "Without question, Operation Understanding was the most critically important public event in our field to reduce the public stigma and misunderstanding of the disease of alcoholism that stands in the way of people seeking help."[12]

With pleasant memories of Operation Understanding still running through my mind, a few days later, on May 14, *Return to Earth* aired and garnered strong ratings. Millions of people watched the movie and empathized with Cliff Robertson's portrayal of me. Suddenly I was fa-

---

[12] Interview with Lisa Cannon, StarBuzz LLC, December 19, 2008.

mous again—this time for completely different reasons. Many people were favorably impressed that an astronaut would admit to his personal struggle with depression, and would seek help. To me, that made it worthwhile. Producers Rupert Hitzig and Alan King received a special award for the film presented by First Lady Rosalyn Carter and the National Association of Mental Health.

● ○ ●

BUT WITHIN A few months of making a public statement in Washington, D.C., that I was a recovered alcoholic, I began drinking again.

Eventually, Dr. Flinn recommended that I enter a twenty-eight-day period of detox and rehab at St. John's Hospital, in Santa Monica, since there was no such program at the UCLA facility where Flinn practiced. While at St. John's, I met Dr. Joe Takamine, a lean, sandy-haired doctor of internal medicine who later became an addiction specialist in California, well known for treating a number of Hollywood celebrities. Unfortunately, I didn't take this program seriously, and after a few days, I simply walked out of the hospital and walked all the way home. The rooms were not locked, so I just left.

After another round of low times, Dr. Flinn arranged for me to be admitted a second time to St. John's to try the program again. This time I stuck it out. Although it was not a mandatory part of the program, I attended several weekly meetings of Alcoholics Anonymous that were held at St. John's.

While I was there, Dr. Takamine cautioned me, "You may not be responsible for your disease, but you sure should be responsible for your recovery—and that is your choice. There is only one real reason for relapse," Dr. Takamine told me. "You want to . . . and you choose to do so." I couldn't disagree with him, but I also couldn't find within myself the power to say no to a drink.

Because of my military background, the St. John's counselors recommended that I meet retired Navy admiral Bud Scoles, a leader in the West Los Angeles Alcoholics Anonymous group. I hit it off immediately with Bud, and he not only encouraged me to attend AA meetings, but offered to become my first Alcoholics Anonymous sponsor. The sponsor's role could take many forms: friend, mentor, motivator, counselor, or simply someone to check up on you to make sure that you weren't sprawled out alone in a drunken stupor. At one time or another, Bud served in all of those capacities for me.

Bud got me going to more meetings than I could count. A typical week included a Wednesday noon stag meeting at Uncle John's Deli in Santa Monica. Thursday nights found us at an AA workshop, followed by a speaker, at the Brentwood Presbyterian Church on San Vicente. Friday nights I attended an AA meeting at St. Augustine's church on Fourth Street. Saturday nights I went to an AA meeting at the Senior Citizens' Center on Ocean Avenue. A Sunday night stag meeting met after supper at a different person's home each week. This meeting was not open to general attendance, but included Bud, Bob Palmer—who would later become my second sponsor—Dick Boolootian, a Ph.D. who taught at a local university, two high-profile lawyers, and me. On Monday nights I attended meetings at Ohio Avenue in West L.A. Bud's plan, which I later learned is basic Alcoholics Anonymous procedure, was for me to attend ninety meetings in ninety days. At each meeting there were men and women (except at the stag meetings) who were somewhere along in the process of staying sober. Some had been sober for only a few days, others a few years, still others for decades. The striking characteristic at almost all of the meetings was the encouragement and positive reinforcement we all gave to each other. The Alcoholics Anonymous groups truly became like a church or a family for many people, myself included.

I responded well to the AA programs, but I still struggled in my attempts to achieve and maintain sobriety. Since my mentor Bud Scoles was a Navy guy, he also frequented the Navy facility in Long Beach, where Captain Joseph Pursch, the psychiatrist, served as director of the Naval Regional Medical Center. The Navy was quite involved in alcoholic recovery programs at that time, and Dr. Pursch was widely regarded as the foremost authority in the field of alcoholism who had never been an alcoholic himself. Admiral Scoles encouraged me to attend some of the Navy recovery programs, and I took his advice, sometimes attending three or four meetings on the same day, when I felt more desperate.

In September 1976, Beverly and I set up an appointment to see Dr. Pursch ostensibly for possible treatment as a couple, but Beverly doubtless went along only to get me into treatment. That quickly became evident when the doctor questioned Beverly and me about our drinking. "I suppose I could eventually become an alcoholic," she said, "but we're not here for me. We're here for Buzz."

Dr. Pursch nodded in understanding and let the matter drop. He agreed to evaluate and work with us on an outpatient basis. I wanted medication for depression, but the doctor wanted me to get sober. I didn't see how that was going to work, and I let the doctor know it. "Thanks, but no thanks," I said.

On Monday evening, September 20, 1976, I spoke to a full house at the Lompoc, California, Civic Auditorium, sponsored by the Mental Health Association. In the course of my speech I described how I had overcome depression and had been treated for alcoholism. "I've been involved in all kinds of races," I told the audience, "but running for happiness is the most important one I've been in." I admitted to the crowd that although I had served as chairman of the National Association of Mental Health, my problems were not solved, and when depression returned, to escape, I turned to alcohol. "I could accept mental health as an illness," I said, "but not alcoholism as an illness."

My speech inspired the audience, and my words must have inspired me, too, because two days later I went back to Pursch, this time practically begging him to take me on as a patient.

On September 22, 1976, Dr. Pursch admitted me to the Navy Regional Medical Center for a full six weeks so he could work more closely with me. While at the Naval hospital, as part of their alcohol treatment program, we boarded Navy vans and drove to attend local Alcoholics Anonymous meetings, such as the one in Bellflower. Attendance was not optional.

In counseling, Dr. Pursch began by trying to build a relationship with me. He spoke with a distinct Hungarian accent. "Tell me why you are here," he began, as if he didn't know, "and by the way, whatever you tell me, I will never tell anyone else without your permission." The doctor stopped and, in an almost whimsical manner, added, "Unless you put me on the spot. If you tell me that you're going to shoot someone, I'll have you arrested."

Pursch and I both smiled. "So tell me," he continued, "what is it that brings you to me? I have to be here, but why are *you* here?"

I relaxed and tried to answer the doctor's questions as best I could. As we talked, I felt confident that I could trust him. *Maybe this can help*, I thought. I began to spill my insides to him. I told him about the discipline and rigidity I had lived with all my life, reinforced by my attending West Point, Air Force flight training, becoming a combat fighter pilot, earning my doctorate at MIT, and culminating in the NASA program, and then back to the Air Force. All along the way, the expected levels of performance grew higher and higher. Then, upon coming back from the moon, I was a news item, going from city to city, riding in parades all around the world, receiving the keys to the city— and anything else I wanted. When I went back to the Air Force, life didn't turn out the way I thought it should. I was passed over for promotion to brigadier general and an assignment that I truly wanted, to be commandant to the cadets at the Air Force Academy. Instead, I was given command of the test pilot program at Edwards Air Force base in California. That sounds like a plum position, but not for me. I was one of the few astronauts in the program at that time who had never been a test pilot. Neil was a former test pilot. So was Mike, but not me. And now, after nearly twenty years in the Air Force, including three and a half at MIT, and seven and a half at NASA, they wanted me to command the test pilot school instead of the Academy.

I explained to Dr. Pursch that since I returned from the moon, I had felt taken advantage of, exploited as people wanted to use my fame for their own purposes.

From then on, any time that I felt the "system" was taking unfair advantage of me and my fame—whether by individuals, companies, organizations, or the military—to deal with those growing resentments, I turned increasingly to alcohol. The demons in my mind tossed up questions such as, *What did I get for serving my country all these years? I'm being relegated to playing the hero, and everyone wants a piece of me. But will they listen to my ideas? Will they value what I can offer for the future?* Then, to keep my life afloat, I would often speak at their conventions and sign autographs, for very little if any honorarium. I felt totally degraded as a person.

I recognized the inherent inconsistency; I didn't want to feel that way, yet in all honesty, I did. I knew that such thoughts were "unacceptable" to the public, to my family, and to myself, and I had a sensitive conscience, so there was no better remedy for putting my conscience to sleep for a while than with alcohol.

I confessed to the psychiatrist that since I had retired, I sensed no purpose and no structure to my life. I wasn't sure what to do next. Pursch listened intently, but he continued to emphasize that my top priority was to get sober and stay that way.

One day early on in our treatment program, I asked the psychiatrist straight out, "Can alcoholics ever drink again?" I was hoping that he would respond positively, that yes, once a person went through treatment, he or she could handle alcohol. Pursch didn't bite, but he did surprise me.

"Of course an alcoholic can drink again. They do it all the time."

"What do you mean?"

"Some alcoholics can drink again, but you, Buzz Aldrin, cannot drink again without getting into problems."

"Well, I don't lose control of my ability to function every time I drink."

"Maybe not, but you have become an unpredictable drinker, Buzz. Some people may have a drink and walk away from the bar. You have a hard time taking one drink without taking four or five more."

I met with Dr. Pursch for about an hour every week, then eventually once every couple of months. We talked about everything from my strict upbringing, always trying to please my father, to being the second man out of the lunar module after Neil Armstrong, and always being known as the *second* man to walk on the moon, and continually being reminded of that fact. At the conclusion of each meeting, Dr. Pursch asked, "Now, how would you summarize what we have talked about and what you need to do? Once you are out the door, you're on your own."

At one point I had a bit of a falling-out with him. I wanted him to meet more frequently with me, to treat me in a psychoanalytic way, and to prescribe some medication for me. Pursch refused. "You will not get well that way," he said bluntly.

I could feel my hackles rising. "May I remind you, Captain, that I am a retired Air Force colonel, and that I am entitled to this care?"

"Yes, I understand that you are retired military, and you are indeed entitled to treatment. And that means you receive the treatment I am prescribing for you, and my prescription for you right now is not pills or psychoanalysis. Right now you need to get sober."

I rose to leave, and walked briskly toward the door, but before I reached it, I stopped and snapped at him, "I won't be coming back. Furthermore, I assure you that I will have no trouble finding another psychiatrist in Los Angeles to treat me."

Dr. Pursch held his ground. "I don't think you'll have any trouble at all finding someone who will give you what you want. All you have to do is tell them who you are."

I left Dr. Pursch and found Dr. Sturdevant, and began going to him for treatment. Pursch was right; I could find treatment with pills and psychoanalysis, but that did not help me. I could handle the depression, but I needed someone to confront me and to help keep me accountable about the drinking. I did nothing but prolong the nightmare.

Eventually I returned to Dr. Pursch again, seeking his help. This time the doctor surprised me. Rather than admitting me again to the naval hospital, he said, "I think you should meet Clancy Imislund. Clancy is a former alcoholic who has been sober for a long time. I think he can help you."

I was insulted and shocked. "You would rather send me to a recovering drunk than to a man of Dr. Sturdevant's caliber?"

"You don't need academics, medication, or psychoanalysis. You are too bright, Buzz, too strong. Granted, your genetic disposition may tend to cause you to be depressed, and that same genetic makeup allows you to drink more than most people without always feeling its ill effects, but if you want to get well, you must seek help in getting sober and staying sober. Clancy can help you do that."

After a while, I met with Dr. Pursch only to maintain my pilot's medical evaluation for the FAA. An Air Force dictum of some sort basically said, "If Buzz Aldrin applies for a medical certificate to fly an airplane again, he must have a psychiatric exam every year." That irritated me because I was doing my best to remain sober, and the psychiatrists still had to verify my ability to fly an airplane. Although I thought it unfair at the time, I now see it as a wise rule, but I sure didn't feel that way then.

By the end of the year I had tired of Beverly telling me what to do—although, in her defense, she was probably simply trying to save my life—and after a loud disagreement, I told her I wanted a divorce. I was on a roll—two divorces in less than two years. In the process, the divorce with Beverly managed to clean out my bank accounts, or what was left of them. But it was worth it to be back on my own again. In retrospect, Beverly loved me as best she could until she could love me no longer. In many ways, however, I will always be grateful to her for encouraging me to seek help for alcoholism, not simply depression. That was worth far more than mere money.

I moved out of Beverly's place to a newly-built duplex on Barry Avenue. While living there, I got a job with the Hillcrest Cadillac dealership, which is a story in itself.

10

TURNING
POINT

I'VE ALWAYS LIKED CARS, THE FASTER THE BETTER. BUT I never dreamed of selling cars, not until I got to the point of needing some form of gainful employment. I was ready to take almost any honest job. I'm not sure what prompted me to try it, other than sheer desperation, especially since I had never sold anything in my life.

While attending Alcoholics Anonymous meetings with Admiral Bud Scoles, I got to know some of the people who were regulars. A guy named Lynch showed up every week and was well thought of because he had a good job as a Cadillac salesman. I talked to him and asked him, "How did you get that job?"

He said that he would recommend me to the owner and maybe I could get a job there, too. Selling cars is a noble profession for many people; for me it was a desperate step. I was trying to save my life, and I needed to be doing something besides sulking alone in my apartment.

I had an interview with Mike Brown, the son of the owner, and the next thing I knew, in July 1977, I was going to work at the Hillcrest Cadillac dealership in Beverly Hills every day. I was a terrible salesman, though. People came onto the lot in search of a car, and as soon as I struck up a conversation with them, the subject immediately turned from the comfort and convenience of a new or used luxury automobile to space travel. I spent more time signing autographs than anything else. Worse yet, I was too honest. I was not a backslapping closer. I could inform the customer, but I could not glibly tell a prospective customer that our cars were his or her best choice, when I knew the weaknesses of our vehicles as well as the advantages. Nor could I sell an expensive Cadillac to somebody who I knew could not afford it, or sell the person a bunch of options that he didn't need. When I told the truth, customers sometimes smiled broadly, shook my hand, and walked away. "Great to meet you, Buzz!" they'd say as they headed out of our lot, smiling, but without buying anything. Mike Brown just shook his head.

H. R. ("Bob") Haldeman, President Nixon's White House Chief of Staff, and a key figure in the Nixon Watergate scandal, came in to the dealership one day. Bob had been born and raised in California, so no doubt he was glad to be out of the Washington, D.C., fishbowl for a few days. I could relate to enduring a media frenzy, and we chatted idly for a few minutes about his ordeal. I showed him some cars while we talked about President Nixon and his Watergate troubles, but do you think that I could sell him a Cadillac? No way. I couldn't sell a car to save my life. In fact, I didn't sell a single car the entire time I worked at Hillcrest. But at least I drove a nice blue-and-white Cadillac for a while.

● ○ ●

LATER THAT SAME month, I ventured out to Edwards Air Force Base to view the first atmospheric "free" flight of the *Enterprise,* NASA's new space shuttle test vehicle, as it landed on its own after being hitched to the back of a 747 jumbo jet. The shuttle was originally intended to be named *Constitution,* but *Star Trek* fans led a write-in campaign urging that it be christened *Enterprise.* It was my first time back at Edwards since my ignominious departure five years earlier. It felt a bit odd to be standing in street clothes among the spectators for the test event, but I also felt relieved on a personal level, and hopeful about the new direction in which NASA was headed.

The space shuttle captured the public's attention with its dazzling display of a different kind of flying spacecraft as it landed on a dry lake-bed runway seven and a half miles long. The winged seventy-five-ton spaceship had already flown piggyback-style, locked to the big jet in a "captive" flight a few weeks earlier. Now, for its first free flight, cars and campers crowded the desert highway that led to the base. Thousands of spectators made the predawn drive over the mountains from Los Angeles to the Mojave plateau to watch the test landing. Already, NASA was planning to send the shuttle on its first flight into space in 1979 from Cape Canaveral, and that mission and the next three to follow were scheduled to end with airplane-like landings at Edwards on the special clay, silt, and sand lake-bed runway.

● ○ ●

THE DAY AT Edwards, exhilarating as it was to watch the landing of the shuttle, was also a bitter reminder that I had been trying to exist on my Air Force retirement pay, half of which went to Joan and the kids, and the new job I was trying out at the Cadillac dealership. Added to that, I was still dealing with periodic bouts of depression. My life seemed a perennial struggle, in which I often wondered, *Where do I fit in after being an astronaut on the moon?* The Technicolor had drained from my life, and I felt discouraged. I couldn't see how anything could change in the near future. The orderly progressive structure of my early years in which I had achieved so much had stalled. Inevitably, it seemed, I would spiral downward when the people at NASA or the aerospace companies for whom I served as a consultant refused to consider my ideas, ideas that I knew beyond a doubt could help forward our space program. When I was "up," I charged ahead, believing that change was possible, and that I could make a difference. But when I was "down," numbness overcame me and after a while I soothed my uneasiness by turning to alcohol.

About that time, Dr. Joseph Pursch reminded me to seek out Clancy Imislund. I had met Clancy while I was still married to Beverly, when I attended one of the meetings recommended by Dr. Don Flinn, but I really didn't become part of his group until Dr. Pursch recommended him as well. Clancy was known as a more rigid recovery group leader. He could be a little rough around the edges, and he shot straight with the people who came to his meetings, sometimes too straight. "Half of you attending this meeting are going to die drunk," he said, partially for effect, and partially as a serious warning. Nevertheless, men and women came to his meetings from far and wide, and from every stratum of society; they knew that he loved them enough to tell them the truth.

Once I got to know Clancy, I understood why the psychiatrists held this nonmedical recovery leader in such high regard. Clancy knew what it was like to be an alcoholic. In our conversations, I discovered that he genuinely empathized with what I had experienced; he understood how I felt. As he described his own inability to cope with alcohol, I thought I was listening to my own inner story. Certainly the details of Clancy's story were different, but his frustration and exasperation at not being able to control his own desires resonated with me. Several decades earlier, he'd drunk so much that he was thrown out of the Los Angeles Midnight Mission, the city's downtown shelter for homeless people, alcoholics, and drug addicts. He had lost his job, his home, and his family, and he had gotten his two front teeth kicked out in an alter-cation. He almost died, but he walked seven miles in the rain to Wilshire and Fairfax, where there was an Alcoholics Anonymous meeting, and the people there saved his life. Years later, after remaining sober, Clancy left a secure job and took a position running that same Midnight Mission from which he had been ejected years earlier. Since then he had worked with all sorts of people, from multimillionaire business tycoons to Hollywood stars to street people. By the time I met him, he'd been sober for nearly twenty years.

One of the things I liked about Clancy was that he treated me just like anyone else. I was not Buzz Aldrin, astronaut; I was just Buzz, an alcoholic.

Clancy was able to get me to do things that I wouldn't ordinarily do, especially since they were not intellectually defensible. For example, early on he invited a bunch of other alcoholics and me to come to his home on the outskirts of Venice for a cookout and an afternoon of vol-leyball in his backyard. Before we could play, however, Clancy passed out some shovels. He stabled a pony in his backyard, so we had to clean up the pony excrement first. The reason was not necessarily to make us nicer or better people, but to gradually change our relationships with the world around us, and our psychological perspectives on our inner worlds. Clancy was also big on humility as an important part of recovery, and few things were more humbling than Hollywood celebrity types—and former astronauts—shoveling pony poop.

I had sworn off drinking several times before meeting Clancy, and had stretched my abstinence to thirty days on at least ten separate occasions. But I'd always found my way back to another bar or another bottle of Scotch. I'd feel almost as though someone had inserted a wind-up spring in my mind while I was sleeping, and that each day the spring was getting tighter and tighter. Before long, I started thinking that a drink might make me feel better. After a while, another drink followed the first, then a second and a third.

With Clancy, I found an "outside" guy who was willing to shoot straight with me. He could see both the problem and me, and he offered advice based on a more objective perspective. When I talked with Clancy about what I was going through, it helped bring clarity to my problem.

Clancy visited me at my workplace at the Hillcrest Cadillac dealership in Beverly Hills. "Leave this job," he told me straightforwardly. "Get out of here. You're not doing anything. You're just sitting in this office all day and people come by to look at the astronaut on display."

Then one day Clancy came in and told the Browns that I should not be working there. "This is not the sort of job for Buzz Aldrin," he told the owners. Clancy felt it was demeaning for a man like me, who was an American hero who had walked on the moon, to be making a living selling used and new cars.

I knew he was right, but I had nowhere to go. In Clancy's opinion, the dealership was simply trading on my celebrity, and I couldn't blame them for that; I certainly wasn't selling any cars for them. I had no desire to sell cars, used or new. I walked into my boss's office and said flatly, "I quit."

I met with Clancy and his group three or four times each week for months, and little by little, my perception of the world and myself began to change. In the process, Clancy and I became good friends. When an opportunity came up for me to go to Lyon, France, to appear in a parade and convocation with a group of other astronauts and cosmonauts, I had no one else to go with me, so I invited Clancy to accompany me, which he did. Good thing, since the event turned out to be sponsored by a wine company!

Clancy was not merely a friend and an adviser to me, he once even negotiated a contract for me, when the New Orleans Symphony invited me to do a dramatic reading as the orchestra performed Gustav Holst's *The Planets*. I gave Clancy a sizable commission for his services, and he relieved me of the burden of having to close a sale.

At Clancy's meetings, I met various women who were also alcoholics. I struck up relationships with several of them, and their company met a variety of needs in my life, but provided no long-term satisfaction. One woman, however, captured my attention—at least for a season. Her name was Kathy, and we met in Clancy's group.

Kathy met more than a sexual need. She and I became close friends, but she kept slipping back to alcohol. I tried to help her again and again, finding in her a deeper addiction than my own. Kathy and I shared an off-and-on relationship, with no real commitment on either of our parts. But when she struck up a friendship with a carpenter with whom she had become codependent, I became concerned. He was not helping Kathy and I knew it.

How low does a person need to go before looking up? Where does an alcoholic need to be before hitting rock bottom? I don't know. I'm sure it is different for every one of us, and the lines are often blurred. For me, I arrived at what I can now look back and see as a turning point, although at the time it was just another in a series of drunken disappointments.

Late one night during a relapse, I started drinking again. When I left the bar, I stopped by Kathy's apartment, but she didn't answer the door. I started pounding on the door in the middle of the night, completely oblivious to the possibility that she might not be home. When nobody answered the door, I broke it down. Before long, two police cruisers pulled up outside the apartment. Kathy's neighbors had called them. The officers subdued me, cuffed me, and led me to their car, "helping" me in a not-so-gentle fashion into the backseat of the police cruiser.

They took me downtown to the police station, and prepared to book me for disorderly conduct. As I looked around the police station, I attempted to do what I always did—play on my celebrity. The officers recognized me, and I could tell that they really didn't want to book me, but they couldn't let me back on the streets in my inebriated condition. "Do you have any friends you can call?" an officer suggested. "Someone who would be willing to take responsibility for you and get you home?"

I called Clancy to come and pick me up, but he refused. "If you want to drink, you are an adult. Go ahead and drink," he said, "but don't bother me." He wasn't angry at me for waking him in the middle of the night, or for stepping off the path he was helping me to follow. Clancy knew alcoholics, and he knew that most of us had a rather sporadic record when it came to establishing a new direction in life. I could hear the disappointment in his voice, but in my semi-inebriated state, I didn't really care.

I hung up the phone and called another good friend I had come to know in AA, Dick Boolootian, asking him to come down to the jail and pick me up. Dick was a brilliant educator, a doctor of science, and a good man. When he walked in and saw me in jail, I thought he might weep. He didn't rebuke me, scold me, or say anything all that profound, but the look in his eyes seared into my soul. He signed me out of the police station and took me home. Dick stayed for a while and tried to talk to me, but I was not conversant. "Go to bed, Buzz," Dick said as he looked at me before going out the door. "Please."

"I will, Dick. I will. I'm just going to sit up for a few more minutes and watch the news. I'll call you later on." Dick nodded and went out the door. After Dick went home, I couldn't sleep, so I started looking around for a bottle. Before long, I found one and downed it. I had hit bottom. Clancy and I stopped meeting regularly after that, and I began meeting with another Alcoholics Anonymous group in West L.A.

I found that the shame of starting over again once I had been sober for a long stretch was a blow to my ego, a process that I did not care to repeat. It takes genuine humility to turn your life over to a higher power, and that may be why it is so difficult for some people to stop their destructive behaviors. Moreover, you can't compromise. You can't say, "Well, I've quit drinking hard liquor, but I'll still have a few beers with the boys." Half-measures are doomed to fail. I've heard of people who quit drinking liquor but literally drank Aqua Velva shaving lotion. Another lady chugged her perfume, all the while claiming that she hadn't had a drink of alcohol.

Many people say, "I just can't help it; I have to drink. I can't get well." I said that, too. The truth is, getting well is a choice. Yes, you can get well; it may take somebody bigger than you to help you, but people in far worse circumstances than yours have gotten well. You can, too.

It is not easy, especially when alcohol and depression are riding tandem on a person. According to the addiction expert Dr. Joe Takamine, the leading cause of suicide is depression; the second leading cause is alcohol. When those two cohorts gang up on the same person, the end result is often not pretty.

During this time, I also met regularly with Dr. Pursch on an outpatient basis. By now Pursch's reputation had grown even larger. Among his patients was Billy Carter, the brother of President Jimmy Carter, whom he had treated for alcoholism. Pursch affirmed that if I could stay sober, the rest of my life would come together. The doctor was right.

Finally, in October 1978, I laid down alcohol once and for all. My willingness to do so was not an act of willpower so much as a coming to the end of my own selfishness. I had always been self-centered, and because of my abilities or my intelligence or my fame, people had let me get away with it. When I began to see myself for what I really was, and had a group of fellow travelers who knew me for what I was—and were not impressed—I began to take baby steps toward getting well. Along the way, I learned that to truly keep something and hold onto it, you have to give it away.

After I had been sober for about a year, Dr. Pursch asked me if I would visit with Betty Ford, the wife of President Gerald Ford. Mrs. Ford was going through the same Navy recovery program that I had gone through with Dr. Pursch, and I was glad to offer her some encouragement. After completing her program at the U.S. Naval Hospital in Long Beach, Mrs. Ford talked to her friends about the need for a treatment center that emphasized the special needs of women. Her good friend Leonard Firestone encouraged Mrs. Ford to pursue her dream, and in 1982 they cofounded the nonprofit Betty Ford Center in Rancho Mirage, California, where untold numbers of people have found help in overcoming alcoholism and chemical dependencies.

Dr. Pursch later asked me to visit with William Holden, which I was glad to do, but Bill didn't respond well. The Oscar-winning actor who had appeared in such films as *The Bridge on the River Kwai, The Towering Inferno,* and *Network* was more concerned about getting back to the set of a movie he was making than he was about taking seriously his own recovery program. Stefanie Powers, his companion at the time, tried to help him, and she meant well, but even she couldn't find a way to keep Bill from walking out on the opportunity to get help. Bill eventually left the program and went back to drinking. Sadly, on November 16, 1981, Bill fell down drunk in his own home, lacerating his head and bleeding to death. When his body was discovered more than four days later, doctors estimated that he had been conscious for more than thirty minutes after the fall, but didn't recognize the seriousness of his injury due to the level of alcohol in his system. When I heard about Bill's death, it saddened me deeply. I knew that could have easily been me had it not been for the turnaround I had experienced in my life.

And I was indeed a very, *very* grateful man.

11

REAWAKENING

A s THE TENTH ANNIVERSARY OF THE APOLLO 11 MOON LAND-
ing approached, I was experiencing a reawakening in my own life.
Following my personal epiphany in October 1978, the milestone
from which I dated my sobriety, I was ready to plunge back into helping America's space program be more farsighted and productive. I also
felt compelled to help others fight their battles with depression and alcoholism. Perhaps they could learn from what I had experienced.

I had once been known as the "best scientific mind in space" according to *Life* magazine. I even carried a slide rule on the Gemini 12
flight in case I needed to correct the computer on the rendezvous maneuvers. That's because I knew if the computer said we were twenty
feet out of plane, I could count on ten of that, but not all twenty. I
could pretty much figure out rendezvous maneuvers in my head.

But the ten years since my moonwalk were not filled with achievements, bold accomplishments, and grand acclamations. It had been my
decade of personal hell. By 1979, I felt that all that was changing for
me. I still suffered occasional setbacks from depression, but overall my
life was on an upswing. What helped me most was following the recommendations in the Alcoholics Anonymous "Big Book"—the book
in which the twelve-step recovery program was originally outlined—to
get my eyes off myself and start helping somebody else. I hoped to do

that by attending classes and seminars in which I could study to become a consultant on alcoholism. I was forty-nine years old when I started a one-week course in June 1979, at the University of Utah's School on Alcoholism and Other Drug Dependencies. I went from there to Rutgers University in New Jersey for a three-week-long-summer-school course at the Center for Alcohol Studies. Both of these courses provided tremendous keys for understanding my own alcoholism and recognizing alcoholic tendencies in others.

As part of our class work at Rutgers, I was assigned to do a project report on some facet of alcoholism. I chose the delicate subject of alcohol's effects on pilots, specifically commercial airline pilots; and the employee programs designed to combat alcoholism at Eastern Airlines. Flying and alcohol seemed to go together for many pilots. I knew that to be true. When I was flying combat missions in Korea and later practicing to deliver nuclear bombs from our bases in Germany and other parts of the world, my first stop after landing was the officers' club. Of course, a smart pilot doesn't dare be impaired when flying, but once out of the cockpit and away from the stress, it is time to relax and let your hair down. Even as an astronaut, I drank regularly and heavily right up to a few days before lifting off for the moon. So I was acutely aware of how pilots tended to relax with the help of alcohol, and I also knew how addictive misusing alcohol could become.

My choice to study the employee programs at Eastern Airlines had not been arbitrary or accidental. My aunt had been a flight attendant with Eastern, and had later married a vice president of the company. Additionally, Eastern's CEO and chairman of the board was none other than former astronaut Frank Borman. I thought for sure I'd be welcomed to do my research with Eastern.

I wasn't. When I went to Eastern's headquarters in Miami to explore what the airline was doing to help pilots who might have alcohol problems, I was informed that Frank had just revised Eastern's procedures. He was very standoffish about me sticking my nose in his programs. Frank and I had always been competitive during our stints at NASA, but I was still somewhat surprised at the lack of cooperation.

Unknown to me at the time, Frank was already experiencing difficulties with his unionized employees, troubles that would eventually lead to the airline being bought out by Texas Air. No wonder he didn't appreciate my asking what treatment programs they offered to help the alcoholics in his planes!

◗ ○ ◗

Shortly after completing my program at Rutgers, I returned to California to join Neil Armstrong and Mike Collins at a private Apollo 11 tenth anniversary celebration at the home of ex-President Richard Nixon in San Clemente. A few days later I headed back to Washington, D.C., to celebrate NASA's version of the tenth anniversary of the initial Apollo moon landing. Other than the party at the Nixons', the tenth anniversary celebration was the first time I had seen Neil or Mike since the fifth anniversary. By July 20, 1979, twenty-four Apollo astronauts had reached the moon, and twelve of us had actually walked on the surface. For the milestone anniversaries of the initial landing, NASA liked to pull all of us back together, and it was always good to see everyone.

Those who attended the anniversary celebration were surprised when I showed up with my former wife, Joan. We were living our separate lives by now, with the only contact between us regarding matters pertaining to our children. I had dated a few women since our divorce, and could no doubt have invited someone to come along to Washington, D.C., but when it came time for the Apollo 11 anniversary, I felt that Joan deserved to be there as much as anybody. For all the sacrifices she made and for the price she paid, she should be able to join in the celebration, too. Besides, she had remained friends with most of the astronauts' wives, so it would be a special treat for her to be reunited with them.

I was pleased people recognized that Joan and I were still friendly toward one another, that we harbored no resentments or bitterness; several remarked that it was refreshing to see a divorced couple getting along so well. Nevertheless, when anyone noticed the two of us together, I was quick to let them know that we had no intentions of reconciling and remarrying.

A lot had happened in our lives since that warm Florida morning on July 16, 1969, when Neil, Mike, and I had set out from Launch Pad 39-A. Our initial landing and the five additional lunar landings to follow ours—the more scientifically exciting trips in my estimation—yielded an enormous amount of information, but, more important, demonstrated to the world the power of American technology once we set our sights on a goal.

Neil was now an aerospace engineering professor at the University of Cincinnati, as well as a consultant to Chrysler. He still liked to dabble in test flights of business jets occasionally, too. Mike Collins had left NASA shortly after our mission to work for the U.S. State Department. He later moved to the Smithsonian Institution, where he directed the creation of the National Air and Space Museum, one of the most popular exhibits in Washington, D.C. By 1979, Mike was one of the top people at the Smithsonian.

And me? I didn't know what I was doing, or where I was going. But I smiled nonetheless when someone at the anniversary would come up and say, "Gee, Buzz, you look great. What's been going on in your life since walking on the moon and experiencing that magnificent desolation?" I had finally come to a great sense of peace in overcoming the struggles I had faced, and the changes I had experienced since Apollo 11.

The space program itself had changed tremendously in a decade. The genius Wernher von Braun, who developed the mighty Saturn V rocket that had lifted us toward the moon, had passed away. Americans had not flown in space for more than four years, and there was some question about when the space shuttle would actually be ready to fly, although NASA hoped that it could make its initial forays into space in 1980. At the time of the tenth anniversary, I knew that we had no plans to return to the moon for at least another decade, if then.

Nevertheless, the festivities in Washington, D.C., were upbeat, warm, and inspiring. President Jimmy Carter honored Neil, Mike, and me at a White House ceremony, followed by a public ceremony on the Mall, where we received a standing ovation from the crowd. In the National Air and Space Museum, we answered the usual questions from the media, including the inevitable "Would you go again?" Neil said that he would take the flight again "in a minute." Mike Collins said he would go again, too, but then quipped, "But it would take more than a minute to get ready." When the spotlight fell on me, my mind quickly flashed back through the stress of the world tour, the subsequent mental depression, alcoholism, and the breakup of two marriages in the last decade, and I said, "I'm not sure I would go again."

In truth, I was more passionate about getting other people into space than going back myself. That was one of the positive aspects I saw in the space shuttle. It held the potential for more than just a few highly trained specialists to travel into space. The shuttle was basically a space truck with a cab that could seat seven and a cargo hold large enough to carry a Greyhound bus and more. The plan was to fly to and from orbit every few weeks, hauling up satellites and other equipment, as well as men and women to a permanent space station. My hope was that not just pilots, scientists, and engineers would go into space, but that one day ordinary citizens—doctors, accountants, musicians, writers, and artists would experience space, too.

That's why in 1979 I got excited about creating a program along with Dr. Dick Boolootian to help United Airlines 727 pilots learn how to fly the space shuttle. The shuttle system was little more than a huge rocket booster attached to a winged orbiter space vehicle that looked and operated much like an airplane once the initial fuel tanks and boosters were gone, so it was only logical that with a little training, most pilots could learn how to fly a shuttle. Although such an idea may seem absurd now, at that time it made sense, especially when the shuttle began to fly in April 1981. I spent hours on end in Dick Boolootian's office bouncing ideas off him, wondering how we could develop space travel for ordinary folks. Others proposed that commercial entities and private enterprises might even want to purchase a space shuttle. Unfortunately, those kinds of creative ideas were quickly squelched after the *Challenger* disaster in 1986. But from 1979 to 1981, my brain was firing on all pistons, and what fueled the engine was my passion to explore space.

I had been sober for several years now, and while I still struggled with brief periods of depression, I was inspired by the possibilities of how I might use my talents to help renew America's passion for space exploration.

In February 1982, I became particularly enamored with the idea of Americans going back to the moon. I attended several conferences at the California Space Institute in San Diego, headed up by Jim Arnold, the same organization led today by America's first woman astronaut, Sally Ride. I had some contacts with General Dynamics regarding the possibilities of establishing a more permanent lunar presence. At another conference in Houston, Dave Criswell made a powerful presentation on the possibility of beaming solar energy back from the moon. Dave got everyone excited about installing rows of solar panels on the moon's surface that would be powerful enough to send power to satellite relays and back to Earth. I was thrilled that creative minds were finally thinking about sound economic and practical reasons for going to another celestial body to do more than simply stomp around, do a few experiments, plant some flags, and kick up some dust.

I knew I could apply my knowledge of orbital mechanics to develop techniques for a spacecraft to travel continually between Earth and the moon in continuous cycling orbits, almost as though it were a trolley on an invisible pulley system drawing the craft back and forth. Now, if we could just keep doing that, cycling back and forth, we could deliver people, products, food and supplies, more technology, and machinery using hardly any fuel for the translunar spacecraft. You just hop on. It's only three and a half to four days away. It doesn't take a rocket scientist to see how easily a system like that could work; well, maybe it does. I called my spacecraft transit concept a "cycler," and I was excited about the possibilities.

On July 22, 1984, in conjunction with the fifteenth anniversary of Apollo 11, I penned an op-ed piece in the *Los Angeles Times* with the title, "Let's Return to the Moon for Good." I felt the time was opportune to send explorers back to its dusty surface, but this time we would establish a lunar base and develop the moon's natural resources in support of space operations. To establish an ongoing method of lunar sorties, I introduced my cycler concept of "coasting trajectories in a translunar rendezvous" space transport system. In one way of looking at it, I saw the moon as one big resource, a natural space station, the ultimate space station orbiting the Earth—and one that already had six American flags on it!

Tom Paine, who had been NASA's chief administrator when I went to the moon, now lived in and operated out of Santa Monica, California. I visited Tom frequently during this period when there appeared to be a resurgence of interest in a return to the moon. I shared my lunar cycler idea with Tom.

Tom liked what he saw, but he said, "Buzz, you know they are thinking about Mars, and there are some interesting ways of getting to Mars. Why don't you think about your lunar cycler and make it go to Mars?"

Oh, I thought, *that's very complicated.*

"Mars?" I asked. "Are you serious? I thought NASA's plan was to support a permanent base on the moon."

Tom raised his eyebrows. "That will never motivate the American people again. We need something bigger, something beyond the moon."

I understood what Tom was saying, so I went to work adapting my ideas. It was only 1985, and a select few were thinking about going to Mars, but I knew that if we focused our minds and technology in that direction, we could achieve that goal. From Mars we could reach other places around the solar system. My basic operating principle was, how can we do it better?

Not surprisingly, most people didn't see the need or the relevance of going to Mars, and I began to get a reputation for proposing harebrained ideas. "Are you serious, Buzz? Do you really think you can shuttle people on a cycler back and forth between the Earth and the moon, much less to Mars?"

"No, I guess not," I'd reply. But I really did.

I started doing basic computations, drawing the relative orbits of Earth and Mars, and by the summer of 1985 I discovered that there was a way to transport people to Mars on what I developed as the Aldrin Mars Cycler. Like space trolley cars, the spacecraft would continue in perpetual cycling orbits between the two planets, picking up and dropping off detachable "taxi" transfer vehicles that could then carry crews and supplies to and from the surface of each planet. The trolley systems could use the planets' gravitational pull as a slingshot propelling the cycler spacecraft back and forth. I estimated that a trip between Earth and Mars could take as little as five months using this technique. The way I figured it, we were halfway there—I was ready to go!

●　○　●

MEANWHILE, I WAS also traveling to various locations on Earth to engage in another of my passions—scuba diving. The first dive I ever took was with my 22nd Fighter Squadron off the coast of Tripoli, Libya, where we were on gunnery training in 1957 while stationed in Germany. Our squadron leader had some diving experience, so on our recreational day he took us to the French Sur Mer Club, where we strapped on some scuba tanks and dove off the pier into the clear Mediterranean waters off the north coast of Africa. Enamored with the underwater world, I signed up for a diving course on my next vacation with my family to a small village between Nice and Cannes on the French Riviera. I bought my first tank and regulator, and it has been a passion of mine ever since. That's why I jumped at the chance to become the first astronaut to train for weightlessness underwater in neutral buoyancy when NASA suggested the idea. In my experience, being able to orient your body in any direction while underwater, without feeling the consequences of gravity, is akin to the sensation of spacewalking.

My oldest son, Mike, was a flight attendant with Cayman Airlines and also an avid scuba diver. At the time, most airlines had what they called "friends and family passes," free or greatly discounted travel tickets. I traveled nearly everywhere Cayman Airlines flew, which included many of the islands in the Caribbean, and sometimes Mike came along and joined me on a few dives. It was probably one of the best seasons in our father-son relationship. The diving trips kept me active and in circulation, but, more significantly, they helped me prove to myself that I did not need to have anyone with me, and that I could stay sober and interact with people without slipping back into drinking. I traveled so much on Cayman Airlines that the airline asked me to become an honorary board member.

On one of my many diving trips, I met the world-renowned oceanographer Sylvia Earle. A born explorer, Sylvia grew up in my home state of New Jersey, in the town of Camden. She received her Ph.D. from Duke University, and later became chief scientist of the National Oceanic and Atmospheric Administration. An outspoken advocate of undersea research, she also hoped to raise public awareness of the damage done to our aquasphere by pollution and environmental degradation. By the time I met her, Sylvia's National Geographic books and films about the sea were considered among the best.

She was smart, sassy, and easy to look at in a bathing suit. We hit it off immediately. I was diving in Nassau at the same time she was there assisting in the underwater scenes for a James Bond movie, *For Your Eyes Only*. Sylvia invited me to help out on the filming of the shark scenes. My job was basically shooting shark "B roll," additional film to be worked in as needed later. It was great fun, and I enjoyed helping.

One of Sylvia's more widely known scientific expeditions took her to the Galápagos, off the coast of Ecuador, an adventure on which she invited me to accompany her. I declined due to other demands on my schedule, and to this day, not going on that extraordinary trip is one of my few regrets.

I did, however, accompany Sylvia on a number of other expeditions, most notably a ten-day trip to the Gulf of Akaba, aboard the *Sun Boat*, a large dive boat that had staterooms below, a briefing room on the middle level, and an upper observation deck. We dove in the northern part of the Red Sea on the east side of Sinai, then flew to Tel Aviv together, and went down to Elat, where we toured their aquarium. Along with divemaster Amos Nakum, Sylvia was collecting specimens for the California Aquatic Museum in San Francisco, where she was on the staff. She was trying to get pictures of a photoflurethicon, a fish that had fluorescent qualities that could be seen underwater at night. We'd do four dives a day, the last one being at night. By the time our crew pulled off our wet suits each evening, we were worn out, but thrilled.

Besides being a meticulous scientist, Sylvia had a quirky sense of humor, too. When she and I were diving together, she loved to sneak up on divers who were close to the caves, intently looking at some strange formation. Sylvia grabbed their fins and frightened the daylights out of them.

In 1979, Sylvia performed one of her most amazing feats, walking without a tether on the sea floor at a lower depth than any human being had ever previously done. Wearing a pressurized suit that looked more like it belonged on the Sea of Tranquillity, she traveled in a submersible down to a depth of 1,250 feet below the surface off the coast of Oahu, in Hawaii. At the bottom, she detached herself from the vessel and explored for more than two hours with only a communication line connecting her to the submersible.

When an interviewer once asked her about feeling alone underwater, she surprised me by drawing a comparison to Apollo 11:

> I suppose some people, many people, are afraid of being alone. But, for example when I go into the forest, I am not alone. There is life all around. If I go into the sea by myself, and I do it a lot, there is life everywhere. I feel sorry for astronauts who, if they were abandoned . . . would be truly, truly alone. When Buzz Aldrin and Neil Armstrong were on the moon, they were alone. The closest living creature was Mike Collins out there in the spacecraft that was orbiting the moon. The next stop was Earth.

Underwater, every spoonful of water is filled with life. You are really never alone, it just depends on your perspective.[13]

I admired Sylvia for her scientific and adventurous mind, and it was refreshing to be around a woman unlike those who unduly idolized my moonwalker status. What she accomplished underwater was in many respects as difficult as what I'd done on the moon. We shared a brief romance, but at the time I was not nearly ready for commitment. Over the years, Sylvia and I have remained friends, and I still see her at the annual Explorers Club dinner at the Waldorf Astoria hotel in New York City. Members range from underwater pioneers such as Bob Ballard, of *Titanic* fame, to mountaineers like the late Sir Edmund Hillary, the first man to climb Mount Everest. And Sylvia is always one of the most respected explorers in the room. She played a crucial role in the reawakening period of my life, and perhaps more than anything, her willingness to explore the unknown prepared me for a shock to my system that would forever alleviate my own sense of aloneness.

---

[13] Sylvia Earle Interview, Academy of Achievement website: http://www.achievment.org/autodoc/page/ear0int-1.

12

FINDING the LOVE
of MY LIFE

I SENSED THE BEAUTIFUL WOMAN EVEN BEFORE I SAW HER. I always had an eye for great-looking women, and since being divorced from Beverly nine years earlier, I had established a bit of a reputation as a "player" in the Los Angeles area. At my age, I was more familiar with the term *playboy,* and although I didn't necessarily see myself that way, I can now understand how those who knew me then may have used such terms to describe me. From my perspective, I simply enjoyed the company of a beautiful woman. I did not enjoy being lonely, so I dated frequently, although never with an inclination toward marriage.

But when I saw the woman conversing with the hostess of the party, Joan Williams, I stopped in my tracks. Bright blue eyes, platinum blonde, vivacious personality with a vibrant smile, she seemed to exude positive energy. She was wearing high heels and a black-and-white-polka-dot designer cocktail dress that highlighted her petite, shapely figure.

Mmm, this could be interesting! I thought.

I was right.

I HAD BEEN invited to the party at the Bel Air Bay Club on Friday evening, October 4, 1985, by a "recovering" friend of mine, Molly Barnes. I was always glad for an opportunity to get out and meet some new people, and it was a casual event at the beach, so I put on a pair of jeans and a light blue shirt with a large embroidered eagle insignia and headed to the club. Somehow, once at the party, Molly and I went our separate ways, and as I circulated among the guests, Joan Williams saw me and grabbed my arm. "Buzz, there's somebody I'd like you to meet," she said as she steered me along.

"Lois, I want you to meet an astronaut who went to the moon. This is Buzz Aldrin. Buzz, this is Lois Driggs Cannon."

Lois later confessed that she was totally unimpressed. Astronauts were not on her list. Bankers, lawyers, tycoons? Oh yes. But astronauts? Hardly.

Lois and I talked for a while, and I was struck by her vitality. When it came time to leave, I impulsively asked her for a date the following night.

"Oh no," Lois said. "You're not going to want to drive sixty miles to Laguna Beach. Besides, I'm going to a black-tie party tomorrow evening." Lois leaned back a bit, eyeing me as if to say, *And you probably don't even own a tuxedo.*

She was right. But I did have some good-looking military uniforms.

"Maybe another time," Lois said.

I looked at this woman and felt strongly that I didn't want to let her go. "I will take you to that party," I said firmly. "What time do you want me to pick you up? I assure you that I will be properly dressed."

Lois seemed surprised, but not put off by my straightforwardness. "What you don't know," I continued, "is that tonight is my last night in Los Angeles, and I'm moving to Laguna Beach tomorrow." It sounded like a good pickup line, but it was true. "I bought a place there about a month ago," I explained, "and I'm taking my final load of belongings to my new home tomorrow. So I will be in Laguna Beach, and I will take you to the party." I wrangled Lois's telephone number and promised to check in with her the next day.

Lois went back to her daughter Lisa's home in Beverly Hills that night and admitted that she had not handled our meeting well. "How could I have allowed him to talk me into going to the party tomorrow night?" she groused. "I wanted to go by myself because I'm sure there will be a number of outstanding gentlemen in attendance."

Lisa laughed and tried to console her mother.

"Maybe he won't really call," Lois suggested.

I did.

The following evening, I wore my Air Force dress white coat, replete with an assortment of medals that I had been awarded, decked out over my left breast pocket area. I rang the doorbell at Lois's home in Emerald Bay, the exclusive, private gated beach community at the north end of Laguna. When she opened the door, I was nearly flabbergasted at her appearance. She looked positively radiant, wearing a Chanel sweater and a long black Chanel skirt. Lois greeted me warmly, and I noticed her eyes roaming up and down my body; she seemed pleasantly surprised that I "dressed up so well."

The event we attended was the opening of the members-only Center Club for the Orange County Performing Arts Center, a rather sophisticated, erudite bunch. As we made what we thought was going to be an inconspicuous entrance, photographers' flashes started going off in our direction. Lois's friends seemed impressed by the moonwalker astronaut tagging along in his dress whites. After making the rounds, Lois greeting her friends and perfunctorily introducing me, she and I danced the night away. Although she tried to remain a bit coy, every so often as we swirled gracefully around the dance floor, out of the corner of my eye, I thought I detected a glint in her eye. When I took Lois home, I politely kissed her goodnight. I wanted to see her again, and it seemed that perhaps astronauts had finally made her list, albeit at the bottom. Both of us, however, had already committed to dates with other people the following night, so we practically stumbled over ourselves in trying to apologize for not being available.

"I have an idea," Lois suggested. "I'm attending a charity event, the Concourse to Elegance, tomorrow afternoon. You could come along with me to that."

"Good," I said. "But before we do, why don't you come over to have lunch with me. My uncle, Bob Moon, is visiting, and I'd like you two to meet."

On Sunday afternoon, Lois and I enjoyed lunch with my uncle and then toured the Concourse to Elegance at the University of California Irvine campus near Laguna. As we walked along, we conversed about my future plans. "What do you want to do in life?" she asked straight-forwardly.

I answered her equally directly, without a moment's hesitation. "I want to serve my country."

At one point, as we were riding in my car, Lois asked me gingerly, "Tell me about yourself." I was uncomfortable in talking about myself, so I simply reached into the backseat of the car and pulled out a copy of *Return to Earth,* the first book I had written following my trip to the moon. "Here, read this," I said. "It will tell you everything you might want to know about me." Lois laughed, but she took the book. By afternoon's end, we were looking for another opportunity to get together.

"How about Monday night?" I suggested.

"Well, I'm supposed to fly to Phoenix to spend a few days with my family, but I could go on Tuesday."

"Great! I have a recovery meeting on Monday evening, and I'd like you to go with me." Looking back, I have to smile at the fact that one of the first places I took Lois was to an Alcoholics Anonymous meeting. Over the course of the weekend, I had explained to Lois that I didn't drink, that I had not in fact taken a drink since October 1978. She seemed impressed, but since she was raised in the Mormon religion, in which alcohol was frowned upon, she could not readily relate to how difficult and significant an accomplishment my cessation of drinking really was. Nevertheless, she was interested in meeting my friends.

Once there, I spoke briefly about myself and my battle with alcohol. Lois was impressed with the "spiritual" tenor of the meeting, and that I would be attracted to such a group and, more important, committed to not drinking alcohol again. Afterwards, I took Lois home and we sat on the couch and talked for quite a while. Before I left, we kissed— really kissed. Something magical happened.

Lois went on to Phoenix to visit her family, and I busied myself preparing for a Sea Space Symposium scuba-diving trip in Egypt. Somewhere in my preparations, it struck me: Why not invite Lois to go along?

I called her in Phoenix, where, I later learned, I had been quite a topic of conversation. "Lois, I'm going to Egypt October 31 through November 11, along with some friends and their wives. Would you like to come along?"

We talked briefly, and I told her about my association with the Sea Space Symposium, and I gave her the flight information. When she asked me about hotel accommodations, I said, "Oh, don't worry, I'll take care of that." Lois apparently trusted me enough to book two rooms at the hotel in Egypt.

Our flight to Cairo included a long layover in Paris, so, rather than remain at the airport, Lois and I took a taxi into the City of Light and did a whirlwind walking tour of the most popular sites, and then we stopped for lunch at Le Fouquet's, a well-known Parisian restaurant. It was November 2, Lois's birthday, and for a few hours we felt drawn into the city's romantic charm as if we were in our own little world.

When we arrived in Hurghada, Egypt, one of the most popular diving resorts along the Red Sea, the men on the trip hustled off to a diving location, while the women planned an excursion to Luxor, the location of King Tut's tomb and other interesting sites, about four hours away. Lois hurried to pack an overnight bag, but by the time she got downstairs, the bus had already left. Ever resourceful, she persuaded an Arab taxi driver to take her to Luxor. Before leaving, Lois left me a note: "All the girls left, but I ran off on a camel with a sheik to catch up with them. See you tomorrow."

On the way to Luxor, the driver spoke no English and Lois didn't speak Arabic. About every twenty or thirty miles the driver was stopped by heavily armed guards at checkpoints. I would love to have heard his explanation for carting a cute blonde on a four-hour trek across the desert.

When Lois was finally reunited with the other women, they received her with open arms. She had made quite an impression with her pluck and verve.

Lois roomed with me when she returned, since I had booked only one room, tempting Lois to abandon her strict religious upbringing to spend the few days with me. Eventually, she joyfully succumbed to my thinly veiled seduction. After that, Lois accompanied me wherever I went, including a long bus excursion to Cairo, where we met and had dinner with President Mubarak. By the time we arrived back in Los Angeles on Monday, November 11, Lois had won my friends' hearts as well as mine.

● ○ ●

NOT LONG AFTER our adventure in Egypt, I took Lois with me to a conference in Houston, where she met a number of former astronauts. All my astronaut peers found her quite charming and put on their best behavior for her. We also had lunch with Merv Hughs, a friend of mine from my astronaut days in Houston. After assessing the situation, Merv whispered to Lois, "Don't get your hopes up. Buzz loves women, and women love Buzz. And he's not about to settle down."

Undaunted, Lois insisted on believing that she and I were a couple with a future. She invited me to go with her to Sun Valley for Christmas, and I accepted. I was not much of a skier, but I figured I could learn. Lois gave me a few pointers, and we were off. Of course, making your way up and down the slopes in Sun Valley is only part of the fun. Skiing there is as much a social event as recreation or physical exercise. Lois seemed to know everybody on the slopes, and they knew her. She introduced me to someone new everywhere we went.

At Lois's condominium, she introduced me to her children, all of whom were in their mid- to late twenties—her son, Bryant, her younger daughter, Brynn, and her older daughter, Lisa, with whom she had been staying the night we first met at the Bel Air Bay Club. Lois had spoken about me in such glowing terms, Lisa was no doubt expecting some suave, smooth-talking bachelor. Imagine Lisa's surprise when I presented a somewhat stiff and reserved demeanor, sitting on the sofa in front of the fireplace and barely engaging in any conversation. Although I was doing much better these days, the effects of depression and alcoholism from years past had taken a toll on my exuberance. Lois sat beside me, emoting over her children and emanating enough warmth and enthusiasm to fill the entire living room. Meanwhile, I barely cracked a smile as I leaned forward and pored over some scientific space papers on the coffee table. No doubt, the kids thought, *Oh my! What has Mom gotten herself into with this guy?* Nevertheless, I enjoyed meeting the people closest to Lois, and her children accepted me immediately and made me feel welcome.

A few weeks later, in mid-January, I invited Lois to accompany me to another event, in Hawaii and Lois readily accepted. The day before we departed, however, Lois called my house, and a former girlfriend of mine answered the phone.

"Who are you?" Lois asked.

"I'm a friend of Buzz's. Who are you?" she asked belligerently.

"Please have Buzz call me," Lois replied, and hung up the phone. When I called, of course, it took some explaining to convince Lois that the woman who answered the telephone was a friend from my recovery group, a feature from my past, rather than a present girlfriend. Lois reluctantly accepted my apology, and agreed to go along to Hawaii for a space conference in Honolulu. Following the conference, we spent a couple of days at a good friend of mine's hotel in Kona on the Big Island. It was the week of my fifty-sixth birthday, and Lois wanted to celebrate, but after a day or two in Kona, for no explainable reason, I felt that I was falling into a blue funk. I didn't want to leave our hotel room; in fact, I didn't even want to get out of bed. In Honolulu, I had presented my Mars cycler concept to President Reagan's advisory panel on the U.S. space program. The members listened attentively, but I came away disappointed, wondering if my words had fallen on deaf ears. That partially explained my emotional turmoil. But perhaps I was also suffering from a guilty conscience, since I had planned to go see a former girlfriend in Florida following this trip to Hawaii.

Lois was baffled. Here we were, in a gorgeous, picturesque, romantic setting in Kona, and I didn't want to go outside. So I didn't. I stayed in bed and watched the news.

One afternoon, Lois returned from the beach and overheard me talking on the telephone: "Okay, Scott, my dear. I just wanted you to know that I'm not coming to Florida."

Lois's interest was immediately piqued. "Oh, are you going to Florida?" she asked. "Who were you talking to?"

"Yes, I was scheduled to go to Florida."

"Oh, why were you going?"

"I have a friend there whom I was going to see."

"Male or female?"

"Scott, an old girlfriend," I answered honestly.

"You were planning to go there, while I'm here with you in Hawaii?" I could see the hurt and disappointment in Lois's face.

"I'm not sure I can handle this," she said quietly. "I think I'll go back to Sun Valley to ski." The remainder of our time in Hawaii was rather cool, and I don't mean the air temperature. Lois was clearly upset, and I couldn't get outside of myself far enough to understand why she was angry. We returned to California, and Lois set off to Idaho. "I'll be back at the end of March," she said, "but don't bother to call."

I had thought that Lois was the love of my life; instead, it seemed that our whirlwind relationship had come to a sudden and ignominious end.

13

The LOIS
FACTOR

ALONE AGAIN AT MY CALIFORNIA HOME, I TRIED TO GET
back into the normal swing of life—life without Lois. I was not
expecting the emptiness, or that gnawing in the pit of my stom-
ach, and I was surprised at the pervasive sense of loneliness I felt without her. I couldn't understand it. I had broken up with women before,
and simply gone on to the next interesting person I met. I mentally reviewed all the usual lines: "There are plenty of fish in the sea." "Too
bad; her loss." "Don't let the door hit you as you leave." I knew I could
go to another party somewhere in Beverly Hills, flash my medals or tell
a few stories about the moon, and leave the party with a beautiful
woman on my arm. But I didn't want to do that. More and more as the
days passed between January and March, I wanted Lois. Strange as it
may sound, I liked *me* better because of her; I liked the person I was
when I was with her. She motivated me, and she jolted me out of my
scientific studies and space dreams long enough to enjoy social gatherings filled with new and interesting people.

I smiled as I thought of her. How had that petite bundle of positive
energy so boldly entered the inner recesses of my psyche and stolen
away with my heart? And how had I been so foolish as to let her get
away? I liked Lois; I didn't want to lose her; Lois was unlike any other
woman I had known. Lois was different. Lois was . . . special.

● ○ ●

Lois's mother, Effie Olena Killian, was a beautiful woman of Norwegian descent, whose family lived in Thatcher, Arizona. Her father, Douglas H. Driggs, hailed from Driggs, Idaho; his family had founded the town, set in the picturesque valley west of the Grand Tetons, that today hosts the popular ski resort Grand Targhee. In 1921 the family traded all of their holdings, including a bank, hotel, and wheat farm for over 300 acres of farmland planted with cotton near Phoenix, Arizona. As cotton prices plummeted, they lost their entire investment and had to start over. But that did not dissuade either of Lois's parents, who were from hardworking, prominent pioneer Mormon families, and who followed their faith with every footstep.

Lois Adele Driggs was born November 2, 1929—just a couple of months before me—in Miami, Arizona, a small mining town. Along with two brothers and one sister, she grew up in the Phoenix area, where her father, an enterprising businessman, opened a bank during the Depression years. Douglas Driggs traveled the surrounding ranching and mining communities, using his trust-evoking and spirited enthusiasm to influence new customers to pay twenty-five dollars to open a savings account. His reputation for honesty met with success, and the bank became known as the Western Savings and Loan Association— eventually becoming the eleventh-largest state-chartered savings-and-loan company in America, with over $5 billion in assets. As the business prospered, the family rose in the social echelons of the Phoenix/Scottsdale area.

Lois's childhood was like a Norman Rockwell painting; everything was perfect. She studied tap, toe, and acrobatic dancing, as well as the popular boogie-woogie and swing styles on the piano. She was an active drama student who participated in several plays in high school and college, and she readily made friends wherever she went.

In her deeply religious family, Lois was sometimes a bit of a black sheep, wishing for more than the cloistered, conservative lifestyle fostered by the church. Her father, however, wanted her to attend

Brigham Young University in Utah, to be in a "Mormon environment." As a compromise, Lois agreed to go to the University of Utah (U of U). In those post–World War II days, college women rarely entered the workforce, so their education often focused on the liberal arts, rather than preparing for a career. Lois's parents hoped that in the Utah environment she would at least by graduation find a good Mormon husband, settle down, and start a family. But Lois had different ideas. She balanced her studies and social life with a special emphasis on learning to ski during her two years at the U of U. Despite the joy of skiing, Lois found Salt Lake City somewhat ethnocentric, and yearned for a more diverse college atmosphere. She applied to Stanford University in Palo Alto, California, and encouraged her older brother, John, to do the same. They were both accepted, and one September day they drove off in a big yellow Chevrolet convertible toward a new world at Stanford.

Life on "The Farm," as Stanford is known by its students and alumni, proved to be everything Lois and John expected, and then some. John was quickly initiated into a fraternity (there were no sororities at Stanford at the time), and introduced Lois to his fraternity brothers, many of whom were football players. The star halfback, Emery Mitchell, grew attracted to Lois. As Emery and Lois dated, the reputation that followed her from high school on through college remained intact: she had high morals and was "hard to get." She never went steady with one fellow, although she could have. Even the beaus she dated on numerous occasions suffered along without a single kiss. But that didn't stop the many Stanford men who saw her as good marriage material, and by graduation, she had several proposals. To their disappointment, Lois was holding herself in reserve for her one true love, her Prince Charming.

Nevertheless, Lois made numerous lasting friends at Stanford, many of whom went on to great success, such as Sandra Day, a bright young woman with whom Lois struck up a friendship that flourished when Sandra and her husband John O'Connor moved to Phoenix to practice law. Years later, Sandra became America's first female Supreme Court Justice.

Upon graduation from Stanford with a degree in education, Lois decided to take her fifth year at UCLA to satisfy the requirement to teach. She had another motivation to stay in California as well, since she was becoming increasingly interested in a young man she had dated during her senior year at Stanford, Bill Edwards, whose family lived in Long Beach. Bill had enrolled at Harvard Business School, so Lois would see him at Christmas and over the summer. Bill's mother talked so enthusiastically about her own teaching career at Hawthorne School in Beverly Hills that Lois applied for a position there, and began teaching third grade the following year. But Lois's romance with Bill did not last beyond the summer. The odds were against them: Bill's father thought Lois was too short, and Lois's father felt that Bill was unlikely to become a Mormon. Indeed, Bill married a tall, beautiful girl who lived next door. Lois finished out the school year at Hawthorne and was offered the chance to renew her contract, but decided her heart was not in teaching. She would take the next year off to tour Europe.

Lois's European travels—with arrangements made by her family to meet and stay with many of their Rotarian friends in cities all over Europe and Scandinavia—combined two of her great passions: socializing and skiing. She met counts and barons and other titled members of Europe's oldest families, as well as many renowned European ski racers. Somewhere between the mountains and après-ski activities, Lois came to know Stein Erickson, a Norwegian ski hero on whom she developed a crush. The relationship never developed, but Lois's skiing did. We are all friends today, and often ski and dine together in Deer Valley, Utah.

Lois returned home after her year abroad, and with the Christmas season approaching, she and her brother, John, decided to drive to Sun Valley, Idaho, to ski. On the way, they stopped over in Salt Lake City, and attended a Mormon fireside singles social event. Lois was introduced to Bryant Cannon, a handsome six-foot bachelor and a former University of Utah football star who worked for IBM. He was seven years older than Lois, and quite dapper. They talked and clicked.

Lois and her brother drove on to Sun Valley the next day, but the skiing conditions were poor, so they decided to return to Salt Lake. That night they had dinner at the home of Lois's college friend Alice Creer. Lois was looking for someone to ski with the next day. During dinner, Bryant Cannon called Alice to confirm his date with her the following night. Alice mentioned that Lois was there, and suggested to Bryant that he take her skiing. Remembering Lois from the fireside singles event, he responded positively, possibly a bit too quickly for Alice's liking.

Bryant picked up Lois and they skied all day together at Utah's Alta resort. The snow glistened in the crisp winter air as they rode the chair lifts, talked, and swooshed down the hill. That night Bryant had the nerve to cancel his date with Alice and take Lois out instead. And Lois had the nerve to accept! Her friend Alice recognized that love was in the air and encouraged Lois to be cautious of this very popular Salt Lake bachelor. Disregarding the advice, Lois skied with Bryant the next two days as well. Already, their budding relationship was gathering momentum.

The following night was New Year's Eve, and Bryant invited Lois to a party at the Fort Douglas Club. It was a gorgeous enchanting evening with mistletoe inside, and light snow falling outside as the couple danced their way out onto the porch balcony. Bryant looked at Lois adoringly and kissed her. Lois responded, and apparently bells rang for both of them. Bryant moved fast, as if he were running for a touchdown. "I think we should get married," he said.

Amazingly, Lois found herself replying, "I think that would be perfect."

As far as she was concerned, this was a match made in heaven. Although they had known each other for less than four days, she felt that Bryant was the man for her. He was handsome, physically appealing, highly intelligent, a great skier, and best of all, he came from one of the most prominent Mormon families in America.

They planned to marry in February, less than two months away, just in time to catch the boat to Europe for Bryant's next assignment with IBM.

Lois and her family spent the short window of time preparing for the large wedding in Phoenix. The Cannon family arrived and everyone began to get acquainted, since few of them had met previously. Lois commented, "I am so happy to get married and raise a family, and I'm never going to teach school again."

"Never?" Bryant asked. "What if we don't have enough money and we need you to teach?"

"Oh, you have a good job," Lois replied. "We'll always have enough money." Bryant's concerns about money should have been a red flag to Lois, but, in the midst of her pre-wedding bliss, she ignored it.

Bryant's brother, Mark Cannon, a Harvard Ph.D. who later developed a career as the administrative assistant to U.S. Supreme Court Chief Justice Warren Burger, unwittingly provided keen insight into Bryant's personality. As he surveyed the Driggs family home, he remarked to Lois, "I guess your reputation is true. You are known as one of the richest and cutest girls in the church."

Lois took Mark's words as a compliment; she should have taken them as a warning.

Lois and Bryant were married in the Mormon church, though in their daily lifestyles neither of them adhered strictly to its religious standards. After a second reception in Salt Lake, they were off to Europe. Lois and Bryant remained married for twenty-seven years. For all that time, she was as happy as a lamb and never suspected that her husband was anything other than faithful and content. Unfortunately, that was not the case.

Lois and Bryant set up their home in Frankfurt, Germany, in February 1955. Ironically, at about that same time, I had just married Joan, and we were expecting our first child in September of that year. We were stationed at Bitburg, Germany, where I flew supersonic jets as part of a nuclear strike force that could deliver atomic bombs deep into Soviet-occupied Eastern Europe.

Lois and I never met during that time, despite Bryant's work on several military computer installations. At a reception for some military personnel for whom Bryant was setting up computer systems, Lois was her usual witty and vibrant self. Bryant, however, was not pleased. After the party, he was irate. "Lois, how could you be like that?"

"Like what?"

"You were too much. Too outgoing. You need to be more subdued." It was the first of many instances in which Bryant attempted to squelch Lois's lively personality. Lois tried her best to hold back and not overshadow him, but felt stifled by Bryant's preference that she restrain her enthusiasm. She became pregnant with their first child in 1955, soon after their arrival in Frankfurt, and a daughter, Lisa, was born in November of that year. From Frankfurt, Lois and Bryant moved to England, where, nineteen months later, in June 1957, Lois gave birth to their second daughter, Brynn.

About four years into their marriage, Bryant informed Lois that he was unhappy with his job, that he had to work too hard at IBM, and that he wanted to get out. Lois was his cheerleader, so she talked with her relatives about Bryant going to work for the family business, and they all agreed that he could come anytime he was ready to join forces. When Bryant quit IBM, however, he accepted a lucrative job with ITT in Brussels, Belgium. The family business could wait.

When Lois's father began to divide up the publicly traded shares of his enormously prosperous business with his children and grandchildren, Bryant suddenly decided he wanted another child. Unfortunately, Lois later felt that Bryant's main motive in having a third child was to secure another batch of stock from her family's business.

Not long after signing on with ITT, Bryant tired of the demanding position and yearned to be free of his work responsibilities. He planned to return to Arizona and join Lois's family business. But first he wanted to take a seven-month sabbatical to travel on an unusual adventure throughout Europe. He bought a twenty-seven-foot Danish cabin cruiser in Copenhagen that he christened *Explorer I,* and navigated the family through the locks, waterways, and rivers of Germany and France, all the way to the Mediterranean, where they visited the ports along the French Riviera. With two young daughters and a pregnant wife, the boating expedition made for some eventful months before they returned to Arizona so Bryant could go to work for Lois's family at Western Savings.

Throughout their marriage, Lois never asked Bryant about their finances, and trusted him completely to handle their investments. They lived well, and Lois enjoyed Phoenix's social life. They now had three children, with the birth of their only son, Bryant Driggs Cannon in 1962. The family business continued to grow, and Lois's father continued to bless them with more and more company stock.

Their comfortable life notwithstanding, Bryant seemed once again restless and disgruntled with his job. Lois arranged an introduction for Bryant to work as a managerial vice president overseeing the computer operations at another savings and loan, Great Western in Los Angeles. Although the company's headquarters was in L.A., Bryant was able to set up the computer center in Santa Ana. The family moved to Emerald Bay in Laguna Beach, Lois's favorite beach community in Southern California, a place where she had spent many a summer day as a teenager during family vacations.

The Cannon family lived in the idyllic private beach community for nearly ten years, and to Lois it seemed like heaven on earth. Eventually, however, dissension at work caused Bryant to be dissatisfied again. He wanted to quit his job, sell the beachfront home, buy a condominium in Sun Valley, Idaho, and in the meantime tour Europe with the family in a Volkswagen camper. The trip to Europe was the beginning of the end.

It was a turbulent time that caused Lois and the three children to propose with great vigor the idea of buying another home back in Emerald Bay in an attempt to regain a sense of the family life they had once known. Bryant finally acquiesced and purchased a small hillside home to appease them, but was absent much of the time with various excuses. Lois attempted to restore some normalcy. By now the children were in college. But where was Bryant? Where had he disappeared to? When she heard from him in early December, he informed her he was now in Sun Valley, preparing for Christmas with the family.

Instinctively, Lois was concerned and decided to surprise Bryant by driving to Sun Valley to find out what was going on. When she arrived and inserted her key in the door, it didn't work. She knocked on the door, and Bryant opened it. "Lois! What are you doing here?" Bryant had no idea that Lois was coming, but then quickly changed his tune. "Come in, come in. Excuse me for a moment, while I make a phone call." Twenty minutes later a man knocked on the door, and served Lois with divorce papers.

Lois was in shock. But Bryant was adamant. He wanted a divorce before the beginning of the new year, and it was almost Christmas.

When Lois awakened the next morning in a separate bedroom from her husband, she gathered her senses. Instead of arguing about the divorce, she decided to go skiing, determined to have one of the greatest days of her life. As she approached the ski lift, she heard a voice call out to her, "Hey, Lois, come ski with me today." Lois turned around and saw a tall, handsome man she had met the previous year in Sun Valley. His name was Clint Eastwood.

For the next four days the famous actor picked up Lois each morning, and they skied together all day long. Clint was involved with Sondra Locke at the time, but became a great ski buddy and friend for Lois. His friendship, along with her other good ski buddies, gave a boost to Lois's morale at this low moment in her life.

Lois and Bryant's divorce was finalized in 1982. Divorce is difficult enough, but in the aftermath of this life-changing parting, Lois awakened to the reality that throughout the marriage, portions of her fortune and her children's had been diverted to her former husband's own purposes, and that he had repeatedly been unfaithful to her. She struggled to regain her confidence and her perky, stylish, enthusiastic self. It wouldn't be easy.

Despite feeling devastated and disappointed, Lois believed in herself. She was a survivor. She kept reminding herself of the ways she had advised her girlfriends about their problems: *Believe in yourself, put a smile on your face, throw away the problems, walk with your head high, and move on! Think about what a great life can be ahead.*

Mustering her stamina to apply this philosophy to herself, Lois marched stalwartly forward, stylish and smiling, even though she didn't feel that way inside. She was, however, secure in her finances following the divorce settlement; her stock and each of the children's stock was valued in the millions of dollars, safely invested in Western Savings. She bolstered her activities and her checkbook by serving as a public-relations figure for her father's company, and received a small stipend of about $35,000 per year to publicize Western's real-estate developments in San Clemente and other locations in Southern California.

As her confidence rebounded, she dated frequently, but refused to get seriously involved with any of her suitors. Often she would go outside on the deck of her home in Emerald Bay, and in the peaceful quiet of a starlit night, as the waves of the Pacific lapped gently against the shore, Lois would look up at the moon and stars, and ask, "Please God, send me my Prince Charming. I know he's out there somewhere." Lois believed it.

Then one night she went to a party at the Bel Air Bay Club, and met a man who knew a bit about that moon.

14

NEW BEGINNINGS

WHILE LOIS WAS PLYING THE SLOPES OF SUN VALLEY, SKIING from January to the end of March, I plunged back into my regular activities, trying to promote space exploration. I had an important meeting coming up in which I planned to present my proposals for the Aldrin Mars Cycler, so it was a busy time for me. I had given my first technical paper on the subject to a handful of engineers at the Jet Propulsion Laboratory (JPL) at Cal Tech in October 1985, just before Lois and I went to Egypt. JPL has been at the forefront of space technology since it created America's first artificial satellite, *Explorer I,* in 1958. The engineers there encouraged me to develop my presentation further. Consequently, I immersed myself in the project. I never called Lois during those months, and she never called me.

Then, on January 28, 1986, I grieved along with the rest of our nation as I watched the fateful launch of the *Challenger,* NASA's second space shuttle. The *Challenger* had already flown nine successful missions from Kennedy Space Center in Florida. Launches had become routine since the shuttle fleet first started flying in 1981. But this *Challenger* flight seemed in trouble from the beginning. It had been delayed several times, and finally lifted off at 11:38 a.m. (EDT). Friends, family, and the world watched in awe as the *Challenger* cleared the launch tower and streaked into the clear blue sky, but no one could see that an

"O-ring" seal in the solid-fuel rocket booster on the *Challenger*'s right side had failed. The faulty design of the seal, coupled with unusually cold weather, allowed hot gases to leak through the joint. Rocket booster flames were able to pass through the failed seal, enlarging the small hole. These flames then burned through the *Challenger*'s support bracket that attached the booster to the side of the tank. That booster broke loose and collided with the tank, piercing the tank's side. Liquid hydrogen and liquid oxygen fuels from the tank were ignited by the flames of the solid rocket booster, and after being in flight a mere seventy-three seconds, the *Challenger* exploded right before our eyes. Few people who saw the horrific sight can ever forget it, as all seven crew members perished. The commander of the mission was astronaut Dick Scobee, who had been a student at the Aerospace Research Pilot School at Edwards Air Force Base during my tenure as commandant. I had been impressed with his flying abilities then. He would be greatly missed.

The tragedy was particularly grievous, since the brave crew members who died included Christa McAuliffe, a schoolteacher from Concord, New Hampshire, who had been chosen from more than 11,000 educators who wanted a chance to participate on a shuttle flight under NASA's Teacher in Space program. She had taken a yearlong leave of absence from her teaching position to prepare for the mission. Through no fault of her own, NASA's first attempt to take an ordinary citizen into space had failed abysmally.

The evening of the explosion, President Reagan paid tribute to the fallen astronauts. "The crew of the space shuttle *Challenger* honored us in the way in which they lived their lives. We'll never forget them, nor the last time we saw them this morning as they prepared for their journey and waved goodbye and slipped the surly bonds of Earth and touched the face of God."

Manned spaceflight is dangerous and dramatic. When an ambitious mission succeeds, as did the moon landing flight of *Apollo 11*, astronauts like me are hailed as triumphant national heroes for doing our jobs, and the flight directors, contractors, and engineers responsible for the success are applauded as visionary geniuses. But when a supposedly routine flight, like the January 1986 mission of the *Challenger,* ends in disaster, the accident assumes the proportions of epic tragedy, replete with victims and villains. The *Challenger* incident certainly had its share of both, and as a result, America's space program was literally grounded until an investigation was conducted into the causes of the disaster. It would be 1988 before the next American shuttle launch.

Leading up to *Challenger,* America had pinned bright hopes on the new shuttle orbiter fleet, with its runway landings and seven- to eight-person capacity, to enable people other than NASA's professional astronauts to fly into space. In 1982, NASA's Advisory Council even established a task force to select private citizens for extra seats that might be available on each flight, and applications soon arrived by the scores. In the year before the *Challenger* accident, NASA flew two members of Congress, Senator Jake Garn and Representative Bill Nelson, on two separate shuttle missions, hoping, I'm sure, that they would bring back glowing firsthand accounts of the shuttle program and how taxpayer dollars were being well spent.

James A. Michener, noted author of the book *Space,* which was later made into a thirteen-hour miniseries for television, had conducted a study group and recommended that NASA include teachers and journalists on space shuttle flights. I was quite supportive of that idea, but wanted to take it one step further, allowing on board creative artists, musicians, singers, movie producers, and anyone who could connect to a large segment of the public. One person who genuinely wanted to fly in the space shuttle was my friend, the singer, songwriter, and actor John Denver.

Denver, who had written such hits as "Rocky Mountain High," "Take Me Home, Country Roads," and "Thank God I'm a Country Boy," was fascinated with space travel. John attended the launch of the first internationally manned spaceflight, *Apollo/Soyuz 1,* as well as the launch of *Apollo/Soyuz 2,* and the landing of the space shuttle. He passed NASA's physical examination to determine mental and physical fitness needed for space travel, and he became one of the leading candidates to be the "first civilian in space." John was planning on writing a song while up in space, but Christa McAuliffe was chosen to make that flight instead. He did, however, get to fly and land the Space Shuttle simulator. An airplane accident took his life before he was able to realize his dream of flying into space. Because of his tremendous support, NASA awarded John its public service medal for helping "increase awareness of space exploration by the people of the world."

Unfortunately, after Christa McAuliffe died in the 1986 *Challenger* accident, NASA lost its nerve for putting civilians into space. In my opinion, barring any accidents, sending somebody like John Denver into space would be much more effective in the long term than putting schoolteachers and journalists into space, as fine as that might be. My reasoning is that artists such as John Denver and others like him reach far more people than do most teachers and journalists. Certainly, I believe in educators, and have spoken at numerous schools in attempts to inspire the next generation of explorers, and I will continue to do so. And of course I know the power that journalists have to get out a message. But to truly touch people where they are, nothing can do it better than a song or a movie or some creative work that lands squarely in the heart. I felt that NASA missed a golden opportunity when they did not include John Denver on a space shuttle mission.

●　○　●

As WINTER GAVE way to spring, there remained an emptiness in my life that could only be filled by one person. I decided to break down and call Lois. Near the end of March, I knew that Lois would be returning to California, and I hoped that she might be willing to see me. I truly missed her. About two days after I thought she might be home, I called and was pleasantly surprised when she answered the phone. Acting just as casual as if our last meeting had ended on a high note, I spoke congenially: "Well, I see you're home. How would you like to go out tonight?"

Lois hesitated a few moments, but then answered, "Okay!"

At the conclusion of our date that night, I kissed her politely, but not passionately as we had before. We went out several more times, and I suggested, "Let's get together more often."

Lois's response surprised me. "No, that won't work," she said. "I'll be glad to go out and have a good time once in a while, but if we are to have any other kind of relationship, I require total exclusivity." She clearly was not going to allow me to break her heart again. "We can still go out, and you can go out with your other friends, and I'll go out with mine, but I don't want to get too involved if you plan to date other people as well."

Something about Lois intrigued me and appealed to me. The woman had class and character. She was unlike so many women that I had dated who spent most of our time fawning over me, or trading on my celebrity. Lois did neither. The basis of any relationship with her, she made clear, was one of equanimity.

In May of that year I presented some of my latest ideas regarding my Mars Cycler in NASA's backyard, when I spoke at the University of Houston–Clear Lake. There was no reason why America, with all its ingenuity, could not begin to plan for lunar and Mars colonies over the next fifteen to twenty-five years. We needed to start thinking about how to get there. No doubt, NASA types in the audience squirmed in discomfort as I readily acknowledged that the Soviets were leading the way to Mars and beyond.

First, I explained my concept of lunar cyclers, spacecraft that travel in a constant orbit between the Earth and the moon, ferrying crews, supplies, and commerce to and from a lunar colony's research and man-ufacturing centers. These cyclers would not land, but would transfer personnel and cargo to "ports" placed in low Earth and low moon orbit. The second phase would be to build a port in a low Martian orbit to serve as a staging area for expeditions to the red planet below, or alter-natively to land on one of the two Martian moons. For travel to Mars, I had designed my Mars Cycler system to fly in continuous orbits be-tween Earth and Mars, with a 400-ton spacecraft rotating at either end of its long struts to create the centrifugal force necessary to produce an artificial gravity environment. The outbound trip to Mars would take about five and a half months, while the return leg would last twenty-one months to take advantage of the relative position of the planets and the natural gravity-assist trajectories serving as an orbital transit-way. The Mars base itself would be staffed by twenty crew members, with half of them exchanged with each cycler arrival, meaning that each crew member would spend more than four years on the planet. The Mars-orbiting "cycla-port" could be maintained with a crew of as few as six, I told the crowd. I was back to the orbital mechanics I loved from my early days as an astronaut, and it was fueling my enthusiasm. To an audience that had grown bored watching American astronauts orbit the Earth, my words were either revolutionary or sheer lunacy.

◐　○　◐

MEANWHILE, I WAS off to the Soviet Union in the summer of 1986. I was accompanied by my youngest son, Andy, who was in the process of earning his master's degree in science technology and space policy at George Washington University. He would later follow that up with a Ph.D. from UCLA in political science, with a focus on Russia's space program. Andy spoke fluent Russian, and he had arranged an invitation for me to meet with Raoul Segdev, the head of Russia's equivalent of our Jet Propulsion Laboratory. I talked to Segdev about my cycler orbits, and the idea seemed to pique his interest. It was clear to me that the Russians were surging ahead of America in space exploration. While we were content to keep orbiting around the Earth in our shuttle, the Russians were eyeing Mars and its moons.

Interestingly, as Segdev showed me around some of the Soviet space facilities, I noticed numerous posters touting the various Soviet space achievements since Sputnik. They had indeed accomplished quite a bit. Strangely, it was almost impossible to find any reference to Apollo 11 or the fact that human beings had ever landed on the moon. The Soviets exhibited posters showing their lunar rovers, vehicles that were far more comprehensive than anything we had used. Their official position was, "It's so expensive to send people to the moon; we can send rovers there and get the same thing done." That was their public line, anyhow. The truth was that the Soviets had tried desperately to beat us to the moon, and to land one cosmonaut, but they just couldn't get their big rocket, the N1, into orbit. They tried three times that we know of, and they failed all three times—the first one less than a month before Neil and I walked on the moon, followed by two more attempts in 1971 and 1972.

In Moscow, we had an appointment with the head of the Soviet space program, who assigned one of their cosmonauts to be our guide, and for a while I thought that we might be able to finagle a tour of Star City, where the cosmonauts trained. As sort of a trade-off, the Soviets wanted me to participate in a future space meeting in Austria that turned out to be motivated by Soviet propaganda. When I realized their intentions, I declined the invitation, and that, of course, ended any possibility of an excursion to Star City. That was simply the Soviet way.

I had several purposes for going on the trip, not the least of which was an opportunity to meet with an Alcoholics Anonymous group in Poland and to encourage them in their work. We also enjoyed a whirlwind detour to Sweden to visit our relatives, and we stopped over in Budapest, Hungary, and Nuremberg, Germany.

I did a few interviews, and once again attempted to answer the inevitable question of how my life had changed after traveling to the moon. There was no sharp edge to my answer, as there might have been ten or fifteen years earlier. No doubt, the German reporters were not prepared for my more subdued yet poignant answers.

Q.—Has your life and attitude changed as a result of being on the moon?

Buzz—It's very difficult to separate out the changes that have come about in me personally, not necessarily from the experiences of being on the moon—which in themselves were very exhilarating and filled with a sense of responsibility—but also a wonderment and thankfulness for being so fortunate to be, as I think I was, at the right place at the right time when opportunity came walking by.

The experiences that caused changes in my life were not particularly because of the technical parts of our mission, or the specific actions of being on the moon, though they do contribute in some way, but they were more the response of me to people, and of people to me that changed totally from before and after. There was a gradual change in being a part of the elite astronaut crew before the mission, but there was the total change in being placed on a pedestal that came about afterward, and trying to live up to that.

Human beings are just many different varieties. And the astronaut group . . . we have the same differences that exist in any segment of people. We just happened to be pilots with the desire to fly faster and higher, and to be involved and to take opportunities as they come along, to seek out areas of achievement. But as far as our personalities go, there's a tremendous variation.

I think that perhaps I had a more sensitive personality that was more susceptible to being affected by the impact of a great change in notoriety.[14]

Unquestionably, the highlight of the trip for me came when we stopped in Feucht, Germany, in the vicinity of Nuremberg, where we visited Hermann Oberth, one of the four early rocketry and space-travel pioneers: the Soviets had Konstantin Tsiolkovsky; America had the brilliant Robert Goddard and Wernher von Braun; and the Germans had the Austrian, Hermann Oberth. Of the four, Oberth was in many ways the most important pioneer of space technology, with his focus on both the theoretical and practical aspects of rocketry. What a thrill it was for me to meet this man who not only believed early in the 1920s that we could travel to outer space, but designed the methodol-

---

[14] This quote is documented on Bill Haynes's personal home movie video of this trip. The interview is with an unidentified German reporter.

ogy to do so. I enjoyed sharing with him some of my space concepts, such as my approach for missions to Mars, and the elderly gentleman nodded knowingly. I think it pleased Herr Oberth to know that someone in the next generation was carrying on his work. We walked and talked, and I held the elderly professor's hand to steady him as we walked in the garden pathway in front of his house, and then on our way to the Hermann Oberth Raumfahrt Museum named in his honor. Just as the efforts of the rocketry pioneers made it possible for me to plant America's flag on the moon, their examples have inspired me to work for the next generation, to enable them to plant our flag on Mars.

To that end, I returned home more inspired than ever to find a way to see my Mars Cycler get into the hands of people who could combine their technological expertise with the political and economic capital to make the cycler a reality. I also had another brainstorm that had been stirring in my mind for some time.

● ○ ●

THE COSTS OF putting people into space were skyrocketing, so to speak, and with the shuttle grounded, we were losing more time every day in our attempts to take ordinary people into space. But what if cost was not an issue? What if we didn't have to depend on Congress to vote the money into the budget? What if we could finance space travel some other way? How could that be done? My mind was teeming with ideas, and the one that I settled on seemed like a plausible approach.

I envisioned a nonprofit venture called ShareSpace, intended to help get ordinary people into space. My initial plan was to sell "shares" at ten or twenty dollars each, with the proceeds going to fund long-term exploration and tourism studies of space travel. Then, every so often, there would be a drawing to award winners with space-related prizes. Initially the drawings could involve more of the public by offering all sorts of prizes including space camps for kids, suborbital jaunts into space, and perhaps, one day, trips into Earth orbit to visit space stations, space hotels and space resorts, and ultimately even trips to fly around the moon. I was convinced, and still am, that by getting more people into space, and giving them that direct experience, the public's involvement, rather than government's, will spur the major advances in space exploration.

Much of my plan was still ruminating in my mind, and I was sitting in yet another mundane meeting discussing these matters, trying to convince another group of skeptics, when somebody said, "Why don't you have a lottery?"

The notion struck me like a lightning bolt. Yes! A lottery is a great idea. Have a lottery in which millions of people contribute money for a chance to win the big prize: a trip into space! We could have other, minor prizes to keep the interest up for those who didn't win the main trip, so I talked with adventure travel groups about providing prizes such as a trip to the North Pole and other exotic prizes. Everyone seemed interested—cautious, but interested.

I attended several national lottery "conferences" in Washington, D.C., gatherings in which people who knew how a legal lottery could be run shared their expertise and advice. Almost immediately, as my mind raced ahead to the possibilities, the obstacles and potential land-mines seemed to pop up. I discovered that lotteries came under the jurisdiction of the attorney general in each individual state, so it would be difficult to have a national lottery. The most significant problem to overcome was that the lottery could not appear to be gambling.

A few years later I went to Las Vegas and talked with Sig Rogich, a casino mogul, and other people who had money and influence; a number of them seemed interested in the ShareSpace lottery. The power brokers in Las Vegas suggested that we come up with a game show in which a person could win a trip into space. That got me thinking about the possibility of a television show similar to modern-day "reality" shows, in which a group of people could compete to win an opportunity to take a short trip into space, traveling as passengers, similar to those wealthy individuals who, as of 2001, started purchasing such trips with the Russians for fees of $20 million and more!

◗　○　◗

GRANTED, WITH THE nation still reeling from the horror of the *Challenger* tragedy, and Christa McAuliffe's schoolteacher-astronaut image firmly embedded in our minds, convincing the public of the possibility and the rationale for everyday folks going into space was no easy sell. Persuading Congress to pass legislation in favor of a national space lottery to be administrated by ShareSpace would be challenging. But I knew a time would come, and when it did, I would be ready. The notion stirred me then, and still does today.

Through a series of connections, I had become a visiting adjunct professor of space studies at the University of North Dakota (UND) in Grand Forks. UND wanted to develop an astronautical curriculum, and I was willing to help structure it with the goal of preparing future astronauts, engineers, and scientists to contribute to the ongoing development of next-generation spaceflight alternatives. John Odegard, a good friend of mine, was the head of the aerospace sciences department, and I was thrilled to help him set up this new program.

At the same time, Jack Anderson, communications director for President Reagan, was announcing in Washington the formation of the Young Astronauts Program, an exciting new venture intended to inspire elementary school-aged children, arouse their spirit of adventure, and help prepare them for the challenges and opportunities in space. I gladly attended the first meeting and took the idea back to John Odegard at UND, and we helped create the first chapter of the Young Astronauts at the Viking Elementary School in Grand Forks, North Dakota. I enjoyed teaching young people about space, but after the first frigid winter in North Dakota, I quickly decided that California was a better location for me. I recruited another fellow from Tom Paine's National Commission on Space to take my place, and that ended my college teaching career. I guess some of the students were listening in my courses; just recently I received an e-mail out of the blue from a former student, who married his sweetheart, also a fellow student in the program, and now they are both Continental Airlines pilots. Perhaps soon they'll be flying Continental Spacelines!

Shortly after I returned from the Soviet Union, I received a call from David Duclon, one of the creators of a popular NBC sitcom, *Punky Brewster*. As he had watched the news coverage of the *Challenger* accident, David wondered how children might be affected who had witnessed the tragedy. Then he heard the next day that his real-life star, Soleil Moon Frye, who played Punky, had dreamed of becoming an astronaut, but, because of the tragedy, had decided to rule out that possibility. That got Duclon thinking about an episode that might help kids all over the country work through similar fears.

Would I be willing to come on the show, Duclon wondered, and help Punky resolve some of her anxiety, and thus hopefully restore an interest in space for some of America's kids? It was an offer I could not possibly turn down.

Working with the advice of several child psychologists, Duclon carefully crafted a story that began with Punky writing in her diary about what she had learned from the space-shuttle accident. Then, through flashbacks, the audience discovers how she came to that understanding—starting several days before the liftoff and then skipping ahead to that afternoon, when Punky comes home from school to talk about the tragedy with Henry (George Gaynes), her foster father. My role was simple: I just had to be myself, as I explained to Punky that all great explorers take risks, but the rewards are worth it. We talked about her desire to be an astronaut, and I encouraged her to pursue her goals. The episode also gave me a chance to get in a plug for the Young Astronauts program, which I had strongly supported since its inception. The show was one of the most widely watched in the short-lived sitcom's run, but it did not prevent NBC from canceling the series the following season. I'm sure it can still be found in reruns around the world.

◉　○　◉

IN THE MIDST of the flurry of activity in 1986, I again raised with Lois the issue of our relationship. "I think we should only go out with each other," I suggested. Lois was glad to date me, but remained cautious.

One day in August, Lois and I hopped in my red Mercedes-Benz convertible and headed from Laguna to Los Angeles along one of the most scenic roads in America, the twists and turns of the Pacific Coast Highway, PCH 1. With the wind blowing in our hair, the blue sky above us, and the blue water to our left, I said, "You know, I'm wearing this male West Point ring, but there's a female version of the ring. Do you think you might like one?" I kept my eyes glued to the road as I drove.

Lois glanced at my bulky West Point ring, and replied noncommittally, "Oh, I might like that."

Still driving and looking straight ahead, I said, "And I thought, for a wedding ring, I might get you a moon rock." I still didn't look at her, but I could almost feel my eyes twinkling.

"A wedding ring, Buzz?" Lois repeated. "Does that mean . . . wedding? Are you talking about a wedding?"

"Well, yeah, that's what I was thinking." I turned and looked at Lois. "Would that be exclusive enough?"

"Yes, absolutely!" Lois affirmed. "I think I'd like that." I could tell that despite my awkward proposal of marriage, Lois was thrilled, although she was still somewhat careful about how she responded.

"Okay," I said, "let's plan to get married."

"Well, let's not tell anybody right away," Lois suggested. "Not until we are sure we really want to do this."

I just smiled. I realized that Lois was thinking that I might back out, and she did not want to be embarrassed publicly. After all, even my friends had told her that I was a ladies' man.

Lois took her time thinking through the matter, and even sought the advice of her dear friend, Sandra Day O'Connor. "Sandra, Buzz Aldrin has asked me to marry him!" Lois confided. "What do you think?"

"I think that is marvelous!" Sandra responded without hesitation. "Buzz is a wonderful man, a true American hero." Sandra's approval of me eased Lois's mind, but she proceeded cautiously nonetheless.

Slowly, over the next few weeks, I convinced Lois that I was sincere. That fall, we attended Lois's Stanford class reunion. Worried that I would become dismayed and call everything off, she still did not want to reveal our engagement to anyone. And she wasn't quite sure how I would react if I knew her real age beneath all that youthful beauty. While in her early thirties, Lois's chestnut brown hair had suddenly and inexplicably turned a striking silver gray. Over the years, it continued to lighten, and from then on she became known as a platinum blonde, even though she never colored her hair in any way. Her hair made guessing her age difficult. As we walked the campus grounds through the many reunion gatherings, several friends waved and called out to Lois from the Class of '61 tent. As we started mingling, Lois said casually, "Well, here we are."

We socialized with many red-clad alumni, some of whom were from Lois's Southern California circle of friends, and realizing the kickoff time for the football game was closing in, I said, "Lois, hadn't we better head over to your reunion tent?"

"Buzz, how did you find out my age?" Lois asked in amazement.

"I looked at your driver's license quite some time ago."

We headed over to the tent for the Class of '51, where I met many of Lois's actual classmates, and we had a ball. Of course none of them could quite keep up with her energy.

When Lois and I first got together, I was still working as a consultant for SAIC, although I rarely went in to the office. I wasn't making a lot of money, but I didn't need a lot. Other than my condo payment, I was debt-free. I did, however, need a challenge to keep my mind occupied. When I visited Lois's family at their home in Paradise Valley, outside Phoenix, it was obvious to me that Lois came from an affluent family, although I had no idea just how wealthy her family was until after we were married. Nevertheless, if I had any doubts, when we stopped by her family's corporate headquarters building, they were dispelled.

At Thanksgiving in 1986, Lois and I announced our engagement at a small private party for family and close friends at the Wrigley Mansion, set upon a hill just above the new corporate headquarters office building of Western Savings in Phoenix. Lois's family had recently ac-

quired the mansion, under the Western Savings umbrella, to hold conferences and other events.

Then, early in December, Lois's family hosted a grand engagement
party for us at the Ritz Carlton Hotel in Laguna Niguel. We sent out
invitations with a picture of the moon, inviting friends to help us celebrate the launching of a "galactic adventure." Since we hadn't as yet set
a date for our wedding, we included a note on the announcement:
"Terminal phase intercept is pending further event sequencing." When
Lois's father stood to welcome everyone, he joked, "I see Lois has four
hundred of her favorite friends here!" His estimate was right on target.
Lois's dad went on to announce our engagement, and that's when the
party kicked into high gear.

People magazine picked up the story of our engagement, and included my whimsical suggestion that Lois's engagement ring include a
moon rock. While it made for a nice story, the truth was, all moon
rocks were government property. For me to have possessed a moon
rock, even a sliver or a chunk large enough for an engagement ring,
would have been illegal. Following the *People* story, I spent several
months trying to convince Federal officials that I did not possess any
lunar material, that I had actually presented my bride-to-be with a diamond engagement ring. When people asked to look at her "moon
rock" ring, Lois would show the ring and say, "Well, don't you know,
the moon is made of diamonds."

Originally, I suggested that we get married on Valentine's Day
1987, but Lois balked. "Oh, I can't pull together a wedding in two
months' time!" she said. "We'll have to wait a year, then."

"Okay," I said. "In that case, I'm going to move in with you."

"Oh no!" Lois cried. "We can't do that." I kissed Lois passionately.

I moved in with Lois at her cozy but elegant home overlooking the
crystal blue ocean of Emerald Bay in Laguna Beach a few days after
Christmas.

15

EVERY SUPERMAN
NEEDS HIS LOIS

F OR THE NEXT YEAR, THE FUEL OF LOVE WAS PRETTY MUCH sending Lois and me into the stratosphere, as we dashed from one event to another, not to mention planning for our wedding.

Amid our activities, I continued to ponder my designs and strategies for space exploration, and kept returning to my Mars Cycler. I could see the spaceship with its trusswork connecting two pyramid-shaped crew modules at either end, spinning around its midpoint to create an artificial gravity environment, and carrying the first humans from Earth to Mars along a pathway of elliptical orbits. I took out my graph paper to chart the most efficient orbital trajectories between these two moving planetary bodies, so the trip could be made with as little fuel as possible, relying on the gravitational forces of the two planets to sustain the orbits.

In July, I headed up to the Rocky Mountains to participate in the "Case for Mars III" conference at the University of Colorado at Boulder where a live satellite link created a "spacebridge" to a group of Soviet scientists in Moscow. The idea being explored was whether the United States and the Soviet Union might go "To Mars Together?" and whether it should be a manned or robotic mission. Former NASA administrator Tom Paine and Cornell University professor Carl Sagan, who popularized science with his TV show in the 1980s and later wrote the book *Contact,* joined me on the five-man panel, and over the course of four hours we dropped any political differences we might have had with the Soviet Union as a nation, and focused on science. We all agreed that Mars was mankind's next destination, but we also knew it was a question of national priorities, and ultimately a question of cost. I knew the United States had the technical capability, and that we could most likely overcome our ideological differences with the Soviets. But I knew there was little hope of such a joint venture without the will of the people to move it forward. As it turned out, the U.S.-Soviet venture never materialized, and it wasn't until nearly ten years later that NASA sent the Mars Pathfinder on its first robotic landing mission.

Besides a few attentive ears at JPL for my cycler concepts, not too many in the space community were seriously interested in planning human missions to our red neighbor. America didn't even have a space station yet, so it looked as though bringing my ideas to fruition might be many years off into the future. Every so often, when these realizations sank in deeper and deeper, I could feel myself losing a sense of what I was shooting for, and how to make it feasible. Without a solid track to move forward on, it seemed I had nothing to do, no real purpose to my efforts, no hope of seeing them realized. The dark mood that I had periodically struggled with over the years reared its ugly head at a very inappropriate time.

Lois had seen a bit of my downside while with me in Hawaii, but after I took up residence with her in Laguna Beach, she got the true, full picture. There I was, with the woman of my dreams, in the beautiful surroundings of her warm and inviting home. And yet I could not find a reason to charge ahead in my normal activities. Mostly I did a lot of catching up on CNN and other cable news programs, getting some serious shut-eye, or reading the space journals to which I subscribed. Somehow I felt I needed to extricate myself from the demands of the world, and on those days I did not want to attend the evening social events with Lois that we had been invited to. On other occasions I went along with her, but I felt subdued and out of place, trying to fit in with the cocktail banter.

Once a reporter came all the way from Spain to do a magazine interview with me, but it was one of those periods where the last thing I wanted was to share myself with the world. I decided I wasn't going to do the interview. I stayed in the bedroom, while Lois talked with the reporter in the living room, but I never came out even to say hello. Lois made excuses as long as she could, but after a while it was pointless, so the reporter interviewed Lois instead. Actually, Lois gave a pretty great interview on my behalf.

Although Lois had read *Return to Earth,* in which I revealed the medical saga I had experienced prior to meeting her, she refused to see me as a depressed person. She simply didn't believe in it. Instead, she viewed my depression as the result of discouragement and disappointment, a lack of confidence in myself, and the lack of a good cheerleader to keep me going. So she began a one-woman crusade to remind me on a daily basis what a good man I was. At first I didn't believe her for a minute, convinced that my down times were beyond my ability to surmount until they gradually dissipated on their own. But I enjoyed hearing what she had to say. Slowly, very slowly, her words began to sink in and have an effect, not just in helping to change my attitude about the blue funk, but often in avoiding it altogether.

Lois loved to look over my shoulder as I spread out my notes on the kitchen table and drew my orbital trajectory sketches of the Aldrin Mars Cycler. To a non-rocketeer my schematics must have appeared more like an abstract pattern of undulating waves intersecting one another in crazy-eight patterns. But she'd exclaim, "Oh, Buzz, tell me about that!" She was loaded with questions, and I enjoyed teaching her about space. Lois had deliberately avoided taking science, math, and astronomy courses at Stanford, thinking that she would never need them in her life. How wrong she was! When we went out on the deck at night and looked at the moon and the stars, she would hardly let go of me, asking me a thousand questions. I enjoyed teaching her about the various constellations and features of the moon, such as the time it takes to reach the moon if you are traveling at the speed of light. About one second!

We spent long hours just walking on Emerald Bay's smooth, sandy beach that stretched more than half a mile between the cliffs that rose up like protective fortresses at either end, and enjoying our togetherness. We watched the sunsets and the phases of the moon. Lois often spent much of her day throwing her positive energy in my direction to make me feel better. She wrote page after page of notes to me, reminding me of all the great things I had going for myself. She quit playing her daily tennis games at the Balboa Bay Club, so she could spend more time encouraging me. She even cut back on many of her favorite social events to care for me, and to do all she could to help lift me out of the doldrums. With irrepressible vigor, she reinforced the feeling that I should be proud of my past accomplishments, and take life as it unfolded.

Lois never wavered in her love for me. That is one of the most stunningly beautiful parts of her character. She was committed to helping me beat depression rather than succumb to it. She made a conscious decision that no matter whether I expressed my love to her adequately or not, she chose to concentrate on loving me. *Concentrate on that which you are in control of,* she told herself, *rather than that which you are not.* She had a boundless well to draw from, and the waters were healing.

Prior to our engagement, I had been seeing a psychologist in Orange County from time to time. Lois wanted to meet with the psychologist, too, to learn how to better help me cope with the depression that still haunted me occasionally. After several months of sessions, however, we both felt that we were spinning our wheels. "Buzz, the medicines these doctors are prescribing are not helping you," Lois told me. "You don't need them. All you need to do is believe in yourself." Lois encouraged me to go without the pills, and she was right. I did just as well without them. My physical system seemed somewhat immune to the medication, anyhow. We realized that we were each other's best support to figure out our problems, and we've never seen a psychologist since.

Lois took me on as her one-person challenge to rebuild my sense of self. Whenever I got down on myself, she wrote more notes to me, page after page, telling me how brilliant, physically attractive, creative, and innovative I was, and how I had so much to offer not just to her but to the world. Sometimes I read her notes, but more often I cast them off, not willing to think of myself in such positive, glowing terms. When Lois realized that I wasn't reading all that she had written about me, she sat close to me and read her notes aloud, reminding me of all the good things I had going for myself. In the process, she was rebuilding the confidence I had lost along the way.

● ○ ●

WE HAD NO financial concerns. I wasn't working at a regular job, but we didn't really need any additional money because I received sufficient income from some consulting fees and my Air Force retirement pay to cover my own minimal expenses, and Lois certainly had no need of money, with her net worth in the millions. Although she was worth a fortune, we never even considered preparing a prenuptial agreement. She wasn't worried about it, and I didn't care about money. Our only "prenup" was an informal verbal commitment, in which Lois promised to learn how to scuba dive, and I promised to become a good skier. Of course, to Lois that meant that I'd be going out of the gate down a race course! As it turns out, we both held true to our agreements.

At times, Lois would ask me, "How do you feel about us? Do you think our relationship is going to work?" She wasn't doubting me; she was worried that I might decide against marrying her. I didn't know how to reassure her any more than I already had, so I simply kept reassuring her. It was probably as serious a statement as a wedding ring when we changed our car license plates. On Lois's red Porsche we put a plate reading MOONGAL; on my Mercedes the plate read MARSGUY.

During this year of our engagement, I felt inspired to resurrect my idea to create a science fiction story about travel between the stars for a book and movie, based on some of my original concepts from the mid-seventies. Lois and I drove to Los Angeles and met with several major talent agents, including IMG and the William Morris Agency, to choose an agent for the project. Coincidentally, I reached out to Tom Clancy in hopes that we could work together on penning the story. With his plate full at the time, he graciously declined, but put in a good word for me with his literary agent, Robert Gottlieb, at the New York office of the William Morris Agency. I soon signed on with Gottlieb, who suggested that I put the science fiction story on hold in favor of a nonfiction insider's account of the dramatic space race to the moon. In view of the approaching twentieth anniversary of Apollo 11, the story was ripe with even more drama as we uncovered recently declassified documents that showed a much closer U.S.-Soviet moon race than had ever before been realized. Gottlieb brought Malcolm McConnell in as a co-writer to work with me, and we were off to a good start.

The more activity, the more Lois liked it. I liked it, too, and felt myself slowly but surely becoming more outgoing in my personality. I began to notice that I was smiling more, feeling more.

In May 1987, Lois and I traveled to our first Cannes Film Festival to attend the premiere of a new French documentary about the *Apollo 11* lunar landing. This was an entirely new world for me, a different crowd. Although I had been around kings and queens, and had met presidents, and I lived around the Hollywood and Beverly Hills crowd, Cannes was something else. I had many friends in high places, but for the most part I didn't socialize with them. Give me a good engineer, a good rocket scientist, and I can talk for hours. But Lois introduced me to a social set that I had only seen on magazine covers as I passed through airports. We met movie stars and producers, pop music artists—every kind of celebrity.

While we were in Cannes, we met the acclaimed Austrian photographer Helmut Newton. "Oh, you are so beautiful together," he said to Lois. "I vould love to take a picture of you; both of you." We told him we would be in Paris in a few days before heading back to the States.

Helmut set up a date to shoot a formal photo at the Georges V hotel along the famous Avenue George V just off the Champs–Elysées. As Helmut prepared for the shoot, he didn't think Lois was wearing a sexy enough dress; he would have preferred her in a low-cut dress, but Lois's modesty prevailed. "Vell, at least show me more leg," Helmut pleaded. Lois complied. The result was a formal—and quite leggy—shot of Lois, and me in my dress whites.

In November, as a surprise for her birthday, and perhaps to make up for the dismal outcome of our first Hawaiian escapade, I took Lois on a trip to the big island of Hawaii where we stayed again at my friend's hotel in Kona. But this time I took Lois to the Keck Observatory, at the nearly 14,000-foot summit of the extinct volcano Mauna Kea, to gaze through the giant telescope. I had called ahead and made special arrangements, so when Lois and I arrived, the astronomers were prepared for us, with the telescopes already sighted on the moon. Enhanced by a perfectly clear night sky, I showed Lois the precise area where Neil and I had landed on the Sea of Tranquillity. This was the closest Lois had ever been to the moon. As she observed the detailed markings of hundreds of rugged craters covering the surface, she could imagine even more intensely what I had experienced when I was there.

◑ ○ ◐

LOIS AND I were married on Valentine's Day in 1988, at the Western Savings corporate headquarters in Phoenix, a cavernous, glass building that more closely resembled the Crystal Cathedral than a bank. The sun's rays streamed down from the sky on this Arizona winter's day, as if straight from heaven. A fountain flowed through waterways at the main entrance; amid the stately palm trees, it made for a magical setting. I wore my dress whites, and Lois looked beautiful, beaming in a long bejeweled gown, her silvery blonde hair sparkling in the lights, dazzling everyone with her fantastic smile. We entered the wedding by descending a majestic upper staircase to the song "Stairway to the Stars," slowly stepping down to the first floor, where 300 guests and family members had gathered. A dear childhood friend of Lois's, a

Mormon bishop, officiated at the ceremony, and was brief and to the point. Then he playfully concluded his remarks, saying, "I hope this marriage will be a new high for you, Buzz." After he pronounced us husband and wife, the building filled with the sounds of "Fly Me to the Moon."

Later, as I sipped Perrier with a lime, I said to the crowd, "I was thinking of a phrase I heard from a guy I took a trip with. He said, 'One small step . . .' Seems to me that Lois and I have launched a giant leap."

◗　○　◗

IF MY MIND wandered up into the clouds before our marriage, I spent even more time envisioning new possibilities for space exploration now that I was enjoying my new married life with Lois. I progressed with my Mars Cycler orbits, but for now, what America most needed was a space station to continue its leadership role in space. At the time, NASA and Congress were struggling with the funding required for building the U.S. space station *Freedom* as proposed by President Reagan. Perhaps if we had a "Starport" facility attached to the station, which could serve as a permanent port for spacecraft venturing back to the moon and cycling ships arriving from and departing for Mars, then the station would greatly expand its usefulness and justify its cost.

I began to think of the best way to design such a Starport. A few years earlier I had met Buckminster Fuller while living in Los Angeles, and was well acquainted with his use of geodesic domes in architecture. Bucky had an inspired sense of engineering, and we used to trade insights on our latest inventions. Playing off his geodesic forms, I used everything from basic toothpicks to elaborate vector and styrofoam modeling materials to experiment with the shape of an external framework that would house tubular habitat modules large enough for a ten-astronaut crew, and multiple berthing ports where spacecraft would be assembled, repaired, checked out for missions, and refueled. The habitat modules themselves would be adapted from spent fuel tanks already launched into space and guided into position rather than falling back to burn up in the Earth's atmosphere. For the framework, I started with triangular pyramid tetrahedral shapes, then twelve-sided dodeca-hedron forms. I finally settled on an eight-sided framework—a "cubo-octahedron"—that would offer the greatest flexibility, strength, and stability to protect the Starport from collisions with docking spacecraft and from harmful movement caused by rotating solar panels. I figured that even if NASA did not go for the design, at least I might adapt it as a set of toy modeling kits for children, to inspire them and get them excited about our future in space. For this Starport design I was awarded my first U.S. patent on a "cubo-octahedron space station," just as America decided to adapt elements of the proposed space station *Freedom* for construction of the newly designed International Space Station.

● ○ ●

SOMETIMES THE NOTORIOUS blue funk still descended over me for no explicable reason, and I would withdraw from the world for periods of as much as several weeks. But Lois continually bolstered me, filling my life with all sorts of encouragement and events. As she did, my mind began to open up, allowing me to be creative once again. I was going to need that creativity for the work I would be doing that summer with Malcolm McConnell on my next book project, *Men From Earth,* a tribute to the pioneering astronauts and cosmonauts from the space race to the moon era. Malcolm had a summer home and kept a sailboat in the ancient, picturesque village of Lindos on the Greek island of Rhodes, so he suggested, "Why don't you and Lois come to Greece? It will be a great getaway for you, and we can work on the book without being disturbed."

We had been married in February, and were scheduled to go to Greece in July 1988, but on the day we were to leave, I fell into a slump and lost all interest and enthusiasm in going. *Why am I writing this book?* I thought. NASA's shuttle fleet had been grounded for over two years since the *Challenger* accident, and our space program was at a low point. Perhaps the public would not be interested in looking back at the story of Apollo and how we won the space race, so why bother? Whatever the reason, I didn't want to go. The taxi was literally sitting out in front of our house, waiting to take us to the airport, and I de-cided that I was not going to get off the couch. Lois was adamant. "Buzz, we are going to Greece!"

I sat staring straight ahead.

"Buzz Aldrin," she said, putting her cute little nose right in front of mine, "you get off that couch right now. Let's go!" Lois literally pulled me off the couch, and started dragging me across the floor, but I re-fused to budge.

"Buzz, if you don't get up, I'm going to go get the taxi driver and have him carry you into the car! We are going to Greece!" This prospect got me up.

So we went to Greece, and had a marvelous time. Malcolm had arranged for us to rent a small apartment near his home, and each day I walked down the colorful village streets to work with him. During our time there, Lois and I visited the Lindos Acropolis. Looking at that structure and recalling the mythology that so epitomized Greek culture, I could envision how modern-day technology had a strange way of fulfilling the "myths" of the people who preceded us. Maybe someday my so-called "fantasies" about space exploration to the stars will be commonplace.

One day, as Lois and I were walking hand in hand down a nearly deserted street, we saw a man approaching us. As he passed, I called out, "Is that you, Walter?" The man turned around, and sure enough, it was Walter Cronkite! Of all places in the world to run into the *CBS Evening News* anchorman, who, with one heartfelt wipe of a tear from his eye before a whole nation, sent us on our way that morning as we lifted off on the great Saturn V on our journey to the moon nearly twenty years earlier.

● ○ ●

IN DECEMBER 1988, Federal regulators clamped down on savings and loan institutions throughout the country, including Western Savings & Loan. The company was working hard to meet new regulatory capital requirements amidst a severe downturn in the Arizona real estate market. Lois's father, Douglas Driggs, founder of Western in 1929, and her brothers, Gary Driggs, serving as president and CEO, and John Driggs, the chairman of the board, had built the family business into one of the most successful savings and loans in the country. Western had survived the Great Depression and prior savings and loan crises in the 1960s, 1970s, and the 1980s, and prided itself on serving the Arizona community's mortgage needs. The Driggs family felt strongly that Western could survive the current crisis as well, but efforts to secure a rescue package and recapitalization did not pan out. Ultimately, in the late 1980s, they could not avert the failure of virtually the entire Arizona savings and loan industry, regardless of the management strategy of the individual institutions. As part of the colossal savings-and-loan debacle throughout the United States at that time, the government seized Western Savings on June 14, 1989, rendering its stock valueless to the bank's shareholders. Unlike the multibillion-dollar bailouts of 2008 to save the investment, banking, and financial institutions of America, in 1989 there was no such bailout, and the entire savings-and-loan industry disappeared.

Overnight, all of Lois's family's resources were gone. Not merely reduced, not like a steep drop in the stock market that held out the hope of rebound. No, in one fell swoop, Lois's and her children's stock assets in the company were gone. Fortunately, Lois and I were relatively debt-free, with no mortgage payments and no real financial stress. Nevertheless, to lose millions of dollars overnight was an awful setback and loss.

The bank managers called Lois and said, "You don't have anything left." She was devastated, and could see no recovery after the S&L mess. Overnight, everything about our financial picture changed, as Lois's fortune and the wealth of her children were quite literally wiped out.

Certainly it upset me that Lois had lost her financial resources, but that sort of change didn't really have an impact on my attitude toward our relationship. Lois was so self-effacing; she said, "Buzz, if you need or want a wealthy woman, I understand if you want to leave."

I thought that was absurd. "Is my course of action going to be any different," I asked, "just because you no longer have your stock?" No. I still had my modest Air Force pension coming in each month, and intermittent consulting fees to supplement it. On my own, that was all I needed. But from Lois's standpoint, she had nothing to fall back on.

For the next few years we had to scramble back from the bottom to build a business of some sort, something that we hoped would allow us to live in a lifestyle at least somewhat similar to the one we had enjoyed during the first part of our marriage. Lois began taking the calls, wheeling and dealing with people or groups that wanted me to come to speak for them or to participate in some special event. Prior to being married to Lois, I had had a secretary come in every so often and simply write a bunch of "thanks, but no thanks" notes, turning down almost every invitation that came to me. I had not wanted to be a public person again.

But when Lois's fortune was wiped out, we had to find some way to survive, and it seemed ridiculous to turn down offers from people who were willing to pay me to speak about what I loved talking about anyhow! So we started accepting a few speaking engagements. Lois and her daughter, Lisa Cannon, a Stanford graduate who had left the music business as a performer to work as an entertainment attorney, took care of the business side, negotiating the contracts, and helped me on the performance side to hone my presentations. Before long, I was busy on the speaker's circuit. That year, with the book advance and a couple of extra endorsement deals that came along, we earned about $250,000. It was a good start, and we felt our lives were rich and full. We didn't see ourselves as older or slowing down; we were healthy and excited about life.

My petite little platinum blonde beauty of a wife suddenly turned into a public-relations dynamo. "The business is Buzz!" she proclaimed, and indeed so it became. Lois encouraged me to do interviews and attend more social functions. She protected my reputation in every way, and just had a knack for helping me to be seen in the right places, at the right times. For my part, I loved it. I was the star performer, who just needed to show up on stage as the curtains parted, and did not need to concern myself with any of the logistics. Admittedly, there

were a few occasions when I balked, but every time we attended another event, it gave me more of a platform on which to talk about my
ideas regarding space exploration. We rarely traveled simply for the
sake of travel anymore. Now it was mainly for business. Lois's father
was delighted to see Lois in the business world—finally making that
Stanford education pay off!

* ◦ *

ON JANUARY 20, 1989, my fifty-ninth birthday, Lois and I went to
Washington, D.C., to attend the inauguration of President George H.
W. Bush. While we were there, Lois's mother passed away, which was a
blow to Lois; her mother was like a best friend. Fortunately, we were
able to return to Phoenix immediately after the inauguration with the
help of our friends Julia and Ambassador George Argyros, who flew us
in their private jet to arrive just in time for the funeral. When Lois saw
her mother in the casket, she fell apart, dissolving in tears. It was one of
the few times since I'd known her that I had ever seen Lois break
down. Her tears were genuine and she grieved for a season, but not
without hope of being reunited in the hereafter, a belief with which she
was raised in her family and church.

Six months later, on July 20, 1989, we were back in Washington,
D.C., at the twentieth anniversary of the *Apollo 11* landing on the
moon. I gave my pitch along with Neil and Mike on the steps at the
Smithsonian in Washington, and listened as President Bush stated that
America would move aggressively forward in space to do three things:
first, complete the space station by 2000; second, go back to the moon,
this time for keeps, by setting up a base there; and, third, begin missions to Mars. I was elated. This was good news indeed.

Unfortunately for the space program, the Democratic majority in
Congress wanted to thwart Bush 41's plans any way they could, and
that included stunting the enthusiasm for getting America's space program back in gear. "How much does all this cost?" we heard over and
over again. "Why should we spend all that money when there are so
many pressing needs on Earth?"

A ninety-day feasibility study was done, with Congress concluding that the president's plans were too expensive, and refusing to fund them. The $400-billion price tag was too outlandish, opponents said. America's renewed thrust into space was dead on arrival.

Naturally, I was disappointed. But because of the lack of government support, I began ruminating more about commercial ventures, including space tourism. As I thought about matters, it seemed to me that ShareSpace, the organization I had envisioned several years earlier, was the way to get ordinary citizens into space. I felt sure that enthusiasm and excitement about the exploration of space were lying latent in American adventurers. All we needed to do was to find a way to help them make their dreams a reality. I had witnessed the United Airlines pilots' excitement over wanting to fly the space shuttle; some companies even wanted to purchase a space shuttle for commercial use. I had known high-profile individuals like John Denver who had a desire to fly into space. I believed that if we could find a way to pay for it, people would want to travel into space and enjoy the experience firsthand. And I was convinced that I had come up with a plan to get them there.

16

OH, the PLACES
YOU WILL GO!

T HE MORE I STUDIED THE COST OF SPACE TOURISM, THE MORE I wondered if there was a better way than just offering seats on the space shuttle to rich people who could afford to spend $20 million or more. The number of those who could afford such an expenditure, while larger than one might think, is still relatively small compared to the people who would be interested in traveling into space if it were an attainable goal.

Even a price tag of $100,000 for a suborbital trip would be exorbitant for most, although I'm sure the seats would be in high demand for those wanting a once-in-a-lifetime experience. Nevertheless, I became more convinced that the lottery was the best way to get the "average Joe" involved, selling lottery tickets at a reasonably affordable price and offering various prizes leading up to the time when we could offer actual spaceflights. I kept talking about it everywhere I went, and increasingly people began to say, "Yes, why not?"

LOIS AND I were still living in Laguna Beach, but we weren't there often. We crisscrossed the United States and hopscotched all around the globe. Traveling as much as Lois and I do sets you up for some unusual experiences. Once, on our way home from Europe, I stopped over in Houston for some meetings. Lois decided to go directly to our home in Emerald Bay to do some catching up on our business with our secretary. It was October 1993, and fires were raging all along the California coastline beginning in the Thousand Oaks area of Los Angeles, and then jumping northward toward Santa Barbara. South of L.A., fires broke out in the Anaheim Hills and worked their way toward Laguna Beach. The line between houses that could be saved and those that were lost was determined often by only a few feet. In Laguna, the fires engulfed one home after another, many of which were valued in the millions of dollars. Fanned by the Santa Ana winds, shooting embers drifted from house to house, setting the roofs on fire and then quickly torching entire homes. Many of Laguna Beach's residents had to flee in the face of the flames.

As the fires crept closer, Emerald Bay's volunteer fire department issued an evacuation order. Lois's secretary left immediately. Lois needed to evacuate, as well. The sky was dark, and Lois knew that fires were raging in Laguna Canyon; yet, she wasn't too concerned or afraid. She assumed the danger was still a good distance away. But when she opened the front door that faced up the hill, she saw huge waves of flames widely surging over the top of the ridge, heading straight toward our home. The fire was only about six streets up from where Lois stood, dangerously close to the highest tier of hillside homes, moving fast, and consuming everything in its path.

Lois grabbed a large box of memorabilia that we had recently filled with some of my more precious items, including some of the envelopes that we had taken to the moon, signed by Neil Armstrong, Michael Collins, and me, and some stamped envelopes that we had arranged to have canceled on the day of our lunar landing. Originally, my fellow astronauts and I had signed these "first day cover" envelopes as a sort of "insurance policy" for our families. When we went to the moon in 1969, NASA had no extra insurance built into its program to cover our families should anything catastrophic happen to us, so, as morbid as it might sound, we signed some of the envelopes and left them behind. Others we actually took with us to the moon. Upon our safe return, we split up all the envelopes between us and signed each other's while in quarantine. For some reason, rather than keeping the valuable treasures in a safe deposit box in a bank vault, Lois and I had simply put them in a box in the closet "for safekeeping."

When it came time to escape the fires, Lois didn't look for money, jewelry, or clothing. She left with only the clothes she was wearing and the one box containing the precious items that had flown all the way to the moon and back. She drove to the Balboa Bay Club where she was a member and could stay in one of the Bay Club rooms for the night.

More than fourteen fires raged around Los Angeles and Orange County. Not one had yet been brought under control, despite firefighters using helicopters to dump huge loads of water and planes to drop chemical fire retardant. The flames burned all around our home, too, gutting expensive houses only a few yards away.

The following day, Lois awakened not knowing whether our home had survived. Logic told her to expect the worst, but she continued to hope for the best. That afternoon, Lois received a call from Stone Philips, a reporter from NBC's *Dateline*. Stone asked if he could pick her up the next morning and take her to Laguna to tour the region and do an interview for *Dateline* in some of the burned-out areas. Lois wasn't thrilled about being on nationwide TV without makeup and in the same casual clothes she had been wearing the day before, but it was an opportunity to check on our home, so she agreed. No vehicles were allowed on the Pacific Coast Highway except those of firefighters and reporters. Once they entered Emerald Bay, to her great relief Lois saw that our home was still standing, with only a bit of roof damage. The two houses next to ours were burned down completely, but our home, with the rest of my Apollo 11 moon paraphernalia inside, was intact.

I arrived back in California the following evening, and met Stone Philips and Lois at our home. He wanted to film me being greeted by Lois with the good news that the house was okay. Our home had been saved, we learned, because the Emerald Bay fire chief had stood on the roof with a garden hose, watering it down to battle the flames. As deeply grateful as we were to him, we were commensurately saddened for our friends who had lost so much—more than sixty homes had been destroyed in Emerald Bay alone, with nearly four hundred lost in surrounding Laguna Beach.

Furniture, clothes, even the house itself could be replaced, but those envelopes and other Apollo 11 items could never be duplicated. One of our first stops the following day was at the bank, where we deposited my moon memorabilia in a safe deposit box.

For once, it felt good to simply stay at home.

Shortly thereafter, I completed my book *Encounter with Tiber,* a science fiction novel of epic proportions involving space travel to the stars. I had been ruminating about the story line and characters since the mid-seventies. In *Encounter with Tiber*, I included in fictional form many of my ideas for space travel in the next millenium. The futuristic spaceships I envisioned, that flew by solar winds close to the speed of light, were actually based on the science as we understood it at the time. No warp-speeding through wormholes. My story line in *Tiber* was what I like to call "science-fact-fiction," incorporating full appreciation for the physical laws of the universe, combined with a healthy dose of imagination. I grew up on Buck Rogers and Flash Gordon stories that seemed outlandish when I first read them, but today might seem terribly blasé. If our minds can conceive it, the possibility exists that we can do it.

◑　○　◑

LOIS WAS COMMITTED to keeping her promise to me, to learn how to scuba dive. On one of our first scuba-diving trips together, she and I were in Australia on Hamilton Island, where she took a five-day scuba-diving course. For her initial dive, we weren't far off Hamilton Island, but it was at night. I thought, *Well, Lois is doing great, and she's a fast learner, and we do have some time, so why not go for a dive?* Lois had never before had on scuba gear outside of a swimming pool or just off the beach, certainly never out in the open sea. But I had confidence in her, and felt she could do it.

We went out on the boat just after sundown, as the moon was coming up. We plunged into the water in the dark with our only light coming from the moon, our flashlights, and some floodlights shining down off the boat.

Lois started out courageously, but under the surface in the darkness she became disoriented. Floundering around for a few minutes was enough for her. Within a short time, she signaled me that she was returning to the boat. It wasn't the longest dive, but it was a great first effort on her part.

On another of Lois's early dives, we were in the Caribbean off the coast of Florida with Jimmy Johnson, former coach of the Dallas Cowboys, and about twenty other people who were treasure-recovery specialists. The group was dredging for rare coins and gold bullion. On one of the days while the others were treasure-hunting, Lois and I went for a dive alone. We dove in a shallow area only about twenty-five feet deep, but the currents were brisk.

We were underwater for about forty-five minutes when Lois looked up and couldn't see our boat. She poked my arm and nodded toward the surface. We both surfaced, and when I looked up, much to my dismay, I saw that the boat was about a mile away. We had drifted in the current during our dive, and hadn't even been aware of it. We tried to get somebody's attention aboard the boat, but with the whitecaps rising higher at the end of the day, our efforts were in vain.

"We're going to have to swim for it, Lois," I said.

"What?" I wasn't sure if it was surprise or sheer horror in her voice, but time was of the essence.

"No time to explain," I said, "but I think we can make better time swimming underwater." We put on our masks, and dove below the surface, swimming as hard as we could, trying to catch the boat. Swimming against the current was extremely tiring. Then our air ran out, and we had to swim on the surface, making it even more difficult. My heart was pounding, and I'm sure Lois's was, too. Our energy was dissipating rapidly. Finally somebody aboard the boat saw us, and realized that we were in trouble. The boat swung around hard, and within a few minutes we were clambering on board. That ended Lois's interest in scuba diving for a while.

When she finally consented to give it another try, we were on a Sea Space Symposium dive off the Mexican coast of Baja, California, in which the guys were off on one dive and the women were on a supposedly tamer version of it. Lois, in her zebra-striped wetsuit, was trying desperately to follow the directions of the divemaster in the heavy seas. They dropped a rope line to the bottom as the women made their way down to where they were going to begin exploring underwater. As Lois and the women were waiting at the bottom, they suddenly saw a school of about ten hammerhead sharks passing by just a few feet away. The divemaster signaled to be still, and the lady divers froze. The moment the sharks passed by, the women made a beeline back up the rope and tumbled into the boat.

When the men returned, I told Lois, "We barely saw a thing."

Lois had seen all she needed to see. Over time, however, she developed a love for scuba diving and became my best diving buddy.

● ○ ●

WHEN IT CAME to skiing, Lois could beat me hands down. Having never skied until I was in my fifties, I might not have had the most graceful style, but I picked it up relatively quickly. Lois was an excellent teacher, with her unmistakable quick-turning, deep-knee-bending style. We did most of our skiing in Sun Valley, where Lois had a home. I became familiar with the slopes, and with all of her ski buddies there. The year before Lois and I met, she had attended a gala celebrity event celebrating Sun Valley's fiftieth anniversary. It was produced by Marjoe Gortner, a onetime child evangelist and movie star, now turned premier event producer. Supposedly named for Mary and Joseph by his minister parents, Marjoe could preach a sermon and quote scripture when he was only four years old. With his angelic yellow curls, he went on to pack revival tents throughout the South until he was seventeen.

Since 1987 he had devoted most of his time to producing several invitational celebrity sports events per year in locations such as Sun

Valley, Lake Louise, Cabo San Lucas, Hawaii, Jamaica, and other resorts. These events often brought together a diverse group of entertainment and sports celebrities to compete in ski races, target snow-golf,
snowshoe races, tobogganing, and water sports, but the weekend always revolved around an auction that raised money for a charity.

Our team leaders were Winter Olympics stars, and at one such
event I was expected to be one of the slalom racers. Spectators didn't
care whether I had ever been on skis before or not, they just loved to
see the celebrities slipping and sliding and tumbling their way down
the mountain. But, thanks to Lois giving me ski lessons that first
Christmas we were together, I fooled them, and although I was older
than most of the competitors, I held my own. I didn't win any of the
races, but I sure didn't lose, and I rarely fell on my face.

●   ○   ●

I'VE BEEN A member of The Explorers Club for years, meeting and interacting with such world-class explorers as the Cousteaus, Sir Edmund Hillary, and many more. At one of the annual galas, Lois and I
met Lady Alexandra Foley, a woman who worked with RMS Titanic,
Inc., the company that had been granted "salvor-in-possession rights"
to the *Titanic*. They had the right to explore the wreck and surrounding ocean areas, to obtain oceanographic material and scientific data
from the area, and to retrieve artifacts from the sunken ship. The RMS
Titanic folks had arranged for two cruise ships, the *Royal Majesty*,
which would depart from Boston, and the SS *Island Breeze*, embarking
from New York in August 1996, to sail to the area above the wreckage.
Among the 3,000 passengers aboard those two ships would be sur-
vivors from the *Titanic*'s maiden voyage in 1912, when, on April 14, it
struck an iceberg and sank with the resultant loss of 1,522 lives.

More than eighty years later, passengers aboard the two ships would
watch the live video feed on giant screens, as a tiny three-man titanium
submersible, the *Nautile*, would descend to the *Titanic* to raise a section
of the ship's hull that was lying in the debris around the wreckage, and

explore the bow section of the ship for the first time. I was invited to be one of the three men to make the two and a half mile dive to the *Titanic*. At the time, I was in the midst of an international book tour, promoting *Encounter with Tiber*, so it probably took me at least half a second to accept that invitation to include the cruise itinerary in my tour and explore the *Titanic*!

Since *Encounter with Tiber* was released to rave reviews, I had been doing a whirlwind tour of the Planet Hollywood restaurants and entertainment complexes across the country. Arthur C. Clarke, the author of *2001: A Space Odyssey*, as well as many other works of science fiction, had started the buzz with his kind comments, lamenting facetiously that although I had written two nonfiction books, I was now moving into his territory. "It doesn't seem fair," Clarke wrote in the foreword to the book, "There was a time when we science fiction writers had Space all to ourselves and could do just what we liked with it. Not anymore. . . . People like Buzz have been there, and can tell us exactly where we went wrong. And now, to add insult to injury, they're writing science fiction themselves. Even worse—it's darn good science fiction." I preferred the term "techno-thriller," but I certainly appreciated such a glowing endorsement from one of the world's best SF writers. We had begun negotiations with Paramount Pictures to do a miniseries based on the book. The script was snatched up by ABC Television. But Disney, ABC's parent company, had already begun production on their *Mission to Mars* feature film and determined that the projects would be competing, so ultimately the *Tiber* series was tabled.

The RMS Titanic organizers planned several special events for Lois and me to meet our fellow passengers aboard the the *Royal Majesty* and *Island Breeze*, and to promote my new book. Then we rendezvoused with the utility ship carrying the *Nautile*. Looking at the tiny yellow submarine, it was almost impossible not to think of the Beatles song by that title. But the Beatles could not have imagined climbing into such a minisub and slowly descending through the darkness nearly three miles below the surface. The submersible was spherical, with small portholes of glass on the left and right sides, built to withstand the enormous pressure of the water at such a depth. It was one of only a few submersibles in the world able to make such a dive.

The inside of the sub was extremely tight, even smaller than the command module *Columbia.* A claustrophobic person would not have lasted three minutes once the hatch was closed. To maneuver the sub, the pilot had to sit and work the controls, while his copilot and I had to lie flat on our stomachs on boards just off the floor to remain dry, due to the wet floor area. If nature called, we had a pail on the floor for collection purposes. It was not a luxurious ride.

My fellow divers were French, so they could speak a bit of broken English to me, but most of the communications with the surface were in French. Although I could probably order a decent meal in Paris, that was the extent of my French, so in addition to the odd feeling of dropping toward the ocean floor through darkness, I felt a bit at a loss to understand the instructions and conversations of my colleagues.

Meanwhile, a British film crew was making a documentary, *Explorers of the Titanic,* that they planned to air on the Discovery Channel. They had asked me to provide the audio commentary as the submersible made its way down to the *Titanic.* Visibility was extremely poor, perhaps less than 150 feet at best, so my live transmissions were rather limited until we got down to within 150 feet of the vessel. Even then, because of the depth, it was impossible to see far beyond whatever was immediately in front of us. But the television folks asked me to describe the lonely darkness on the bottom of the ocean as compared to what I had experienced on the moon. I gave it my best shot.

It took us more than an hour to descend to the *Titanic.* We were not attached to the ship above us by a tether, but moved under our own power as we dropped through the darkness. I was on the right of the pilot, with my face pressed against the porthole-type window, straining to see as we made our way down. I caught sight of the eerie remains of the sunken ship, like a ghost rising through the hazy darkness. The *Nautile*'s pilot eased the sub forward until it hovered just above the *Titanic*'s bow. We were 12,500 feet below the surface. I grabbed a camera and started snapping pictures of what I thought was probably a place where passengers had once stood and looked out over the sea. The algae and other organisms covering the rusty bow gave it a strange whitish, surreal appearance, almost as though it were made of crusty gingerbread covered with frosting. We continued all the way down to the ocean floor. Color means nothing on the ocean's bottom, since no sunlight ever makes it that far down. But in the lights from our submersible, I saw a sight almost as fascinating as the *Titanic* itself. Some pure white sea creatures that looked like a cross between a crab and a starfish were swimming all around the vessel. They had no eyes, which made sense to me, because there was no light to see anything by. In all my diving experience, I had never seen such unusual creatures.

The pilot maneuvered the submersible around the *Titanic*, searching for the items we hoped to raise. We were planning to float a fifteen-ton section of the *Titanic*'s hull to within 215 feet of the surface. We had six lift bags filled with diesel fuel, which we pulled to within 100 feet of the wreckage. Each of the bags was capable of lifting more than three tons of material. Diesel fuel does not compress under the water's pressure, and is lighter than water, so ostensibly the lift bags would cause the *Titanic*'s hull to float. The *Nautile*'s pilot used the sub's manipulator arms to connect the bags to the hull section with strong cables. But as we began to lift the hull, one of the cables connecting the lift bags snapped, and another would not release, causing the assembly to become unstable. We tried cutting the rope with a knife in the manipulator arm. But even though we cut the rope, nothing happened. One of the bags had somehow disengaged, so nothing we did was going to bring up the hull. The rough seas had caused the *Titanic*'s hull to sink into the ocean's floor. We had already been down about nine hours, and still needed another hour to ascend to the surface. Although the mission itself was scrubbed, the experience for me was truly worthwhile. To have traveled to the moon, Earth's new frontier, and to the ocean floor, Earth's deepest frontier, in a span of less than thirty years, was an extraordinary pair of adventures.

● ○ ●

In 1998, I traveled to the North Pole on the Russian nuclear-powered icebreaker *Sovetsky Soyuz,* on a trip scheduled by Quark Adventures, organized by The Explorers Club, and headed by Mike McDowell. My longtime friend and ABC network news personality Hugh Downs, and his wife, Ruth, were also aboard. Hugh had a film crew on the ship for the ABC television program *20/20.* I had asked Lois if she would like to accompany me to the North Pole, and she said, "No way, but you go and have a good time. Then you can come back and tell me all about it." If Lois planned to be cold, she preferred to have skis attached to her feet. She didn't relish the idea of spending a week on a Russian icebreaker. She did, however, find a camping store in Paris where she bought my French couture cold-weather red-orange mountaineering outfit. I felt very warm and quite fashionable—and later wore this same outfit for my "Final Frontiersman" photo shoot with photographer Annie Leibovitz for *Vanity Fair.*

We flew to Murmansk, Russia, and from there it was a fascinating trip across the Arctic Ocean, slowly crunching our way through the thick ice as we moved northward. The nuclear vessel, with 75,000 horsepower, made the trip without a problem. My fellow passengers numbered about a hundred people from every continent, including a group of Japanese tourists who were among the first to own GPS devices and were constantly trying to figure out where we were. Everyone seemed to get along well, and except for comments about the cold, I got the sense they were inspired by the surroundings.

During the day as we traveled, the president of the Explorers Club presented lectures along the way. He had been a Navy captain who commanded submarines during the Cold War, and had charted the northern coast of Russia for American spy subs. Once he had actually surfaced a U.S. sub at the North Pole, bringing it up through a break in the ice.

I enjoyed the lectures, but I spent just as much time sketching out new rocket ideas on a *Sovetsky Soyuz* scratch pad. I knew that at some point the U.S. space shuttle program would come to an end, and we would need some sort of program to get us back to the moon and on to Mars, so I constantly doodled ideas for new rocket designs. Perhaps because I was on a Russian ship, I thought a lot about the Soviet five-engine rockets, wondering how we might be able to adapt those ideas for American rockets. Some of the configurations I scribbled on those scratch pads later formed the basis of my StarBooster rockets, developed by the band of engineers at my rocket design company that I had formed a few years earlier.

Despite the freezing temperatures, all of the passengers were on the bridge when we reached 90 degrees north, the latitude of the North Pole relative to the Earth's equator, and 180 degrees east-west, where the Earth's longitudinal lines converge. There's nothing like being "at the top of the world, looking down on creation," and I could almost hear the soulful voice of my favorite singer, Karen Carpenter, as I took in the wide, frozen expanse. When we had gone as far as we could aboard the icebreaker, two helicopters flew the passengers over to where we were served a meal on the ice. We set up a baseball diamond and played a game of softball at the North Pole, and a group of younger passengers even took an extremely brief swim.

The photo of the bright red-and-yellow "North Pole" sign planted on the 90N spot surrounded by the nondescript sea of white ice, with our red-and-black Russian nuclear icebreaker in the background, was worth far more than a thousand words. The experience was priceless, causing me to become even more excited as I thought about all the adventures I wanted to share with others by sending them into space.

I came home invigorated and inspired to formally organize my non-profit foundation, ShareSpace, with a team of advisers to build upon my lottery concept. It was time to take regular citizen explorers, or "Global Space Travelers" as I would come to call them, up into space for the adventure of a lifetime. We just needed to find the spaceship to take them, and a legal lottery mechanism. But that's what the American dream is all about, right?

17

ADVOCACY for
AMERICA

As THE WORLD WAS APPROACHING A NEW MILLENNIUM, I seemed to catch fire myself, with renewed energy and passion to promote space exploration. Thanks to Lois's upbeat attitude and positive influence, I felt like a totally changed man, with a beautiful wife and a new life. I was miles above where I had been when I landed on the moon. Certainly, being sober helped me think more clearly, and the organization and comfort Lois provided in our business and at home allowed me to be more creative, all of which gave me more confidence to stand up in public and express my ideas about returning to the moon, creating workable spaceports, and moving on to Mars.

What I wanted people to understand was that we needed to be talking about a comprehensive vision, a master plan. It wasn't an either-or proposition—either we go to the moon or we go to Mars. Instead, everywhere I went, I presented an integrated plan showing that my ideas were not the disjointed ramblings of a once-and-forever moon guy, but that at each step along the way, we could chart our course in an evolutionary way. We could be improving the program—and life—for all concerned. By getting more people into space by means of my ShareSpace concepts, and by using renewable rockets, we could lower the costs of space travel for all.

That was one of the reasons why, in 1996, I started a rocket design company to develop the StarBooster family of reusable rockets, based on some of my hand-drawn schematics and sketches of new rockets that I had been making for some time. My plan was to use existing rocket reliability and transform expendable rockets—the kind we've all watched burn up and plunge into the sea or disintegrate in space—into recyclable rockets, including "fly-back boosters" that would be fueled by liquid rocket fuel and return to Earth, land on a runway, to be used again and again, providing significant savings.

As it stood, not enough viable work existed to justify NASA making weekly or even monthly flights into space with the space shuttle. But if more people wanted to go, and good old American ingenuity and the forces of competition were encouraged, the result would be more efficient and affordable space travel for all, with more opportunities for exploration at less cost to the government.

I was so passionate about these ideas that I willingly testified before a House congressional committee, chaired by Congressman Dennis Hastert, in May 1997, the first committee hearing ever to take place at the National Air and Space Museum. Our charred *Columbia* command module from *Apollo 11* served as an appropriate backdrop. I presented my ideas promoting space tourism as one of the key ingredients to jump-start America's dawdling space program, and for sustaining and expanding the future exploration of space.

After a brief introduction, I quickly got to the thrust of my argument:

My chief message is this: America must dream, have the faith to achieve the dream, and develop the fullest possible knowledge of the possibilities that await us. Even the best-trained and the brightest engineers, scientists, businesspeople, and political leaders, if they have no vision, are mere placeholders in time. We must dare again to take risks as a nation. And we must see again that this generation of Americans—those alive today—have at their fingertips the technology and the recent history necessary to trigger a cascade of vast new discoveries for this living generation and those that will follow.

Several of the congressmen nodded in approval as I spoke—while others were simply nodding—so I stoked the fires even more. I talked about how the successful Apollo program had led to technological breakthroughs that we now take for granted, such as satellite-driven communications. Other goals, such as routine commercial flights to and from space, space tourism, settlements on the moon, and the human exploration of Mars, had not happened yet, but I encouraged the committee to press forward and accomplish those goals within our lifetimes.

But each of these advances requires three things: knowledge, faith, and commitment. Knowledge that we can achieve these feats for all mankind, faith in ourselves, in things larger than ourselves, and in the importance to mankind, that we use the opportunities at our fingertips, and a newfound national commitment to do what God has given us the power to do. In short, I'm here today to issue a call for national action.

I felt almost as though I were a "space evangelist" as I attempted to inspire America's leaders to get back in space:

We have within our grasp the technology to get everyday citizens into space routinely and safely for the thrill of a once-in-a-life-time ride and adventure. We also have the technology to cost-effectively return to the moon again. We're even at the threshold of being able to affordably get to Mars with manned missions.

I knew that the members of Congress were already seeing dollar signs in their minds, so I sought to remind them of the incredible potential that was lying untapped on the moon and in space.

"Imagine having space-based solar energy assets and space-based resources that truly keep this planet pollution-free and make budget deficits literally unthinkable by their sheer richness," I said slowly, looking from committee member to committee member as I spoke.

That's what awaits us if we make the right investments. The future I allude to has yet to be built. But all this is not fiction. It's very close to being fact. A clean, green, non-polluted Earth drawing on abundant space-tapped energy from our sun, passenger travel to and from space for commercial and adventure activity, the step-by-step advance to Mars, even low-cost cycling missions to and from that planet and then beyond. All these goals are worth pursuing and well within our grasp. Once more, they will reenergize this nation, and, if Apollo is any example, spur rippling economic growth.

I knew that my points were being well received, and even the committee members were getting excited. I wanted to lay out their role in my vision for them.

You know the Apollo program's miraculous achievements were built on a dream by this nation's leaders and our people. Let us take stock of ourselves and our place in the history of mankind. And let us not be timid or content to rest on our laurels. Already a generation has passed since we walked on the moon. I will say it again, and pray, as I did when we sat on the moon, that we can start this engine.

I knew that time was limited and I needed to bring my remarks to a close, but I wanted the committee members to realize that we were not merely talking about energizing our economy or kicking up some more dust on another celestial body. No, these ideas were much bigger than that. So I made an impassioned plea:

The one argument that I feel is most compelling is, the mission is larger than ourselves. We were called together as a nation and as a species by the Apollo missions to the moon. And there is simply no measure of the good that these explorations brought to us all, not least by bringing the global community closer together.

I closed my statement by issuing a final word of inspiration: "As I like to say with my feet firmly on the ground, on Earth today, as surely as they were on the moon nearly thirty years ago, let's join together and shoot for the stars, *ad astra*."

For a moment I thought the committee was going to give me a standing ovation. They didn't, but they were obviously moved by my presentation, and I breathed a sigh of relief that it was done. But I wasn't going anywhere just yet. The congressmen had questions for me. I answered them as straightforwardly as possible, continuing to lay out the vision for America's getting back into space in a big way.

After a while, the committee chairman, Dennis Hastert, started to pull the meeting to a close. "First of all, Dr. Aldrin, let me just say that this is an interesting hearing we're having. Usually we're looking into the problems in government and somebody breaking the laws and where dollars are misspent and all these types of things. In a sense, you bring us today some vision that we don't usually get to look at and . . . as a backdrop for where we go in the future, as politicians and members of Congress and just the nature of our work, we don't do the vision thing enough."

Several other congressmen had more questions for me, and Chairman Hastert did not seem to be in any hurry to get me out of the hot seat. The questions naturally turned to what value there would be in going to Mars. I had been thinking of my answer for nearly twenty years. "Let's look briefly at the value of going to the moon," I began.

In the last twenty-seven years, one thing has stood out that, as I meet people, they want me to know where they were when we were on the moon, and they remember vividly that particular day. They are almost obsessed to come up and tell me where they were. And I am trying to understand what that means. I am convinced that what it means is that there was value added to a human's life on that day, and I multiply that by the millions of people that experienced that, and I think we are getting close to understanding the value of human society challenging itself and carrying out a commitment successfully.

More nods from the committee members kept me going.

It's not the value of the rocks that we brought back, or the great poetic statements that we all uttered. Those things aren't remembered. It's that people witnessed that event.

We are not going to justify going to Mars by what we bring back. Whether there is life or not shouldn't be a determining factor in whether we go to Mars. We are going to make a commitment and carry that out.

And what is that commitment going to do to this world today that is so focused on the immediate payoff—the attitude of "What's in it for me right now?" Everything around us, fed by the communications industry, focuses on fixing today, and it doesn't focus on where we are going to be in the next twenty to fifty years. We need something that draws away from today, and internationally supporting a thriving settlement on Mars and all the benefits that it is going to bring back here on Earth, and the feel-good attitude that people are going to have, that's going to be the value of going to Mars.

I took a breather as Congressman Jim Turner jumped into the conversation. "It is exciting just to listen to you speak," he said to me. "I guess as I listen to you lay out your vision, Dr. Aldrin, it seems to me that one of the biggest challenges we face is trying to figure out a way to get that common commitment."

I thought I knew where the congressman was going, so I followed his lead, and said:

People want to journey into space; they want to share that participation. Just ask them. I go around and they want to know when they can get into space. And it is doable. The tourism industry worldwide is a multibillion-dollar industry. Let's just unleash that into space, and not just for the affluent, but with wisely worked-out lottery principles. You can form a corporation and issue shares and distribute the dividends by random selection for thousands of space-related prizes, including a ride into orbit. And that could develop the rocket and the spacecraft systems needed to go to the moon. Not the other way around. We are not going to make a commitment to go to the moon and then use those vehicles for tourism; it should be the other way.

There. I'd done it. I'd actually laid out my ShareSpace concept in front of a congressional committee. Either they'd think I was nuts, or they could recognize that the future was staring them right in the face.

Whether or not Congress got the message, the media certainly did. One newspaper called me "a traveling evangelist for cost-effective manned space travel to Mars and maybe beyond." The *Washington Post* said something similar: "Aldrin pitches a space race renaissance. He sounds like a high-tech preacher hustling a mega-billion-dollar gospel of the stars."

Maybe so. I was glad to point out features of the replica *Eagle* lunar module used in 1969 and on display at the Air and Space Museum. But my real focus was on the future and convincing people to dream space dreams once again. I did not want "a giant leap for mankind" to be nothing more than a phrase from the past.

In May 1998, I introduced my newly formed nonprofit ShareSpace Foundation to the public in the National Space Society's magazine, *Ad Astra* ("to the stars"). I was currently chairing the NSS Board of Directors, and I couldn't think of a better audience to share the genesis of my hopes for ShareSpace than the space advocates and enthusiasts who comprised the membership of this grassroots organization. I called out for citizen participation in a lottery-type program, where for a nominal price of say, ten dollars, they would gain access to prizes in a range of space-tourism experiences. The purpose of using the lottery approach was to strengthen and accelerate the growth of commercial space, along with furthering opportunities and activities for people in space. And besides, lotteries are as American as apple pie and space exploration. ShareSpace may have initially been conceived in fictional form in my 1996 space novel, *Encounter with Tiber*, but the message of the novel's character Sig Jarlsbourg pretty much said it all: "If you want that better world, we need to see space tourism take off right away, and it can't be as a plaything of a tiny group of super-rich people. It's got to have broad-based public support and enthusiasm right from the start."

◑　○　◐

EARLY IN 1998, the news was released that Senator John Glenn would be returning to space as a passenger aboard the space shuttle. I thought that was fantastic. John was a wonderful candidate for "civilian space travel" since he had such high visibility and he was still in great physical shape. Of course, it was not lost on the public that John was also the first American astronaut to have orbited the Earth. John flew on the *Friendship 7* Mercury capsule on February 20, 1962. The mission lasted a mere five hours, and Glenn was strapped to his seat the entire time, never experiencing weightlessness. For him to get a second chance to orbit the Earth at seventy-seven years of age was a great coup for civilian space travel.

On October 29, 1998, Lois and I traveled to Titusville, Florida, to attend the launch of the space shuttle *Discovery* on which John Glenn was a nonpaying passenger. A crowd of more than 200,000 people—more than usual, these days—had gathered to view the spacecraft attached to the giant rocket booster rumble off the launch pad. It felt almost like a party atmosphere as Lois and I watched along with other celebrity onlookers, including President Bill Clinton and the First Lady; a number of U.S. senators; baseball Hall of Famer Ted Williams; Hollywood entertainers Tom Hanks, Bruce Willis, and Ron Howard; and musician Jimmy Buffett. With a deep roar that practically shook the ground three miles away, and a billowing cloud of fire and smoke, *Discovery* slowly inched off the ground, headed into the perfectly clear blue sky.

The press was quick to point out that John's journey was the most elaborate and expensive political junket ever. The mission lasted for nine days, during which time he participated in some experiments designed to ascertain the affects of spaceflight on the elderly, particularly in the areas of equilibrium, muscle loss, and sleep disturbances. John later quipped that he'd wanted to do a spacewalk, but NASA had feared that at his age he might wander off.

While John was still in orbit and the nation followed his progress, I received an invitation to appear on the CBS television program *The Late Show with David Letterman.* I've always enjoyed David's quirky sort of humor—it reminds me of my own—so I said, "Sure, I'll be glad to come on."

It was great fun, and David and I spoke at length about space tourism, and how it is technically feasible and is likely to become a highly profitable business. We talked about some of the new developments under way, and I even told David about my own projects, ShareSpace and my new rocket development company's StarBooster rockets. It was a great opportunity to pitch the idea of space tourism to a younger audience that would be the primary clientele for future adventures.

David was quite interested in the feasibility of space tourism. "How much will one of those seats cost?" he asked.

"Initially about eighty to one hundred thousand dollars," I replied, eliciting chuckles from the audience.

"Oooh," David responded. "But you get complimentary cocktails once you get on board, don't you?"

That led into a perfect opportunity to tell David and the audience about ShareSpace, and my plan to get the private sector into space. I had been on David's show several times before, most notably prior to the twenty-fifth anniversary of the Apollo 11 lunar landing. David loved to introduce me as the first guy named Buzz to walk on the moon. His rapier wit was always only a second away, but he really did get it whenever I began describing space tourism, putting up clusters of modules as space hotels, and launching tourists on spacelines carrying as many as eighty to one hundred people at a time to an orbiting hotel for week-long vacations.

David wanted to know what the tourists would do all that time.

"They'll float around, and enjoy zero gravity, just like John [Glenn] is doing now," I told him.

"Will there be games and activities?"

"Yeah, yeah!" I said. "We're going to play checkers."

For all of his joking, David understood the vision for space tourism, and I appreciated having the opportunity to share my ideas about it with his audience. On other occasions when I've been on David's program, I have done some rather quirky things myself. For instance, once in response to a letter from a viewer, David had me "live" in a New York City cab "about thirty-three inches above the big blue marble we call Earth," doing important "space experiments" such as dropping my astronaut's pen, which dropped like a rock, of course. "This is America's finest hour," I said. On another show, I was on top of the studio roof of the Ed Sullivan Theater building, dressed in full spacesuit regalia, in the pouring rain. As another of David's ridiculous experiments, I was to hit a golf ball off the roof, to supposedly determine the gravitational pull of the roof. The golf ball was teed up on a mat, and I could barely swing the golf club in the bulky spacesuit, but I hit it with a good stroke and the ball sailed off the roof. "It's so serene, so tranquil, looking down on the Earth from the roof," I said. Of course, as usual, my tag line was "This truly is America's finest hour!"

On another of David's shows, I participated by reading his "Top Ten List." The topic was "The Top Ten Other Things to Say When Stepping on the Moon." Dressed in a bright orange "NASA" jumpsuit, I deadpanned lines such as, "Set your phasers for fun; the Buzzmeister has landed!"

David said on one show that if he was running NASA, we'd have a shopping mall on Neptune by now. I wouldn't doubt it a bit.

Over the years, I have appeared on numerous news interview shows, but I've especially enjoyed the lighter moments playing off the space themes, such as on *The Tonight Show with Jay Leno*. Working with Jay was great fun, as well. We both wore brown trench coats, *Casablanca* style, and Jay drew comparisons between life on the moon and life in Hollywood, where the real space exists.

While promoting *Encounter with Tiber*, I appeared on Rosie O'Donnell's talk show during the week of Elton John's birthday, so, as a special tribute, Rosie was having all of her guests sing one of their favorite songs by the prolific pop artist. Mine, of course, was "Rocket Man." In my estimation, there was no better Elton John song, and who better to sing it but me? I didn't even pretend to try to sing it seriously. I stood on stage with a deadpan expression and droned, "I'm just a rocket man, and I think its going to be a long, long time . . ." The audience laughed uproariously.

I also did an "interview" with Ali G, alter ego of Sacha Baron Cohen, star of the movie *Borat*. For our interview, Cohen played his Ali G hip-hop journalist character to the hilt, with a British gangster street accent, dressed in a yellow jumpsuit, and adorned in heavy gold jewelry and a black skull cap. His shtick was to go around to distinguished people under the pretense that they were giving serious interviews. In fact, when he came to my home, we were expecting British Channel Four to show up. Instead, Ali G walked in, and commenced his litany of nonsensical questions. He asked me, "What was it like not being the first man on the moon? Was you ever jealous of Louis Armstrong?" The funny thing about Cohen's zaniness was that many people he interviewed would get upset and storm out, but when he did the bit with me, I caught on rather quickly and had a great time with him, playing it straight.

I love humor, so maybe that's why when an invitation came to "appear" as myself in an episode of *The Simpsons*, I couldn't resist. The episode was called "Deep Space Homer," in which Homer went into space with me. I had warned Homer about the effects of weightlessness, and in typical *Simpsons* style, he flubbed up. Homer and I were in the capsule and we were listening to James Taylor's song, "You've Got a Friend," when Homer opened up some potato chips.

"No, Homer," I cried. "They're ruffled!"

I had a ball doing the show, and to this day, it is one of the most popular episodes of *The Simpsons* ever aired.

Of course, with all this publicity and commercial effort, I opened myself to a great deal of criticism by my detractors, including a number of my fellow astronauts. Their big gripe was that I was drawing too much attention to myself. Their criticism hurt, but I took it in stride. The truth was, no other astronaut, active or inactive, was out in public trying to raise awareness about America's dying space program. None of them. They were all content to sit back on their laurels, while the Russians, Chinese, and just about anyone else surged ahead of us in space. All the while, we had the technology and the wherewithal to keep space exploration alive; the question was whether we had the will.

Beyond that, what my critics never acknowledged was that what I was selling was not myself. I was selling the future of spaceflight—hoping to pave the way for ordinary citizens to explore space, for financiers to see the viability and the profitability of permanently orbiting space hotels and "sightseeing" trips to the moon and other destinations in space. NASA was not paying me to promote the space program, nor was anyone else. Fortunately, my commercial ventures made it possible for me to work on space promotions free of charge.

One of the more interesting and enjoyable of those commercial ventures came to me as a surprise.

18

POP GOES
SPACE CULTURE

FOR SEVERAL YEARS, LOIS AND I HAD BEEN SPENDING A LOT of time driving up to L.A. on business and to attend a variety of Hollywood events in the evenings. To avoid having to drive back the sixty miles to Laguna at night, we sold my old home at Table Rock and used the money to buy a small apartment in Beverly Hills that we could use as a pied-à-terre. Eventually we sold that apartment, as well as our home in Emerald Bay, and bought a luxury high-rise condo along the Wilshire Corridor of Los Angeles, just west of Beverly Hills, because so much of our business was now connected to the entertainment industry. It was a good move for us, making it much easier to meet with agents and publicists, and to participate more readily in Hollywood's celebrity events. From my perspective, I liked the high security, and there was no yard work; also, we have a beautiful panoramic view stretching from downtown Los Angeles to the Palos Verdes Peninsula and the Pacific Ocean.

A little-known Hollywood fact is that my name had already been firmly ensconced in Hollywood lore long before Lois and I moved there. On the famous Hollywood Walk of Fame, at the corners of Hollywood and Vine, Neil Armstrong, Michael Collins, and I have not one star but four, one on each corner of the intersection. Actually, our "stars" are in the shape of moons. Other celebrity stars lining the popular stretch of sidewalk include the very first person awarded a star on the street, Joanne Woodward, wife of the late Paul Newman. Cary Grant, Audrey Hepburn, Gene Autry, Clark Gable, and even Rin Tin Tin and Lassie have stars embedded in the sidewalk on this famous street. But Neil, Mike, and I are the only ones with four "stars," Hollywood's tribute to the first lunar landing.

Lois and I loved being in Los Angeles, if for no other reason than that we could better keep up with all the entertainment news. When the animated Disney movie *Toy Story* was released featuring a character named Buzz Lightyear, I naturally noticed the play on my name. I called Howard Green, a vice president at Disney, and Howard invited me to come up to Burbank and meet Tim Allen, who had done the voice for Buzz Lightyear.

We took some pictures with Tim, as well as with Tom Hanks, who provided the voice for Woody, the "star" of the movie. But when the studio wanted me to pose with a Buzz Lightyear action figure, I thought they were taking advantage of my willingness. "Maybe my representative should talk with your representatives before you use these pictures," I suggested.

Disney didn't pay me a penny for associating my name with the Buzz Lightyear character, but I've had a good relationship with the Disney organization over the years, and we've had a lot of fun together. And of course, Buzz's motto—"To infinity and beyond!"—is one that I could heartily endorse, albeit tongue-in-cheek.

I got to the place where I started referring to the Buzz Lightyear character as my cousin, and people loved it. Often, when I am in the middle of a speaking engagement, I will draw a twelve-inch-high Buzz Lightyear action figure out from behind the podium, and no matter how erudite, scientific, intellectual, or academic the audience, Buzz always gets a good response. It also creates a moment when I can talk about inspiring the next generation of children to explore space.

When Disney managed to secure a spot on the space shuttle *Discovery* for Buzz Lightyear to actually travel to the International Space Station in 2008, it was big news. We did an "instructional" video piece, to be disseminated on YouTube, in which I coached Buzz Lightyear on some of the finer points of space travel. "I know where you are going," I told Buzz. "I've been in space two times. I've walked on the moon. Before we can let you go into space, you have to pass a battery of tests. Are you ready?"

We then put Buzz through his tests: the antigravity test, in which we plunged Buzz into a home aquarium filled with water and live fish; the fitness test, in which I put Buzz on a treadmill and turned it on, which sent him tumbling across the room; the centrifuge test, in which I put Buzz in the clothes dryer along with a load of clothes and turned it on. Poor Buzz was sent tumbling again. For the crash-landing test, we hung Buzz from a tree by his parachute cords; and for the rocket test, we attached a firecracker to Buzz's life support pack and blasted him to infinity and beyond. After all these tests, I held the Buzz Lightyear action figure close to my face and said, "Congratulations! You are cleared for launch." Then, in a grandfatherly tone, I looked at Buzz and said, "Just remember one thing: I'm the real Buzz." We had great fun doing the video, and when Buzz Lightyear actually flew on the *Discovery*, a live "Woody" character was at Cape Kennedy to see him off, along with hundreds of Buzz Lightyear fans.

Buzz's journey was part of NASA's "Toys in Space" initiative. The program was designed to encourage students to pursue studies in science and mathematics, subjects that are vitally important in sustaining U.S. economic competitiveness and technological leadership. Buzz stayed in space at the International Space Station for several months before returning to a hero's welcome and, of course, a new "Toy Story Mania!" attraction at the Disney theme parks.

I've enjoyed working with Disney to inspire older kids and adults to think more about space as well. When Disney opened its "Mission Space" attraction at Epcot Center in Florida, then-CEO Michael Eisner invited me to test it out for accuracy and authenticity. The attraction launches visitors into a simulated space adventure, complete with a pulse-pounding liftoff followed by the sensation of weightlessness in outer space. After testing the ride, I was quite impressed. I told

Michael, "This is the closest thing to spaceflight that most people will ever experience. When those rockets ignite for liftoff, you feel an increase in g force, just like the real thing." Of course, through Share-Space, I hope to allow people to actually experience the real thing in the near future.

I'll take almost any opportunity to share space with the next generation. I've written two children's books, *Reaching for the Moon* and *Look to the Stars,* and have spoken in schools all over America, but I've discovered that I can also be effective, and often reach many more children, by working through television. That's why I was excited when the producers of *Sesame Street* called me to appear on the show with the Muppets, the lovable puppet characters originally created by the late Jim Henson. I had a great time working with the Muppets, although I hated disappointing Cookie Monster when he asked me if the moon was really one big cookie.

"My name is Buzz Aldrin," I told him, "and I'm an astronaut."

"Astro Not?" Cookie asked.

"That's my job. I explore space."

Cookie Monster was intrigued. "You got to tell me truth. Is moon a big, yummy cookie?"

"I'm afraid not, Cookie Monster," I consoled him, "but if you ever got there, you would still love it. The stars all around are even brighter than they are here."

Indeed, I have worked with many television programs and have even appeared in a few movies over the years. As early as 1976, I appeared in the made-for-television movie, *The Boy in the Plastic Bubble,* starring John Travolta. More recently I played myself in the first animated feature film to be produced in 3-D, *Fly Me to the Moon,* about three flies who stow away in the helmets of the Apollo 11 astronauts to make the trip to the moon. It was a very creative production, and I especially liked the way they reenacted the whole launch, staging, and rendezvous sequences of our spacecraft—a must-see for all budding astronauts.

I've had a few other brushes with pop-culture fame. For instance, when the Music Television network (MTV) debuted in 1981, their network identification used a photograph of me with the American flag on the moon. In place of the stars and stripes, however, the network substituted their MTV logo. From day one, every time MTV went to their network identification, there I was, holding the MTV flag. Additionally, MTV labeled their hip new music videos as "Buzz-clips."

When the music video genre caught on and MTV in 1984 began handing out Video Music Awards for the best video productions of the year, the award received by winners was a silver statuette in the shape of an astronaut holding a flag, originally called the "Buzzy," named after me. Playing off of the original space-themed station ID logo, the astronaut statuette stands nearly twelve inches high, weighs more than seven pounds, and is made by R.S. Owen, Inc., the same company that makes the Oscars for the Academy Awards. Later, MTV changed the award's name to the "Moonman," but the statue is still modeled after my image. A few years ago I had the pleasure of getting to know Tom Freston, one of the original founders of MTV, who personally presented me with the MTV statuette, inscribed TO THE ORIGINAL MOONMAN.

Neon-colored original "Moonwalk" screen prints were created by Andy Warhol in 1987, based on the "visor shot" photo that Neil took of me on the moon. Warhol added the American flag into his art, and made two versions in contrasting color schemes, one in neon yellow, red, and blue, and other in a deep neon pink and violet palette. If you look closely at the visor of my helmet in his prints, you can see how he inscribed his initials "AW" in abstract strokes. Lois and I are fortunate to have one of Warhol's "Moonwalk" prints hanging in our home.

Promoting myself as a potential commercial pitchman while protecting myself against the unauthorized use of my image sometimes created a tenuous balance. One of the more awkward instances came about as a result of the wristwatch I wore on the moon. As Omega did with all the astronauts, I was given one of their Speedmaster watches as a Gemini astronaut, which I had worn during my Gemini 12 flight. I also wore an Omega Speedmaster during the Apollo 11 mission. The watch is clearly visible in many of the pictures of me on the moon, so it could easily be assumed that my timepiece was the most famous wristwatch in the world. It was optional to wear while we were walking on the surface of the moon. Neil chose not to wear his. And few things are less necessary when walking around on the moon than knowing what time it is in Houston, Texas. Nonetheless, being a watch guy, I decided to strap the Speedmaster onto my right wrist around the outside of my bulky spacesuit.

For years, although I did not realize it at the time, the Omega watch company used photos of me on the moon in their advertisements. They paid nothing for the use of those photos, neither to NASA nor to me. But they were certainly getting a lot of bang for their buck on that donated watch.

Later, at Omega's invitation, Lois and I accompanied some of their company representatives to Riyadh. On the plane, I talked with one of the Omega executives about my recent discovery that Omega was using my picture in a print ad promoting Omega watches as the first watch on the moon. I suggested to the Omega representative that we should strike some sort of agreement under which we could promote their watches, and I could receive some compensation for their using my image. I had no intention of suing; I was hoping to strike up a business deal. The Omega representative surprised me. "You'll probably have to sue us," he said bluntly.

Upon my return, I realized that he was probably right. I hired a lawyer to send some letters, still hoping to work out a deal, but Omega wasn't willing to budge. After a long season of lawyer runarounds, I dismissed the lawsuit, deciding it wasn't worth pursuing any longer. At the same time, I would think that Omega had to pay something to other celebrity spokespersons for wearing Omega watches in far less conspicuous places than the moon.

Not one to harbor ill feelings, I can see two positive results that came from the Omega situation. First, thanks to my efforts to negotiate with Omega, new standards were put in place as to how commercial companies should compensate astronauts for their photos when used in advertisements. Astronauts now benefit more fully from the "right of publicity" to control their image as shown in photos taken of them during spacewalks and moonwalks, even though their faces may not be visible behind the helmets of their spacesuits. More personally, I later struck up a venture with Bulova to create two outstanding Accutron watches—the Eagle Pilot and the limited edition Astronaut—which include features I found helpful in space, and which both have my signature engraved on their casebacks. In fact, Bulova Accutron provided the original timepiece in the *Columbia* command module for our trip to the moon, so the relationship has been a natural one.

Forty years after I stood on the moon's surface with my Omega Speedmaster watch on my wrist, Omega made a great effort to overcome any problems we had in the past. They invited me to Basel, Switzerland, to attend a celebration of our moon landing along with some of the other Apollo astronauts at the BaselWorld watch fair. They were very gracious hosts and presented me with a beautiful new limited edition Speedmaster watch that commemorates Apollo 11. This was a welcomed gesture since my original Omega Speedmaster was stolen on the way to the Smithsonian.

A much more sticky situation arose, however, when I discovered that the Bermuda-based liquor company Bacardi-Martini was using the "visor shot" in its advertising campaign to promote Bacardi rum. In the print ad, a bottle of rum was shown splashing its contents onto the image of me standing on the moon, and as if to suggest that rum transforms everything to a party atmosphere, the lower half of my spacesuit had turned into a pair of swimmer's legs in swim trunks and fins. It made a mockery of this iconic image. What's more, I was just about to celebrate twenty years of sobriety at the time.

I had a new legal team in place thanks to Lois's daughter, Lisa Cannon, who brought in entertainment litigation attorney Robert (Rob) C. O'Brien to help her handle my business affairs. It turned out that this was Bacardi's second attempt to use the visor shot in its campaigns. The first time, a few years earlier, Bacardi's ad agency had claimed that since the photograph was in the public domain, they thought they could use it freely. When informed of my right of publicity in the photo, they agreed not to use it. Apparently the current advertising arm of the company was not aware of this prior agreement.

Rob O'Brien went to work, and the local media soon picked up on the case. When we both appeared on the nationally syndicated entertainment news program *Extra,* Rob told the viewers, "Whatever the legal merits of the case are, this is a terrible way to treat an American hero." The show's host then asked me how I felt about my image being used by an alcohol company.

"I don't want to become Bacardi's version of a Joe Camel," I replied.

The case was settled successfully, and Bacardi even made a public statement: "By using a portion of the visor shot in the advertisements, Bacardi did not intend to cause the public to recognize Aldrin in the advertisements nor believe that Aldrin endorses, or has ever endorsed, Bacardi products. . . . Bacardi has a great amount of respect for Aldrin, is sympathetic to his concerns and, therefore, has apologized to him for publishing the advertisements."

Because of the success of my cases, I was able to help out other astronauts in protecting their images. In one such instance, a toy company, Action Products, was using the photographs of *Apollo 12* commander Pete Conrad and *Apollo 15* lunar module pilot Jim Irwin, along with some of my photos, on the packaging of their Apollo spacecraft and rocket toy models. Since both Pete and Jim had passed away, their widows, Nancy Conrad and Mary Irwin, were trying to protect their rights. So Rob O'Brien represented all of us, and we proceeded on a united front. At one point, intimations were made in the settlement discussions that Action Products was willing to settle only with me and not with the others. But we stuck together, and after a ruling in our favor by the federal judge in the case, our efforts had a successful outcome. Actually, Action Products came around full circle, and Nancy and I ended up settling the case for Mary, her, and me over dinner with the company's president. Later I even licensed my image for the company's handsome three-foot-tall model of the Saturn V rocket.

As a footnote to the Omega story, all of the astronauts were required by NASA to return their Speedmaster watches after their missions, which I did. The watches are housed in the vaults of the Smithsonian Institution in Washington, D.C., and several are on display at air and space museums around the country. All but one of the watches are accounted for. The Omega Speedmaster I wore on the moon has been missing ever since I entrusted it, along with other artifacts, to NASA's Johnson Space Center to be packed and shipped to the Smithsonian. The box and artifacts made it, but not the watch. At least one person claims to have discovered the original watch on a California beach, and sued me and the U.S. government to obtain title to the watch. As part of the case, the experts at the Smithsonian examined the watch and compared it against the watches in their possession. Lisa, Rob, and I also participated in the procedure. Wearing white cotton gloves, I was able to hold my watch from Gemini 12 for the first time in 35 years, as that timepiece and others were compared against the purported Apollo 11 watch. I understand that the Smithsonian determined that the plaintiff's watch was not one of the NASA watches, and the case was dismissed. People have told me that the Speedmaster I wore on the moon is the Holy Grail of watches for serious collectors, and I assume that the search for it will go on.

● ○ ●

FORTUNATELY, MOST OF my commercial endeavors were about building positive relationships, rather than chasing after infringements. And while I enjoyed all of these ventures and remained constantly on the lookout for more good opportunities, as we neared the thirtieth anniversary of the landing of *Apollo 11*, I seemed to get a second wind when it came to the development of viable options for civilian space travel. I was sixty-nine years of age, but I felt more energized than ever. Lois handled the business, while I poured myself into space projects.

"Buzz, you have found your niche," she said with a laugh. "You work as if you are still on assignment for NASA, trying to develop better rockets, a better space station, and spaceships to take us to Mars."

Lois was right; I was thrilled with life, and excited about the possibilities of promoting adventure space travel as a logical extension of the world's $3.5-trillion tourist industry. I got even more fired up when I heard that a wealthy friend of mine was willing to put up whatever it might cost to become America's first space tourist—even if that meant flying into orbit in a Russian spacecraft.

19

GOOD-BYE BLUES,
HELLO SPACE VIEWS

O N SATURDAY, APRIL 29, 2000, LOIS, LISA, AND I WERE preparing for a trip to Hong Kong, where I was scheduled for two important speaking engagements, one keynote speech for the Pacific Asia Travel Association, and one presentation for a British company's campaign to enhance computer education in China. Both of these engagements had been booked by the Harry Walker Agency, with whom we worked on high-end events.

We were scheduled to fly from Los Angeles to Hong Kong that very night. The evening before, Lois and I had joined a couple for dinner at The Grill in Beverly Hills, during which I broke off a front tooth in my lower jaw. It was more irritating than painful, but it definitely bothered me. Lois dropped me off at the dentist early Saturday morning, but the dentist could only perform a stopgap measure, and I would have to come back the following week. I was frustrated that the dentist could not adequately repair the tooth in time for the trip.

My son Andy stopped by later that afternoon to visit, and he and I talked space for a while. We reviewed some of the roadblocks that StarBooster was facing when it came to attracting the substantial investment needed to develop our rocket designs. Andy worked in the aerospace industry and was constantly trying to help me find a way to bring my ideas to fruition.

"I wish I could help you find the funds," Andy said, "but Boeing has their own designs to get their new contracts from NASA. Everybody is trying to come up with the next big idea for the next generation of spacecraft after the space shuttle is retired."

Andy seemed convinced that although the United States had led the world into space, NASA was dragging its heels when it came to space tourism, and the Russians were most likely going to start taking paying passengers into space. Many of those passengers would be Americans. I knew that Andy was right because a friend of ours, Dennis Tito, was already planning to travel into space on a Russian spacecraft.

Andy and I talked further about the latest rocket designs I had been working on with Hu Davis, a former NASA engineer, who now was my co-designer for the StarBooster family of rockets. In light of NASA's decision to continue flying the shuttle for at least another twenty years, there was an opportunity for my StarBooster design team to submit a proposal to NASA for our reusable fly-back boosters, along with our designs for the StarCore heavy-lift reusable launcher, and the StarBird reusable orbiter. When Andy left, for some reason I became discouraged. I was glad that the Russians and, more recently, even the Chinese were pursing space exploration, but I just couldn't comprehend why America had to allow the Russians and Chinese to leapfrog ahead of us in space travel when we had all the elements we needed to be clearly superior in technology. We just weren't using them in the right combination. I knew that my StarBooster team had a design for a reusable rocket booster that could lead to airline-style tourism, while also taking care of future launch needs for NASA. But I couldn't get NASA's attention. The more I considered it, the more depressed I became, and thought, *Aw, what's the use?* I went into our bedroom, turned on the television, and flopped down on the bed.

After a while, Lois came in, and when she saw me lying on the bed, just staring at the screen, she said, "Buzz, come on, we have to get ready to go to China. I need to get your suitcase packed. I have several nice suits here. Which would you like to wear for your speeches? Do you like the blue suit with the light blue shirt—"

"I'm not going," I said, interrupting Lois's wardrobe check.

"What? What do you mean, you aren't going?"

"Just what I said, Lois. I'm not going to Hong Kong."

"Buzz, you have to go to Hong Kong. You have two very important speeches to give."

"I'm not going!"

Lois could tell by my demeanor that I was serious, but she kept trying to encourage me, to get me up and ready to go. "Buzz Aldrin, you *are* going on the plane tonight!"

"Lois, I'm not going," I said emphatically. I got up and walked out of the bedroom, out into our living room, and kept right on going. I walked out of our condo without telling Lois where I was heading, and let the door slam behind me.

One of the reasons I didn't tell Lois where I was going was that I didn't know. I just knew I had to get out for some air. I pressed the elevator button, thinking at first that I would head down to the ground level and walk, but then, when the elevator door opened, I pressed the number for the top floor instead of going down. At the top floor, I went over to the fire-escape door, pushed it open, and climbed the stairs to the rooftop of our building. From the rooftop, ahead of me, I could see all the way to the Pacific Ocean, several miles away to the west, and to the east, the lights of downtown L.A.'s skyscrapers. Behind me, four lanes of busy Saturday afternoon traffic on Wilshire Boulevard whizzed by the condo tower. I walked over to the edge of the roof and looked down. It was certainly a long drop to the street. Heights had never bothered me, so I simply stood along the edge and looked out at the sights below.

How long I stayed on that rooftop, I'm not really sure, but it must have been longer than I thought, because when I finally went downstairs, Lois's daughter Lisa was there, and the women were in a tizzy. Apparently Lois had called Lisa when she realized that I was adamantly refusing to go to China, and Lisa had raced across town from Santa Monica, a good twenty- to thirty-minute drive. Both had been frantically looking for me, in the lobby, in the exercise room, everywhere.

"Buzz, where have you been?" Lois implored. I could tell she had been worried about me.

"I was on the roof," I replied.

"On the roof!" Lois and Lisa practically shouted in unison. Apparently my answer did nothing to allay the women's concerns.

"Buzz, what were you doing on the roof?" Lois wanted to know.

"Getting some air."

Lois was troubled by my going up on the roof, though she continued packing for the trip nonetheless, and I remained equally as determined. "I'm not going. I won't go, not with my tooth like this," I said. The tooth was a problem, but it was a lower tooth, so it didn't really look bad, but it was a good, legitimate excuse. I went back into the bedroom and crawled in bed. The blue funk was back.

I told Lois and Lisa I just "couldn't do it in my current state of mind." I couldn't control the way I was feeling. Lois knew, however, that this could be devastating to my reputation as a professional speaker. In all the years since I had met Lois, we had only canceled one previous high-end speaking engagement because of illness, and while everyone understands that cancellations by speakers, musicians, and other performers can always be a possibility, it is never a good thing when it happens, and it is always inconvenient for the sponsor and disappointing to the audience. Just as in the space program, the slogan "Failure is not an option" was well known, so in working with speakers' bureaus, the adage could be adapted to "Cancellations are not an option."

Lois and Lisa started scrambling. I knew that my refusal was a self-destructive act, and at that moment I didn't care. I tended to give myself permission to do that which was not in my own best interests. But Lois refused to give up. She felt sure that I would get on that plane the next day, if I could just have a little time to mull things over. Lisa called the agency and explained that I had a problem with my tooth, and asked if they could reschedule my speech from the first part of the event to the last part, to allow me enough time to get there. Because it was a three-day conference, and I was slated to open the conference, Lois suggested that my speech be switched with that of the closing speaker. The agency agreed to try to make such a change with the event sponsors.

Lisa went back home, and Lois scheduled another dentist appointment for me early Monday morning. But on Sunday she simply left me alone. She and Lisa went house-hunting, looking for a new home for Lisa. Lois didn't call, she didn't prepare any meals, she simply left, and stayed that night with Lisa.

When Lois and Lisa returned on Monday, Lisa gave me a hand-written letter she had penned to me over the weekend. "Please read this," she asked. In the letter, Lisa expressed her heartfelt support of me, but also her honest concerns. Basically, her letter said, "Buzz, it is your choice; if you don't want to be involved in this sort of activity, you don't have to be. If you don't wish to participate in speaking engagements and other events that give you an opportunity to promote your ideas, we don't need to pursue this sort of business, and I can go find another job." Lisa had been a rock musician and a successful entertainment law attorney before coming to work full-time for Lois and me, and had refocused her entire career to help me in all my commercial endeavors. In her own way, Lisa was making it clear that the choice was mine, that nobody was imposing the family business on me. Perhaps just knowing that my independence was not being squelched made my acquiescence to Lisa and Lois a little easier.

Lois changed our flight to China to Monday night. The sponsors had shifted my speech from the opening to the closing. But as a consequence, they couldn't get the first-class tickets that they had originally arranged for us. We would fly business class all the way to China.

"We'll be there with you and for you each step of the way," Lois encouraged me.

"Okay, fine," I answered. "But after the speeches, I'm not doing anything, no sightseeing, no social events, nothing. I just want to relax in the hotel."

"All right, that is okay."

We boarded our flight to Hong Kong on Monday, May 1, and on Wednesday afternoon I fulfilled the first engagement, enjoying my time on stage, and speaking extemporaneously for most of my keynote. The audience and the sponsors seemed to love it, and gave me a great ovation. During the second engagement, I stayed closer to a more scripted presentation, and that event had a very successful outcome as well. We stayed a few extra days in China, flew to Beijing, and I actually conceded to do a bit of sightseeing, especially when our hosts arranged a private tour of the Forbidden City, where we viewed the inner sanctum of the City and entered the royal bedchambers that few other Americans have been privileged to see. That night our hosts treated us to an elegant dinner at the China Club. We were treated royally, and what could have been a disaster turned into a trip of a lifetime because of Lois's absolute confidence in me, and her dogged determination to overcome any actions that might be self-destructive on my part.

One of the important realizations for both of us that came out of this experience was that I could rise up and perform in spite of feeling blue—and even be inspiring to others. I was beginning to realize that I could transform from a downward spiral to my usual energetic and productive self. Sure, such challenging moments may arise in the future. But the good news is that such occurrences have become rare, and have not interfered with my productivity. Lois and I have learned to recognize the symptoms of approaching depression, and we are committed to making sure that every day is a good day, no matter how external events affect our lives.

● ○ ●

OF ALL MY endeavors, I am happiest when working on space projects—especially space tourism. I want everyone to enjoy the thrill of space travel. That's why I was very pleased when I learned that Dennis Tito, a former aerospace engineer at the Jet Propulsion Laboratory who had amassed his self-made fortune by applying his methodical approach to building an investment firm, was pushing hard to become the first American space tourist. The ticket was to be brokered by Space Adventures, Ltd., the premier space tourism agency to which I had coincidentally lent my name over the last several years as an advisory board member. The destination was the International Space Station. The only difficulty I had with the itinerary, in spite of my general support of international cooperation in space, was the mode of transportation. He would be hitching a ride on board the Soyuz spacecraft, at a cost of nearly $20 million. Dennis would have to go to Russia to make his American dream come true.

Dennis moved from his 30,000-square-foot Pacific Palisades mansion located on a hill overlooking the ocean to a tiny, bare apartment in Star City, the Russian cosmonaut training headquarters outside Moscow. He completed his training with two Russian cosmonauts, and on April 28, 2001, they launched from the same pad from which *Sputnik,* history's first flight into space, had lifted off. It was also the same pad from which Yuri Gagarin, the first man to travel in space, took off forty years earlier, on April 12, 1961.

A couple of months after Dennis returned from his mission, both he and I appeared before congressional subcommittees to answer questions about space tourism. Dennis had successfully opened a door to space tourism; now I just had to find a way to make it affordable to more people. The committee asked me to address three questions specifically:

1. What types of activities will be enabled or enhanced by space tourism?
2. What are the major hurdles that must be overcome before the space tourism business can be self-sustaining?
3. What role should the Federal government play in promoting space tourism?

For me, these three questions were like a volleyball hanging over the net, just waiting to be spiked. I began by explaining to the congressional committee that space tourism was the key to generating the high-volume traffic that could bring down launch costs. NASA's own research had suggested that tens of millions of U.S. citizens wanted to travel to space, and that the number would increase immeasurably if the global market were included. This volume of ticket-buying passengers could be the solution to the problem of high space costs that plague government and private space efforts alike.

I emphasized, though, that if we were to avoid the mistakes of the past, it was imperative that we involve the private sector. The needs of the commercial space tourism business must be central as we define the next generation of reusable space transportation. The next vehicles must be designed with the flexibility not only to satisfy NASA's needs, but to meet high-volume commercial tourism requirements, and the private sector must be responsible for operating the system.

I admitted quite candidly that I had an ulterior motive for promoting space tourism, that my goal really was to get the United States back in the space exploration business, to begin again to discover what was "out there" in the final frontier.

"My passion about this," I acknowledged, "springs from the way that large-scale space tourism leads to space infrastructure that enables broader national goals—such as a return to the moon and the exploration of Mars."

In answer to the committee's first question, I expressed my strong opinion that if the government would get out of the way, space transportation could evolve into a normal industry. "It will become like the rail, pipeline, ship, highway, and air traffic systems," I told the committee members. "They all have vast markets, low costs, high reliability, full reusability, and routine operations. Today, space transportation is characterized by small markets, high costs, high accident rates, wasteful expendability, an inability to operate on a routine schedule, and continuing loss of market share to foreign suppliers."

I knew this was not the message the committee wanted to hear, but it was the truth they needed to hear, so I pressed on, reminding them of the benefits of space tourism. Properly planned and implemented, space tourism could help cut the cost of space access by 50 to 70 percent, I told them. This lower-cost system will deliver several benefits:

- The United States will recapture the lion's share of the global satellite market.
- NASA's planetary probes will become far more affordable.
- Space hotels will become feasible, providing greater volume at far lower costs than the International Space Station.
- The launchers for space hotels and space tourists will be equally ideal for expeditions to the moon and Mars, as well as to launch massive military payloads like space-based lasers and future solar-based satellites.
- Perhaps the greatest long-term benefit will be the mass production of spaceflight, the high-flight-rate, high reusability, and high reliability. The nation that establishes a two-stage fully reusable heavy-lift launch vehicle will lead the world for the next thirty to forty years in charting the space frontier.

I contrasted these positive effects with the current situation in which the exorbitant cost of the space shuttle and the International Space Station operations have become a millstone around the neck of our space exploration programs and the American taxpayers.

I knew I had the committee's full attention now, so I proceeded to answer their question about some of the hurdles that had to be addressed before space tourism could become self-sustaining. I'm sure I surprised the members when I said, "Actually, it may be self-sustaining already. Some Russian officials have said that Dennis Tito's check covered the entire out-of-pocket cost of launching the Soyuz rocket that took him to the space station. If space tourism already makes financial sense when you fly Russian expendable rockets—what happens when their technology becomes reusable—when Russian launch costs suddenly drop and their safety goes way up?"

I went on to point out something that many of the committee members probably didn't know: "We Americans have spare seats for rich tourists, too. The space shuttle often flies with only five or six people, when it can hold seven to eight. The United States could be learning about space tourism, using the assets it already has. Flying passengers on the shuttle can be part of the research that leads to new vehicles, based on first-hand experience with the shuttle tourists. So I have to say that NASA's refusal to actively encourage passengers on the shuttle is a major hurdle."

Ouch. I could almost feel the committee members wince as they came face-to-face with the truth that one of the biggest hurdles to advancing in space is our own space administration.

I talked a bit about the difficulties in raising capital for space tourism, or even accessing loans to finance the business. I knew from my experience with StarBoosters that lenders were skittish about loaning money to what they regarded as a highly speculative start-up industry.

Since the gloves were off now, I figured I might as well lay it all out candidly before the congressional committee:

Another hurdle is the current structure of the space transportation industry. Two major private companies, Boeing and Lockheed Martin, formed a monopoly [United Space Alliance] to operate the space shuttle. Even monopolies have good ideas from time to time, and one idea was to turn the *Columbia* orbiter into a commercial vehicle, one that might take passengers. NASA's reaction was to have the president of the monopoly fired.

On the military space side, the two major companies were both given contracts for the Evolved Expendable Launch Vehicle. With the 20/20 clarity of hindsight, we can now see that this was a mistake. Now neither of them has any incentive to develop reusable vehicles, despite what may be said for public consumption, at least until they've recovered their considerable costs sunk in the new systems.

I could see on some of the committee members' faces that they didn't quite catch the significance of this, so I spelled it out specifically:

We have a civilian space agency that's been hostile to tourism, and the two major private companies left with no incentives to move on to reusable systems that could greatly serve our national interest and the waiting tourism market. In the meantime, the Russians just announced at the Paris Air Show that they are moving ahead with their reusable first-stage system, the Baikal. Making matters worse, they have found a market for their vehicle in Europe, where they are now attempting to team with the European Space Agency to use it as a reusable booster on the *Ariane 5,* replacing the more costly and accident-prone, expendable solid rocket motors.

Until NASA becomes an advocate for space tourism, or Congress intercedes and mandates the Department of Defense or NASA to develop reusable space transportation—and it can be done during this administration—the current establishment structure will not produce what we need.

When it came to answering the committee's third question—what should the government do to help—I grew even more direct:

First, it should keep its promises. Speaking very personally, I want you to know what NASA has done directly to my ShareSpace Foundation. At the end of March, after great effort, we responded to a NASA request for cooperative research proposals on the Human Exploration and Development of Space. We offered to compile detailed and sophisticated market research on the potential demand for passenger space travel. Two months later, NASA told us our proposal was exactly what they wanted. But in the same letter, it said the money to fund the entire program had been hijacked by other budget needs. This, unfortunately, has become more of the norm for doing business with NASA, not the exception.

I doubt that NASA has congressional approval for this maneuver. I hope you tell them to put the money back where they found it.

Next, NASA should immediately set up the mechanism for flying paying passengers on the space shuttle. My ShareSpace Foundation has been proposing this to NASA for two years now. We offered to create a scientific research program on what's required to safely train passengers for space travel, and what medical standards should be developed for screening passengers. The passengers' own ticket money would pay for all the research, and my foundation would make the results freely available. This would be a tremendous help to all the companies planning space tourism ventures, and to the government agencies that would regulate them. Leftover ticket money would go back into NASA to support other space tourism initiatives.

Since the shuttle was declared operational, more than 100 seats have gone unused. If the value of a seat is $20 million, that amounts to $2 billion in lost revenue for the space program.

The ShareSpace Foundation proposal for shuttle seats would see the chance to fly to orbit made available in many different ways. Some seats would be sold to the highest bidders to determine just how much early pioneers are willing to pay for space travel. This is important market research data. Some seats would be offered via sweepstakes or lotteries, so every American could have a small chance of flying to space. Others might be sold to television networks, so professional communicators could educate the public about the nature of the experience. It also would be good to have an independent journalist or two check in person on the space station's progress. As things stand now, the taxpayers will pour up to $95 billion into a government construction project, and the only people who will report on how it's going are employees of the federal agency in charge of construction. This strikes me as very unusual for such a massive expenditure of taxpayer funds.

I reminded the committee that Russia already had established a lead in the area of space tourism, but it didn't have to be that way. "If NASA continues to be hostile to using the space shuttle, all space tourists will be forced to use Russian companies, as Mr. Tito did. This makes no sense to me. We have spare seats in the shuttle, and using them doesn't cost NASA a cent. Instead, it brings in extra money."

I concluded with what I hoped was a challenge to the members of the committee. "As I hope you recognize by now, space tourism is not just a cute idea," I said. "The country that leads in space tourism will reap a tremendous drop in launch costs and far greater vehicle reliability. Its exploration initiatives and its military space activities will dominate the twenty-first century. As you can see, the United States is way off course on this subject, and it desperately needs Congress to firmly set a new pro-tourism policy."

I reminded them that many people were looking forward with great anticipation to traveling into space, and that once the restrictions and impediments were removed, people would be lining up for the possibility of a trip. "I know of two individuals, a well-known Hollywood producer and a well-known television correspondent, who are ready to go right now." I was referring to my friends, the film director James Cameron of *Titanic* fame, and CNN newsman Miles O'Brien, with whom I have had the pleasure of being interviewed on many occasions.

Since Dennis Tito's flight in April 2001, five space "tourists" have followed suit to join this exclusive orbital flight group, most recently paying over $30 million for a seat on Russia's *Soyuz* spacecraft to fly for a week up to the International Space Station. These have included: Mark Shuttleworth, a South African computer software entrepreneur; Greg Olsen, an American entrepreneur and scientist in the optical sensor field; Anousheh Ansari, an Iranian-American cofounder of Prodea

Systems and title sponsor of the Ansari X PRIZE; Charles Simonyi, a Hungarian computer software architect and developer of Microsoft's office applications, who was also the first space tourist to make a return trip to the ISS in March 2009; and Richard Garriott, an American computer game designer and son of Skylab astronaut Owen Garriott. I have met all of these spirited adventurers—or "Global Space Travelers" as I like to call them—and I herald their commitments to expand the human spaceflight experience. They all trained diligently for their respective flights and activities on board the ISS, and they have all brought back inspiring stories, photos, and new perspectives and insights on how space travel can be shared with more people.

● ○ ●

In 2002, I was appointed by President George W. Bush to serve on the Commission on the Future of the U.S. Aerospace Industry, where I emphasized the importance of NASA partnering with privatized efforts to develop alternative spacecrafts and rockets. Our final commission report strongly urged the creation of a new space imperative for America, and that NASA look to private industry to accelerate commercial space endeavors in the twenty-first century.

But once again NASA put off any action that might open the doors to a paradigm shift regarding access to space. I had been trying for years to transform the U.S. government's approach to the space program, trying to get members of Congress to replace short-term thinking with a long-term, forward-looking perspective, planning for where we want to be thirty to fifty years from now, instead of getting back on the budget treadmill every year, perpetually debating the same issues regarding the space program year after year. Inevitably those issues revolved around the perennial question, "How much is all this going to cost?"

That's why ShareSpace was (and remains) such an exciting concept for me and for others who are able to share the vision of what we could do. One of those people was Les Moonves, president and CEO of CBS television. Les and I engaged in serious conversations regarding the possibility of a *Survivor*-type television program in which contestants could compete in various astronaut-training ordeals over the course of the season, with the winner receiving the grand prize of a trip to the International Space Station on the Russian Soyuz spacecraft, since commercial suborbital flights were not yet feasible in the United States. Our only stumbling block was the price tag.

In recent years I've been approached by as many as ten separate television production companies and high-profile television producers who want to develop a space "reality" show or a competitive game show similar to *American Idol,* along the lines of *Who Wants to Be an Astronaut?* If we can put the right ingredients together, who knows? I might get back into space yet! But, even better, I'm working to find a way to give *you* a chance to travel in space!

20

A BLOW HEARD
'ROUND the WORLD

Like most Americans, I'm quite skeptical about con-spiracy theories. I'm someone who has dealt with the exact science of space rendezvous and orbital mechanics, so to have someone approach me and seriously suggest that Neil, Mike, and I never actually went to the moon—that the entire trip had been staged in a sound studio someplace—has to rank among the most ludicrous ideas I've ever heard. Yet somehow the media has given credence to some of the kooky people espousing such theories, and my fellow astronauts and I have had to put up with the consequences.

This is almost a no-win situation. If you ignore the panderers of nonsense, they say, "See! Buzz is afraid of the truth." If you attempt to correct their error, you automatically lend undeserved credibility to their ridiculous suppositions. I am passionate about passing down accurate history to the next generation, so I must confess that I've had little patience with the conspiracy nuts. To me, they waste everybody's time and energy.

Nevertheless, since I'm probably the most publicly visible of all the astronauts who walked on the moon, I get more of the close encounters of a kooky kind than my colleagues, although any one of them has a collection of stories they could share as well.

Because of the publicity the hoax theorists have garnered, occasionally even in a serious interview a reporter will broach the subject. One September morning in 2002, I was in Beverly Hills at the Luxe Hotel, filming a television interview for a Far Eastern TV network, when the interview began going in a direction that I knew was out of bounds. At first I tried to be cordial, adroitly answering the question, assuming that the interviewer would recognize my reluctance to talk about inanity, and bring the focus back to a bona fide space subject. Instead the interviewer began playing a television segment that had aired in the United States on the subject of hoaxes, including a section suggesting that the Apollo 11 moon landing never happened. I was aware of the piece and had been livid when it originally aired. I did not appreciate the interviewer's attempts to lure me into commenting on it. Lisa had accompanied me to the interview following her early morning triathlon training in the Santa Monica Bay, and she immediately recognized that this was a flagrant violation of our willingness to conduct the interview in good faith, so she called a halt to the production. We weren't belligerent, but we did not linger long over our good-byes, either.

We left the hotel room and walked down the hall to catch the elevator, only a matter of seconds away. I pressed the button for the ground level, and Lisa and I looked at each other and smiled. It had been a strange morning already. When the elevator doors opened on the ground level, it got worse.

As we stepped out into the hotel foyer, a large man who looked to be in his mid-thirties approached me, attempting to engage me in conversation. "Hey, Buzz, how are you?" He had his own film crew along, with the camera already rolling to document the encounter.

I greeted him briefly, acknowledging his presence, and kept moving— standard procedure for life in Hollywood. As Lisa and I walked through the foyer toward the front door of the hotel, however, the man kept getting in my way, peppering me with questions, none of which I answered. Lisa took my arm and glared at the man. "That's enough," she said, as I could feel her pressure on my arm guiding me toward the door. "Please let us alone; we're leaving now."

We stepped outside under the hotel awning, and the film crew continued right along with us. Lisa's car was parked across the street on Rodeo Drive, but there was no crosswalk nearby, and the traffic was brisk.

Meanwhile, the "interviewer" had taken out a very large Bible and was shaking it in my face, his voice becoming more animated. "Will you swear on this Bible that you really walked on the moon?"

I looked back at the man and gave him a look as if to say, *Will you swear on that Bible that you are an idiot?* The man was becoming more virulent, inflammatory, and personally accusatory in his outbursts. I tried not to pay any attention, but he was saying things like, "Your life is a complete lie! And here you are making money by giving interviews about things you never did!"

Lisa approached the cameraman and insisted, "Please turn off that camera! We're just trying to get across the street to our car."

I'm a patient man, but this situation was silly. "You conspiracy people don't know what you're talking about," I said.

Lisa spied a break in the traffic, so she grabbed me by the arm again, and said, "Buzz, let's go." We started walking across the street, but the large man kept getting right in front of us, standing in the middle of Rodeo Drive, blocking our path as his cameraman kept rolling film. Lisa seemed nervous about trying to go around him, while searching for her keys to unlock the car with the man in such close proximity, so we turned around and walked back to the bellman's station outside the hotel.

"Okay, this is ridiculous," I said to Lisa and to the bellman. "Call the police. This guy is not letting us get to our car."

I was under the awning, and Lisa turned away from me to approach the cameraman again. "Please turn that camera off," she said. Meanwhile the large man was nearly screaming at me, "You're a coward, Buzz Aldrin! You're a liar; you're a thief!"

Maybe it was the West Point cadet in me, or perhaps it was the Air Force fighter pilot, or maybe I'd just had enough of his belligerent character assassination, but whatever it was, as the man continued to excoriate me, I suddenly let loose with a right hook that would have made George Foreman proud. *WHAAP!* I belted the guy squarely in the jaw.

While I prided myself on staying in relatively good shape, it was doubtful that my septuagenarian punch did much damage to the fellow, except perhaps to his ego. But he was not at all concerned about the punch, anyhow. It was obvious that he had been goading me in that direction, and he seemed ecstatically happy that I had finally grown exasperated and hit him.

"Hey, did you catch that on tape?" he called out to his cameraman. That was all he cared about.

Lisa turned around and walked back to me. She cocked her head slightly, looked up at me, and asked quietly, "Buzz, what happened?"

I looked back at my stepdaughter rather sheepishly, and said, "I punched the guy."

"You what?" Lisa's hand instinctively flew to her mouth in disbelief, as though already postulating in her mind any potential legal ramifications.

The film crew and "interviewer" hastily packed up and headed for their vehicle. They had gotten what they were hoping for—and more. Before the night was over, the film of me punching the guy was on the news and all over the Internet. The interviewer went to the police, threatening to file assault charges against me.

In the meantime, Lisa contacted our legal representative, Robert O'Brien, and told him everything that had happened. Robert suggested that we hire a criminal lawyer, just in case the encounter actually led to charges.

On the following *Tonight Show,* Jay Leno included the incident in his standup routine, cheering, "Way to go, Buzz!" They doctored up the video of my punch, and edited it to make it appear as though I had given the guy about twenty rapid-fire punches instead of the one.

David Letterman also came to my defense in his opening remarks for *The Late Show,* and threw in a double feature on the story the next night, since they had "dug up" some old archival footage of a reporter accosting Christopher Columbus, accusing him, "You didn't really cross the ocean and land in the New World. You're a liar!" And of course, Columbus decked the guy.

By then, television networks and evening entertainment news programs were calling, suddenly wanting me to appear on their shows. Ordinarily I would have been delighted, but our legal advisers said, "No interviews." Eventually the matter died down. The city of Beverly Hills did not bring charges against me, and there were witnesses to the harassing behavior that provoked my response. It still cost me money to hire a lawyer to defend myself, and the hoax advocate received the publicity he sought, so I suppose, in the end, he won. But the punch provided me with some satisfaction, at least, and I was gratified by the calls and notes of support. CNN *Crossfire* commentator Paul Begala gave me a thumbs-up, and many others sent encouraging messages. Ironically, some of the most supportive words came from my fellow astronauts, to the effect of, "Hey, Buzz, I wish I'd punched the guy! Finally, somebody has responded to these hoax theory perpetrators." More than my knowledge of rendezvous techniques, more than my actions under pressure during the initial lunar landing, more than anything in my career as an astronaut—it seemed as if nothing elevated me more in their estimation than "the punch." From that day on, I was a hero to them.

◗ ○ ◗

ON JANUARY 29, 2003, I was in New York to celebrate General Electric Plastics' fiftieth anniversary of the invention of *Lexan* at its "Innovation Day," held at New York's Grand Central Terminal. Lexan is the highly durable polycarbonate material used in everything from plastic water bottles to space helmets. I donned a replica of my *Apollo 11* space helmet with a visor made of the Lexan resin, and shared my space stories with more than 500 sixth graders. As part of the anniversary celebration, I made a spotlight appearance on NBC's *Today* show, and talked about the space shuttle *Columbia*, which was due to land in a few days, and of course how excited I was about the progress we were making toward getting ordinary citizens into space.

Back home, I arose early on the morning of February 1, 2003, and turned on the television. I had penciled into my handwritten calendar the time that the *Columbia* shuttle was expected to return from its mission to the ISS for its runway landing at the Kennedy Space Center at around 9:00 a.m. (EST), 6:00 a.m. (PST). I brewed some coffee, poured myself a cup, and sat down to watch the reentry. But I could tell that something wasn't right; it was suddenly too quiet, and at this point in the landing, such a silence was highly unusual. Normally the radio transmissions between ground control and the shuttle would be constant back-and-forth confirming critical data and readings. I turned the television's volume higher, thinking it might be something malfunctioning on our set, but the interruption of communication from the *Columbia* was real—and alarming. Unknown to me or to most of the world at that moment, the space shuttle *Columbia* had already begun to disintegrate as it streaked high above Texas during reentry into the Earth's atmosphere. All seven crew members died in the catastrophe.

Apparently the shuttle had been damaged either during or shortly after launch when a piece of foam insulation, no bigger than a small briefcase and weighing slightly more than a pound, broke off from the main propellant tank. The debris struck the edge of the left wing, damaging *Columbia*'s thermal protection system, which guards it from the intense 3,000-degree-Fahrenheit temperatures generated during reentry. Making matters worse, it was later discovered that NASA engineers suspected the damage the entire time the shuttle was in flight, but it was determined that there was little that could be done to repair the problem. Nobody bothered to tell the *Columbia*'s crew of the danger they were in as Commander Rick Husband, an experienced shuttle pilot who had flown one of the first missions to the International Space Station (ISS), ran the spacecraft through its final burns.

The *Columbia* spread bits of debris across parts of Texas and as far away as Arkansas and Louisiana. My heart sank as I watched the television coverage of the tragedy.

I had little time to grieve, however. Within minutes, all six telephone lines in our home and office were lighting up, with what seemed like every television network and news agency in America wanting to ask me about the chain of events. Several television networks wanted me to sign on as their exclusive news commentator to help viewers understand more about this horrific incident.

I knew I couldn't help everybody, but felt compelled to do what I could. I decided to work exclusively with NBC, and within two hours I was on the air with various NBC commentators, discussing the catastrophe. I tried to remain stoic and scientific in most of my comments, but at one point during my appearance on NBC's *Nightly News*, while discussing the disaster with Brian Williams, I could no longer hold back the tears welling in my eyes, as with trembling voice I recited a lyric from the song, "Fire in the Sky," written by Dr. Jordan Kare that seemed so appropriate to me:

Though a nation watched her falling
Yet a world could only cry
As they passed from us to glory
Riding fire in the sky.[15]

I knew the natural result of such a tragedy would be for NASA to pull back, to say, "We aren't going to do anything until the investigators' report is released and we find out why this horrible accident occurred." That was understandable, but we dared not put life on hold as we waited.

Months later, when their report came out, the *Columbia* accident investigation board mandated that the remaining three shuttle orbiters in the fleet, *Discovery, Endeavor,* and *Atlantis,* be permanently

---

15 Jordan Kare, "Fire in the Sky," © Jordan T. Kare, Seattle, WA, 1981, 1986; used by permission.

retired by the year 2010. NASA had been struggling with the issue of how long to fly the shuttles; some claimed they were never meant to have a thirty-year lifespan when they began flying in 1981. This mandate made it all the more urgent for America to put into effect a strong new vision and start building the next generation of spacecraft to replace the shuttle program. The report also recommended that the astronaut crew be separated from cargo in the launch vehicle in future space transportation systems. I saw this as a red flag that might prove a costly limitation as we moved forward.

With that premonition in mind, I initiated a conference call between two key admirals to raise the issue, Admiral Hal Gehman, who chaired the *Columbia* accident investigation board, and Admiral Craig E. Steidle, NASA's associate administrator in charge of exploration systems. I told them that the separation of crew and cargo would restrict and limit the flexibility of configuring our future launch systems. We reviewed the issues, but in the end the accident board was not going to change its position due to underlying crew safety considerations. As it turns out, NASA implemented the board's report by developing two completely different launch vehicles (the *Ares I* and the *Ares V*) to launch crew and cargo separately in its new Constellation program. Though it may take a rocket scientist to understand the ramifications, in my opinion—one shared by many others—NASA's development of two completely different launch vehicles has strayed far from the shuttle-derived designs that make the most sense. This approach is what lies at the crux of our space program's challenges today.

It saddens me to know that we have fallen short on our progress as a nation to lead the world in space. As I write these words, we do not have in place a new space transportation system to take over when the shuttle orbiters are retired. At NASA's current pace with the Constellation program, America will experience a gap of at least five years in which we will have no capability of launching humans into space. We will have no direct ability to send our astronauts to the $100-billion investment in the International Space Station. We will be completely dependent on the Russians to fly to the ISS, or possibly the Chinese, once they are invited to participate in the station. Moreover, we will have no capability to get back to the moon or on to Mars.

Although the space shuttle would fly again following the *Columbia* disaster, NASA's position regarding the future use of the shuttles has not changed. I have suggested stretching the existing schedule to retire the shuttles by one-year intervals, and flying at least one of our shuttles back to the International Space Station and docking it there as a permanent part of the structure, but so far these ideas have not been well received.

We have experienced hiatuses in human space launch capability in the past, following Apollo and Skylab, before the new shuttle fleet was developed. It was a fallow period in which we could not venture into space. After the Mercury program, NASA might have faced a gap before fully developing Apollo, but instead, we filled it with the Gemini program. We have existing technology today to prevent another pause in exploration, but only if NASA partners with commercial aerospace companies currently developing such spacecraft. Furthermore, it would indicate true progress if after almost thirty years of landing the shuttle fleet on the runway, NASA were to adopt a gap-filling technology of a heavy-lifting spacecraft with wings that could land on the runway, rather than the simpler, nonprogressive way of landing space capsules in the ocean to be recovered as we did in the early days of Mercury, Gemini, and Apollo. Development of such a spacecraft is still barely possible to bridge the gap, but time is running out.

◐ ○ ◑

PARTIALLY TO TAKE my mind off the *Columbia* disaster, and partly because it was something that I had never previously done, I accepted an invitation to be a celebrity participant in the Twenty-seventh Annual Toyota Grand Prix, held in Long Beach on the first weekend of April 2003. The event pits celebrities against professional drivers in a high-speed race for charity, with proceeds benefiting children's hospitals in Long Beach and Orange County, California. I've always loved cars, and I love speed, and I love driving fast. But I had never really raced cars, and I couldn't pass up the opportunity, even though I was seventy-three years of age. I was assured of having at least one distinction: being the oldest driver on the course.

Lois didn't really want me to drive in the race, because it was not a staged event; it was a real speed race and it was dangerous. The race circuit was nearly two miles long, winding through the streets surrounding the Long Beach Convention Center. On the straight stretches, a driver could reach speeds of close to 100 miles per hour. But the course is especially noted for its last section, in which it runs through a dangerous hairpin turn followed by a slightly curved section that follows the length of the Long Beach waterfront and is lined with palm trees, making for quite a challenging and scenic track. More than 200,000 race fans turn out annually for a weekend of racing, food, and music. Professional drivers who have won the Toyota Grand Prix include Mario Andretti and Al Unser Jr. Past celebrity participants have included Hollywood actors and actresses such as Cameron Diaz, Queen Latifah, Gene Hackman, William Shatner, Dennis Franz, Tony Danza, and Kim Alexis, and athletes such as Bruce Jenner, Lynn Swann, Walter Payton, Mary Lou Retton, Joe Montana, and rocker Ted Nugent.

For two weekends prior to the race, the celebrity drivers practiced on a makeshift track out in the Mojave Desert. The sponsors always invited both male and female celebrities to race, so it was quite a rowdy bunch. It was fun to hook up again with Olympic skiing gold medalist, Picabo Street, whom Lois and I had come to know in Sun Valley, Idaho, and whom I saw at a number of ski celebrity events. For the Toyota race, professional drivers Shawna Robinson and Jeremy Mc-Grath, as well as actor Josh Brolin, were breathing down our necks. It was an exhilarating but humbling experience; it had been a long time since I'd driven a car with a manual transmission. My eye-hand coordination wasn't quite as quick as when I was flying fighter jets in Korea, so almost every day during our test runs, I crashed a car into the wall. Comedian Adam Carolla loved making fun of me for my crashes. "Buzz's best friend is the wall," Adam joked.

During the actual race, I was doing great and holding my own until nearly the end, when swimsuit model and actress Angie Everhart crashed into me and knocked me into the wall and out of the race. Afterwards, Angie came over to me and got down on her knees, begging my forgiveness. "Oh, Buzz, I'm so sorry. Please, I'll do anything to make it up to you!" I just smiled as the photographers flashed pictures of us. Peter Reckell, star of the daytime television series, *Days of Our Lives,* was the celebrity winner and Jeremy McGrath the pro winner.

●   ○   ●

ON DECEMBER 17, 2003, Lois and I traveled to Kitty Hawk, North Carolina, for the nation's celebration of the "Centennial of Flight"— one hundred years to the day since Wilbur and Orville Wright successfully got their 1903 Wright *Flyer* off the ground and into the air. But unlike their "first in flight" day, this December 17 was pouring buckets. In spite of it, the crowds still gathered, huddled together under tarps for the beautifully staged ceremony in honor of the first powered flight. President Bush came from Washington, D.C., to speak to the crowd. Our friend John Travolta served as master of ceremonies for the morning events, and I delivered the formal prayer at the opening. The security guards held an umbrella over my head as I went up to the podium. I decided on this occasion to share the words that had helped me through so much of my life over the last twenty-five years:

"God grant us the serenity to accept the things we cannot change, courage to change the things we can, and wisdom to know the difference."

It was a sentiment I thought we would all do well to remember, having come so far from the first powered flight and in the context of looking to our future challenges in space.

As the rain abated, the celebration was honored by a 100-plane flyby spaced throughout the day. All sorts of dignitaries, celebrities, and aviation legends were on hand to commemorate this occasion, including Apollo 16 astronaut Charlie Duke, as well as Neil Armstrong and Apollo 10 astronaut Tom Stafford. One of the highlights for me was being named as one of the top 100 aviators in history. Somewhere, I hoped my father was smiling.

The celebration culminated with a re-creation of the Wright brothers' first heavier-than-air powered flight, which took off at precisely 10:35 a.m. and lasted twelve seconds, covering a mere 120 feet. Think about that—only twelve seconds in flight, but they were twelve seconds that changed the world. Naturally, I couldn't help but think how far we had come—from Kitty Hawk to the moon in sixty-six years— and how far I dreamed of going.

To that end, the very next day after the Centennial of Flight, our ShareSpace Foundation held a one-day symposium to usher in the next century of flight. We called it "Next Century of Flight Space Imperatives," held at the Ronald Reagan Center in Washington, D.C. Our goal was to inspire a new vision for America's space exploration program. With a small, overworked staff, we secured sponsorships from Boeing, Lockheed, American Airlines, and others. We partnered with Aviation Week (publisher of the magazine of the same name) to host the conference, which also included an elegant gala affair the night of December 17 at the National Air and Space Museum. The conference took six months to put together, and was attended by numerous movers and shakers in the space and aviation world, including Senator E. J. "Jake" Garn, a former U.S. senator from Utah, who had been the first member of Congress to fly on the space shuttle; the astrophysicist Neil deGrasse Tyson, director of the world-famous Hayden Planetarium in New York; Elon Musk, cofounder of PayPal, now turned aerospace entrepreneur with his space transportation startup, SpaceX; and no fewer than five of my fellow Apollo astronauts.

"To me, this is a culmination and a beginning," I said in my opening remarks. "It's the culmination of many years, months, weeks of efforts that I've attempted to put into building a coalition, to building a consensus. United we stand. Divided we kinda circle the wagons and shoot inward instead of accomplishing what we're after."

I was convinced that at this juncture in history, America was lost in space. I hoped that through the symposium we could stimulate some ideas. "We have to push forward," I told everyone I met. "We've got to set out a new vision for our country's space program." NASA didn't seem to have a clear goal or vision. Moreover, the Chinese had just entered the space picture in October, becoming only the third nation in the world to launch humans into space—*taikonauts*, they dubbed them—as well as a satellite and probes to the moon, with plans for future probes to Mars. There was some concern that we might be on the verge of new space race in which we were handicapped by the upcoming retirement of the shuttle and the lack of a clear objective.

The futurist Alvin Toffler, whose once-controversial book *Future Shock* now reads like history, spoke at the conference and encouraged us to look forward to even more astounding developments in flight over the next hundred years. That set the tone, and by the end of the day, our hopes were soaring. The symposium might not have changed the world overnight to get our space program back on track for the next 100 years, but it was a productive exchange of forward-thinking ideas. Best of all, a few weeks later, on January 14, 2004, President George W. Bush announced a renewed "Vision for Space Exploration," a fresh agenda for NASA and others related to America's space program, with a goal of returning to the moon to set up permanent lunar bases, and then to initiate human exploration of Mars and beyond. It appeared at the time that the "moon, Mars, and beyond" statement would marshal the nation in a new concerted effort. I'd like to think our symposium lent some extra impetus to that decision.

I smiled as I read about the President's initiatives. I had much I wanted to accomplish, and the announcement by the President of the United States gave me hope that my dreams could yet come true within my lifetime.

21

WEIGHTLESS
AGAIN

IN 2004, ZERO-GRAVITY FLIGHTS BECAME AVAILABLE COM-
mercially in the United States for the first time. Prior to that, the
only place the average American citizen could experience a zero-
gravity flight was by flying with the Russians. Occasionally NASA extended zero-gravity flight privileges for educational purposes, or for
unusual requests by Hollywood filmmakers for scenes in space, such as
the scenes inside the capsule for the movie *Apollo 13*. Now anyone who
is healthy, and a bit wealthy, can enjoy a zero-gravity experience at a
cost of about $3,500 per person. Of course, if you are really wealthy, you
can rent the entire plane for your family reunion or company retreat.

During my astronaut training in preparation for my first mission on
Gemini 12, we affectionately referred to the plane in which we performed our weightless training as the "vomit comet." Actually it was a
hollowed-out, fully padded Air Force KC-135, the military version of a
Boeing 707 jet, that pulled about two g's each time it flew up in a steep
angle into the atmosphere, where it would linger for about forty seconds before pulling another two g's when we came down. At the top of
these parabolic maneuvers, I floated free in a weightless world. Imper-
vious to the Earth's gravitational force, I traversed the mockup of *Gemini* with its open hatch in a simulation of my upcoming spacewalk. In
one of my last zero-gravity training flights, we flew eighty parabolas at

once. On rare occasions, a few members of the astronaut corps lost their breakfast. But my inner ear never seemed to fail me or sense the conflict between the g forces and the weightlessness. You might say I have a steady orientation when it comes to up and down.

When Zero Gravity Corporation commenced a nationwide tour in key cities across the United States to fly its "G Force One" plane and promote this new adventure, the National Space Society (NSS) offered a special deal on discounted tickets to its members for the first of two flights to be launched out of Burbank, California. The NSS is a great grassroots organization for space advocates and enthusiasts, of which I was privileged to serve as chairman for several years in the 1990s. The organization has grown and expanded under the excellent guidance of its young and knowledgeable director, George Whitesides. They asked me to join the flight to publicize the event. I hadn't been weightless in thirty-five years, so I thought it would be a good chance to brush up on my technique. Lois wasn't quite up for this adventure, so Lisa came along in hopes that there might be an extra seat available. I also invited along former Los Angeles Mayor Dick Riordan, though ultimately he couldn't stay through the delayed takeoff schedule.

I was asked to offer some words of encouragement to the participants, and share a few thoughts with an ABC newscaster covering the event. As the twenty-five NSS novices went through their brief training session, I could see this was a good first step toward exposing the public at large to the adventure of space travel. Their eyes lit up with excitement and a sense of anticipation as I shared with them a bit of my ShareSpace philosophy:

> The phrase "tourism in space" is no longer the giggle that it was about ten years ago. And I can say that not only do I want to be alive to see humans walk on the moon again, but I also want to be alive to see things like lotteries selecting people to go into space. My interest, eventually, is orbital travel, and I know that the interim step is suborbital activities, and I applaud all the efforts that are being done on that behalf. I want to accelerate the movement

from suborbital flight to orbital as soon as I can. That's very difficult to do. And only governments have been able to do that so far,
so it's quite a challenge to get the private sector and the entrepreneurs somehow to do what until now only governments with a lot
of money have been able to do. We need to open it up to a vast increase, and that's why I think the use of sponsors that are involved
in supporting this activity can also be instrumental in helping to
select the participants who get involved in it.

It was time for the flight. All the participants and I donned our blue
flight suits, provided by Zero Gravity, and accented with sponsor Diet
Rite space patches on the pockets. Buckled into a few seats in the back
of the specially modified and padded Boeing 727 plane during takeoff,
we soon unstrapped as the plane rose to a sufficient elevation to begin
its parabolas. The pilot would fly about ten of these maneuvers—a
far cry from the eighty I once endured in my training—but probably
more than enough for newcomers. The participants would experience
parabolas that produced a Mars gravity (one-third Earth gravity) environment, then a lunar gravity (one-sixth Earth gravity) environment,
and then complete zero-gravity weightlessness. On the mark, the zero-g
guides gave us a countdown as we approached each twenty-five-second
period of weightlessness, and issued a warning as we were about to
come out and hit the g forces.

"Three. Two. One. Get ready for lunar gravity!"

In pure delight, the participants, guides, and I suddenly found ourselves lighter than air. For me it was like riding a bicycle, but this time
it was purely for fun rather than training on equipment in bulky spacesuits. For the NSS participants, it was a brand-new sensation as they
pushed off from the floor, glided and wafted in a freer movement than
they had ever felt before. It was less than a minute, but felt like forever,
until the warning for pull-out came and we all assumed our stationary
positions lying on the floor on our backs to evenly distribute the g's,
making each of us feel twice as heavy as our real weight.

By the time we got to zero-gravity, I was having the time of my life, somersaulting with ease, propelling through the air like Superman, and giving the ABC newscaster some great sound bites. But the interview questions didn't last long, since the brave female reporter found herself succumbing to the effects of nausea. Of course each flight suit came equipped with a little plastic bag for that purpose.

About one hour and ten parabolas later, we landed on the tarmac. All the participants, even the reporter, were now officially initiated zero-g flyers, and each was presented with a certificate of weightless flight. The next group for the second flight was in training, being prepped for their first experience.

"Hey, Buzz!"

I heard my name being called out by one of the Zero G marketing guys. He took me aside to say, "We've got a bit of a problem. All the footage ABC shot of you on the flight didn't turn out because the camera wasn't working properly. Would you be willing to go up again on the second flight?"

"Why not?" I said. "But this time I want Lisa to join me."

Lisa had a blast, doing all kinds of cheerleader gymnastics from her youth, and learning pretty quickly some of the acrobatic movements I was showing her. We somersaulted together, cartwheeled in pairs, and even pulled off a human windmill with each of our hands stretched upward and out, spinning as we held on to each other's ankles. She had no side effects, though she may have overdone it for her first time, admitting that if the pilot had performed an eleventh parabola, she might have lost it. As for me, the second flight was even more fun than the first. My seventy-four-year-old body felt thirty-nine again!

Since those two flights venturing into weightlessness, I have participated in several others—most recently at seventy-eight years of age—to help promote the experience to the public, and as the featured Apollo astronaut on the "Platinum Zero G Experience" for Zero Gravity Corporation in flights out of the Kennedy Space Center and Las Vegas. It has been a real thrill to see the enthusiasm with which the participants have embraced the experience, and I recommend it highly. Just make sure you eat a light meal before you go!

◐ ◯ ◐

I WAS HOME in Los Angeles when Burt Rutan, founder of the aerospace development company Scaled Composites, called and invited me out to the Mojave Desert. He was about to have another of his test flights of a new suborbital spacecraft he was developing. I had been out a few times earlier during the development phase, and had enjoyed seeing the progress he was making with the unique winglet design. His approach to liftoff was also unique. The suborbital craft would not be launched vertically or horizontally on its own, but would be carried under the belly of a larger, broad-winged, jet-powered carrier airplane called the *White Knight*. At an altitude of about ten miles, the suborbital craft, christened *SpaceShipOne*, would separate from the *White Knight* and fire its rockets to continue another fifty-two miles upward and reach the sixty-two-mile mark where the blackness of space begins and the curvature of the Earth is clearly visible, and the pilot would experience weightlessness for about five minutes before reentry.

On the day that I joined Burt to watch the test, a large crowd was expected, including media, since *SpaceShipOne* was a key contender for the $10-million award being offered by the X PRIZE Foundation for the first privately developed craft to be piloted on two consecutive suborbital flights within a two-week period. In creating the prize, the foundation took a cue from the Orteig Prize, a $25,000 award created in 1919 by the New York hotel owner Raymond Orteig, to the first aviator to fly nonstop between New York City and Paris. For nearly eight years nobody claimed Orteig's prize, but then, in 1927, Charles Lindbergh won it in the *Spirit of St. Louis*. To stimulate competition, ingenuity, and innovation in the fledgling space tourism industry, the $10-million X PRIZE offered a huge incentive. More than a dozen companies worldwide took the challenge seriously.

Backed by financier and Microsoft cofounder Paul Allen, Burt's efforts were looking very promising for winning the prize. But on this occasion they still had a few kinks to work out. As a crowd of hundreds gathered in the area surrounding the hot desert landing strip, we all gazed up as the graceful *White Knight* took flight with *SpaceShipOne* fastened securely to its fuselage. After separation, Mike Melvill, the sixty-three-year-old test pilot, continued speeding upward, followed by a thick white contrail that made it easier to be tracked by the naked eye. Suddenly the spacecraft went out of control into a roll, as the contrail now turned into a series of curlicues. With a great deal of skill, and a bit of luck, Mike was able to keep the roll symmetrical until the rocket burned out, and then fully regained control to make it back for a successful and safe landing. Averting a potential disaster, both he and the craft escaped injury.

We all congratulated the pilot for the great recovery, even though he had failed to achieve suborbital distance. In the crowd I ran into my friend, Richard Branson, flamboyant founder and CEO of Virgin Galactic, who was on hand for the flight. Richard is an English billionaire with more than 300 companies under his Virgin logo. He has a knack for building businesses, so I was glad when he expressed interest in suborbital space tourism. He was considering an association between Virgin and *SpaceShipOne* to adapt the technology for a fleet of suborbital craft. By the time *SpaceShipOne* won the X PRIZE, it bore a Virgin logo. Richard was never one to miss a good opportunity to market and promote his companies.

On September 29, 2004, Mike Melvill became the first civilian pilot to fly into suborbital space, successfully qualifying *SpaceShipOne* for the first round of the two requisite X PRIZE flights. To celebrate en route in his brief moments of weightlessness, he released a bag of M&Ms that floated around the cabin in a colorful display. I wasn't able to be there in person for this first, but was thrilled with the outcome. Days later, on October 4, 2004, *SpaceShipOne* made its second qualifying flight to win the $10-million Ansari X PRIZE, as it was now called, since the prize was primarily funded by the Ansaris, a wealthy entrepreneurial Iranian family from Texas. Anousheh Ansari became so enamored with space that she eventually flew as the first female space tourist, traveling to the International Space Station on a Russian Soyuz rocket in September 2006.

In November, Lois and I went to London for a meeting with Virgin Galactic's Stephen Attenborough, Alex Tai, and others at their Kensington offices, to discuss a potential collaboration between Virgin and my ShareSpace Foundation. I knew that Richard wanted to design his own spacecraft for suborbital tourism and hoped to be operating regular flights by 2008. That date has since been revised, but there is little doubt that the world will see Virgin Galactic taking people on suborbital rides in the near future.

While my friends were developing fresh ideas for making suborbital travel feasible, safe, and profitable, I focused my attention on my StarBooster family of rockets and spacecraft that could carry larger numbers of passengers into orbital space with each trip.

There are enormous differences between launching a suborbital craft and launching an orbital craft. One of the easiest ways to understand the relative degree of difficulty is the speed needed in both instances. A suborbital craft may top out at about 2,500 miles per hour to perform the sixty-two-mile lob to the edge of space, whereas the thrust and speed required to take a vehicle into orbit is exponentially greater, on the order of 17,500 miles per hour to reach about 220 miles above the Earth and sustain ninety-minute orbits encircling the entire globe. It's a whole different ball game.

NASA's missions were never intended to maximize the number of people sent into space, but to maximize the scientific or exploratory aspects of each journey. But for space tourism to be profitable, and thus more inviting for private-sector investors, we must take more people into space on each launch. I wanted to design a spacecraft to carry forty, fifty, possibly even eighty to one hundred passengers into Earth's orbit each time it launched, a "space bus," if you will. To do so would require a massive spaceship.

But I wondered, *What if we could launch more than one crew, each in its own spacecraft, on one launch vehicle? That has never been done before!* I went to work on that concept, designing one heavy-lift launch vehicle, but one that could carry up to six separate spacecraft or "crew modules" attached to it, similar to the way in which the space shuttle orbiters have previously been attached to a launch vehicle. But in my design, there would be six separate eight-person crew modules, rather than one shuttle orbiter. That way, we could launch nearly fifty people into space at one time! Following liftoff, each of the crew modules would separate from the launch vehicle to embark on their own respective missions, and then return to the Earth for a runway landing. In addition to taking more people into space with each launch, the flexibility offered with multiple crew modules would make it feasible for NASA's scientific missions and private-sector missions to be launched at the same time, on the same launch vehicle, from the same launchpad, thus saving money, while opening the space frontier to public travelers. It was a win-win idea, so I put my thoughts together in a formal proposal, and on December 7, 2004, I was awarded a U.S. patent for "Multi-Crew Modules for Space Flight."

At the same time, I was unwilling to give up on the idea of developing a heavy-lift launch vehicle that could serve as a workhorse similar to the Saturn V rocket that we used for Apollo launches. The Saturn V was capable of carrying enormous weight, as much as 260,000 pounds, into Earth's orbit, and as much as 104,000 all the way to lunar orbit, nearly a quarter of a million miles away. But after launching us to the moon nine times, and hoisting America's first space station, Skylab, in 1973, the Saturn V was inauspiciously "retired" from NASA's transportation vehicles.

Instead, NASA focused on developing the space shuttle program, with its initial launches in 1981 using a transportation system that carried only 55,000 pounds and could travel only about 215 miles above the Earth, within the area referred to as "low Earth orbit." Since the shuttle was partially reusable, it was thought that it would replace the need for the Saturn V, reducing costs and making spaceflight more routine. Unfortunately, those goals turned out to be more elusive than NASA originally thought.

Consequently, back in 2002, I started encouraging my StarBooster design team to work on a "next-generation" launch system that would once again power a spacecraft with human beings beyond low Earth orbit. We needed something bigger, a heavy-lift launch vehicle that could carry an expanded crew, have greater cargo capacity, and also have on board an escape pod that could be a "space lifeboat."

We named the vehicle we were developing Aquila, the Latin word for *eagle*, and obviously a term that meant a great deal to me. The Aquila was a heavy-lift rocket system that would carry twice the payload of the space shuttle's capacity, with the goal of accomplishing large missions such as building a space station, space hotels, or space ports along the route between Earth and Mars. All of this could be done at lower costs and lower risks, since fewer flights and less assembly in space would be required.

As 2004 drew to a close, I could see that people were catching on to my vision of space travel, and entrepreneurs were developing new technology that could take us to the final frontier, or, as my cousin Buzz Lightyear is fond of saying, "to infinity and beyond!" Except this is no movie; the commercial exploration of space is becoming more certain every day. Soon the images we have always perceived as being a part of the "future" will be our present-tense reality.

22

FINAL FRONTIERS

ᴇARLY IN OUR MARRIAGE, Lois CONFIDED TO ME THAT SHE always wanted to be a movie star and to interact with the interesting and famous people of the world. Imagine how tickled she was when none other than Robin Leach, of the *Lifestyles of the Rich and Famous* television show, contacted us to do an interview. "But, Robin, Buzz may be famous as a result of walking on the moon," Lois gently protested, "but we're not rich." Robin didn't mind; he seemed to know instinctively that our marriage would take Lois and me around the world and into the presence of not only the rich and famous, but presidents and royalty as well.

One of our royal encounters occurred when I was asked to speak at a university in Madrid, Spain. After the event, we had a little extra time, and wondered what to do. Lois asked, "Do you know anyone in Madrid?"

I thought for a moment, then said, "The only person that I know in Madrid is the king." Lois looked at me and cocked her head, uncertain whether I was joking or not.

"I think I'll give him a call," I said. I looked in my address book, found the phone number for the king and queen, and called Juan Carlos, the king of Spain. I had met Juan Carlos, of course, during the Apollo 11 world tour, so when I called and told him we were in

Madrid, the king said, "Come on over." We did, and we enjoyed the marvelous hospitality of the Spanish royalty. Lois loves meeting world leaders, and I don't think she has ever doubted me on such matters since that trip to Madrid.

Over the last twenty years, Lois and I have had a lot of fun growing the "business of Buzz." We have worked with some of the world's leading innovators and their enterprises and have enjoyed every minute of it. More recently I have been honored to collaborate with some well-known companies to create and develop space-inspired products in connection with the launch of my Rocket Hero™ brand. Perhaps through these efforts we can generate excitement and interest in space.

Throughout all our activities, Lois and I have maintained a travel schedule that most twenty-year-olds would have a hard time matching. As Lois likes to say, "They may be in full swing, but we are in full orbit." And like anyone who travels frequently, Lois and I have experienced our share of travel nightmares, ranging from canceled flights to the time when I lost my passport while on a trip out of the country. Perhaps the most memorable close call occurred in a way we least expected.

In February 2005, Lois and I were in Brussels for Earth and Space Week, where I was to speak at the space conference. The next day we were scheduled to have dinner with two ambassadors—Rockwell Schnabel, the U.S. envoy to the European Union, and Chris Korologos, the American ambassador to Belgium. But when I woke up that morning, I found I could hardly speak or pronounce any words clearly enough to be understood. Alarmed, Lois called the ambassador's office, and they sent an ambulance for me right away. We spent the rest of the day in a Belgian hospital, where the doctors ran all sorts of tests and it was determined that I had suffered a kind of mini-stroke. Slowly, before the day was over, my speech returned and I felt fine. We went on to Gstaad, Switzerland to stay with our friend Heidi Chantre-Eckes in her ski chalet, and enjoyed an energetic day of skiing. But as soon as we returned to the United States, I was subjected to a series of intensive medical examinations.

After seeing a number of doctors, I was led to Dr. Willis Wagner, a classmate of Lisa's from Stanford and one of the top vascular surgeons in the country. The matter was urgent, he said. "You're going to the hospital tomorrow morning." He performed a successful operation, removing a large blood clot. If the blood vessel had burst, it could have caused a major stroke that would have impaired me for the rest of my life, or possibly even killed me. Fortunately, the problem that occurred in Brussels sounded an alarm. I had been the picture of health, and passed my physicals at NASA every year with flying colors, but I'd never had an ultrasound that might have revealed the clot. Sometimes those experiences that we think are mistakes or misfortunes turn out to be lifesavers. Had I not had the forewarning in Brussels, we might not have averted a potentially life-threatening situation later. Could be I've got some good guardian angels watching over me. I'd just like to know more about what star systems they live in.

● ○ ●

OVER THE YEARS I've received a number of awards and recognitions from many fine organizations, but one that I have especially cherished is from the Horatio Alger Association of Distinguished Americans. Each year the association inducts new members into its prestigious group, chosen because of adversities they have overcome. Our friends Diane and Harry Rinker nominated me for membership, and I was inducted in 2005. The Horatio Alger Association of Distinguished Americans culls hundreds of nominations to make the selections for each award, so I was deeply honored. Moreover, the organization comprises mostly multimillionaires who started from humble, sometimes destitute, beginnings, but are now living the American dream. Members of the association sponsor more than $5 million in need-based scholarships for aspiring college students.

In my acceptance speech, I acknowledged that most people in the association had experienced trying circumstances before achieving success. I, however, achieved the greatest success, universally acclaimed as one of mankind's most extraordinary achievements to date, and then found adversity crouching at my door, waiting to trip me up. Once entangled, I didn't unwittingly fall into depression and alcoholism; I took willful steps in the wrong direction, thinking I could turn around at any point. But like a motorboat idling on the Niagara River, I soon found myself being swept along, past the point of no return, out of control, drowning my sorrows and disappointments in alcohol, and heading for the precipice and ultimate destruction.

Having been to the moon, I plummeted into my own personal hell on Earth. Had it not been for some friends who cared enough to call a drunk a drunk, even if he had walked on the moon, I might have perished. I will always be grateful to Alcoholics Anonymous for saving my life, and for helping me to sustain now more than thirty years of sobriety.

But, thankful as I am to my friends in AA, it wasn't they who motivated me to see the best in myself. For that, I will be forever indebted to a petite little bundle of loving energy, my wife, Lois. She helped me to believe in myself, and she believed in me so much that she was willing to do whatever it took to help me fulfill my dreams. As I accepted the Horatio Alger Award, I looked over at Harry Rinker and said, "Thank you, Harry, for nominating me for this great honor and for being a true friend."

Then I looked at Lois, and I could feel the tears welling in my eyes. With great emotion, I expressed what anyone who has known me already knew, that she was not merely the wind beneath my wings, she was the wind behind me, under me, and in front of me. "And thank you, Lois, for standing behind me and supporting me and leading me these last nineteen years."

I went on to express one of the key facts of my life; I have been most fortunate to be consistently at the right place at the right time. "I am truly humbled and honored to receive the Horatio Alger Award, not only for what it signifies, but also because I respect and revere so many of the members who have come before me. One in particular who has gone before me in aviation is General Jimmy Doolittle, who led the bombing raid on Tokyo and was inducted into this association in 1972.

The title of his autobiography is *I Could Never Be So Lucky Again.* And that's exactly how I feel about so many things in my life. My talents and motivations combined to put me in the right place at the right time and propelled me into a career that far exceeded my boyhood dreams of becoming a pilot."

I looked out at the group of young men and women that the association had invited to receive scholarships based on their need and academic abilities, their faces bright with anticipation and potential. Although I certainly didn't qualify as a wealthy man in dollars and cents, I was rich beyond measure with a treasury of life experiences that I hoped might inspire them. More than anything, I wanted to encourage them to believe in themselves, the way Lois had encouraged me. "So, scholars, open your arms wide," I said. "Pursue America's abundant opportunities and reach for the stars. Who knows? You just might get to your own moon landing."

I wasn't merely spouting tripe to those teenagers. I truly believe that we have the universe at our fingertips. We were on the right track when we took the challenge laid down by President Kennedy, and we will continue on the right track if we expand upon that commitment.

I remain passionate about my vision for space exploration. In September 2007, when Google cofounder Larry Page wanted to make a media splash with his company's $30-million Lunar X PRIZE—an award to be split between the first two private-sector teams that can soft-land on the moon, robotically roam for at least 500 meters, and transmit a mooncast back to Earth—I stood at the podium with him to help sell the idea.

I believe that space travel will one day become as common as airline travel is today. I'm convinced, however, that the true future of space travel does not lie with government agencies—NASA is still obsessed with the idea that the primary purpose of the space program is science—but real progress will come from private companies competing to provide the ultimate adventure ride, and NASA will receive the trickle-down benefits.

Millions of people get excited about the possibility of going into space; something about space travel intrigues and inspires. And a few of them are movie moguls who have shown a great interest in space, like my friend Ron Howard, who directed *Apollo 13* and who lent his name to promote the Sundance Award–winning documentary film *In the Shadow of the Moon*. It's the story of the Apollo landings told by the astronauts themselves, starring several of us moonwalkers. Of course I've enjoyed conversing with my fellow explorer, Jim Cameron, the famed director of *Titanic*, at a number of film festivals and space events. He shares my passion for missions to Mars (and has even expressed interest in going there himself), and we also share an interest in exploring the oceans of the Earth.

I recall one evening when Lois and I went out to a charity event in Los Angeles at the Beverly Wilshire Hotel in support of breast cancer research. The event was hosted by Tom Hanks, who produced the HBO series *From the Earth to the Moon*, starred in *Apollo 13*, and has always been supportive to us and all of the astronauts. Coincidentally, it was an evening when we were experiencing a lunar eclipse. As Tom was making his introductions, in addition to talking about cancer research, he couldn't resist talking about the moon. "Tonight we have a lunar eclipse, and we happen to have a man who actually walked on the moon." Ironically, at this same event in 2009, Tom introduced and extolled the strength and courage of a breast cancer survivor close to me—my wife, Lois. I really appreciate guys like Tom, who have given so much of their time in support of such worthy charities, as well as our space program. And I don't mind it at all that he titled his IMAX film on space exploration to the moon *Magnificent Desolation*, after my words.

On another occasion we were at the Beverly Hilton with Clive Davis, of Arista Records fame. I had only met Clive a few times, but Lois wanted to go to the pre–Grammy Awards party, so we attended. When Clive came out on stage, in a room full of famous celebrities, he said, "I want to recognize somebody really special who is here tonight—Buzz Aldrin!"

I was honored by both Tom's and Clive's kind words, but what it tells me is that space exploration holds a fascination for many people that is much bigger than Neil, Mike, or me traveling to the moon. There's something within us that says, "Me, too! I want to discover what is out there."

That's why I know that one day my vision will come to pass. Share-Space will indeed find a way to manage a lottery or some other method of giving ordinary people a chance to travel into space. Space hotels will be constructed, providing the opportunity for people to take a truly "out of this world" vacation. One day my Mars Cycler will be put into practice; spaceports will be built along the way between Earth and Mars, and mankind will set up camp on Phobos, one of the moons of Mars, and then eventually on the red planet itself. Why? Because it is there, just waiting to be explored.

I look forward to seeing these things happening during my lifetime, but if they don't, please keep this dream alive; please keep going; Mars is there waiting for your footsteps.

Exploration is part and parcel of who we are as human beings; it is wired into our brains, and although I don't completely understand this, it is wired somehow into our hearts as well. If we can see the horizon, we want to know what's beyond. If I can do it, so can you.

Today as I write these words, Lois and I are nearing eighty years of age, and both of us are still going, stronger and faster than ever, traveling around the world, attempting to inform future generations, and inspire them to venture outward in creative exploration of our universe. Indeed, the final frontier may well be human relationships, one person interacting with another. Lois and I believe in marriage, but we have no illusions about it. We both know that a great marriage takes enormous sacrifice. Marriage can eliminate a large measure of loneliness in life, but we've learned that the challenge of compatibility will always be there. On the other hand, we are convinced that our marriage has created a multiplication of purpose, that in our case at least, one plus one equals far more than two. We can say that confidently, because our marriage has been based on a great love and respect for each other, but also on a firm commitment to each other.

Perhaps even we did not realize how inextricably we were linked together until our friend, and my fellow astronaut, Pete Conrad, died of internal bleeding as the result of his motorcycle accident a few weeks before the thirtieth anniversary of Apollo 11. Pete was the third person to walk on the moon and, as he claimed, the first person to dance on the moon. After his first step off the lunar module onto the moon's surface, he quipped, "That may have been one small step for Neil, but it was a long one for me!"

Lois and I attended Pete's funeral, and went to Arlington National Cemetery for the interment. After the ceremony, I took Lois's hand and said, "Come on, I want to show you something." We walked up through the grass a short distance away, and I stopped and pointed at two gravesites. "There are my parents," I said to Lois. "And that's where you and I will be," I said, pointing to the adjoining plots.

Lois was overwhelmed. "Oh, Buzz! That's one of the nicest things you've ever said to me!"

Okay, so I'm not too big on mushy words, but it meant a lot to Lois to know that I was committed to our marriage for the long haul. In my own inimitable way, I was saying to her, "Lois, no matter what happens, we are in this thing for keeps." When all is said and done, I'm grateful to the space pioneers, Tsiolkovsky, Goddard, von Braun, and Oberth, but I will always be most thankful to my wife, Lois, for coming into my life in 1985, and boosting me far beyond where any rocket could take me, or anything I could ever have achieved on my own.

In truth, the real heroes of Apollo 11 were not Neil, Mike, and me, but the teams of thousands at NASA and across America who magnified their efforts and believed we could do it. Along with this concerted undertaking, it came down to individuals who were willing to say, "Maybe there's another way, a better way, to do things."

One of my heroes in particular was John C. Houbolt, a little-known engineer at the Langley Research Center in Hampton, Virginia, who came up with a daring and ingenious alternative to fly to the moon. It was 1961, and NASA officials were debating two approaches: launching two Saturn V rockets to rendezvous in Earth orbit, versus using one direct rocket to take us there. John's idea was to send two spacecraft, and to rendezvous at the moon. Initially, John's idea struck many people—myself included—as dangerously complex, even bizarre. But Houbolt stubbornly kept pushing his plan, and thanks to his persistence, that is how Neil Armstrong and I walked on the moon and then were able to rendezvous with Mike Collins in the *Columbia* orbiting the moon above us to come home to Earth.

We need some men and women like John Houbolt today, individuals who can learn from the past, and then devise new ways of taking us into the future.

● ○ ◐

MAGNIFICENT DESOLATION? Maybe so, but over the years, I've been able to fill in a good many of the craters in my life. What a great life I've had! Schools are named for me in Virginia and Illinois. Planetariums bear my name. I've written nonfiction books, novels, and scientific papers, and worked on screenplay treatments. A music award still bears my likeness, and a popular toy character with my name inspired an animated film series and a ride at Disney World. I was an ace fighter pilot in the Korean war, earned a doctorate from MIT, and, oh yes, I was the second man in the history of the human species to set foot on a celestial body other than Earth. I feel that I've been able to accomplish quite a bit in my short time on this planet, and I'm not done yet!

Oh sure, I still get frustrated at times because I am a visionary often stymied by a bureaucratic maze. But I keep a forward-leaning attitude, looking up the road, always wanting to do something for the betterment of America's space program.

My fellow moonwalker Alan Bean says:

Buzz is the only astronaut, the number-one person, who is still trying to help NASA do their missions better. No other astronaut is doing that. Many are running boards, sitting on panels, etcetera, but when you want to talk about ideas, how to do something, how to go to Mars, how to cycle back and forth, how to get a rocket to travel to the space station, nobody phones me up and says, "Here's an idea for something we could do better at NASA." Nobody but Buzz. I'm trying to figure out which color to use on my new painting, but Buzz is trying to help the country and the world. Buzz has the good ideas. He just needs somebody to understand them and get them into the right hands. If you are working on anything to do with space, and you don't talk with Buzz, you are making a huge mistake. Buzz doesn't give up, and thank God he doesn't.[16]

When I finished my doctoral thesis at MIT on the subject of orbital rendezvous, I dedicated it "To the crew members of this country's present and future manned space programs. If only I could join them in their exciting endeavors!" For nearly half a century now, I have been one of them; I'm known as an astronaut, and I am still thrilled with that designation. But I don't want to live in the past; as long as I am here on Earth, I want to be contributing to the present, and I want to stride confidently into the future.

I believe mankind must explore or expire. We must venture outward. And one way or another, when men and women first set foot on Mars, I will be there, whether watching on my flat-screen television in my Los Angeles home, or looking down from the stars.

---

[16] Interview with the author, November 17, 2008.

Everyone Needs Space—ShareSpace Foundation

I am often asked to describe why I founded the nonprofit Share-Space—what my vision is for the organization, and what I hope to accomplish through it. The essence of my plan involves three key areas: exploration, experiences, and education.

1. **Exploration.** Lunar Renaissance.
   a. To enhance public understanding of the benefits of past exploration and the expected benefits of future paths of exploration.
   b. To encourage astronaut and space program workers' reunions on the anniversaries of Apollo flights, as reminders of our achievements and inspiration for future exploration of the moon, Mars, and beyond.

2. **Experiences.** ShareSpace Awards.
   We plan to present (nontransferable) awards to randomly selected winners (lottery-like) from $100 donations for space-related adventure experiences including guaranteed suborbital flights. Startups will be limited to space advocacy membership

groups, people who have already shown an interest in space exploration, but the general public will be included soon after the initial offerings. We plan to create even greater publicity through nationally broadcast TV contests, with the winners receiving ever more expansive prizes, progressively leading to prizes of possible orbital flights.

3. **Education.** Science Education Ambassadors.
   These ambassadors could be parents or retired teachers of K–12 students, in all state and federal political districts, who will inspire students to see space in their futures, to encourage studies of math and science, and to help ensure that education policies are carried out. We must begin with the children to educate the next generation on the importance of space exploration, and the knowledge that will be necessary to get us there and to keep expanding and exploring new horizons.

You can become part of ShareSpace at www.sharespace.org or receive more information about our activities at www.buzzaldrin.com.

● ○ ●　Acknowledgments

JUST AS LAUNCHING a rocket to the moon requires many dedicated people working behind the scenes, this book is the result of a tremendous team effort by numerous individuals working together from the inception of the ideas to the finished product. As such, I want to express a heartfelt thanks to all who helped launch *Magnificent Desolation*, who worked with me each step of the way and brought this book in for a successful landing.

My deepest appreciation to Lisa Cannon, President of StarBuzz LLC, for her indefatigable and invaluable efforts in overseeing every aspect of the writing and editing of the project. I could not have told this story without her.

Day in, and day out, I thank Ken Abraham for his exceptional writing talents in shaping the story and putting my words together in a dramatic and enjoyable style. No small task!

I must extend an extraordinary thanks to my agent, Dan Strone, CEO of Trident Media Group, for catching the vision for this project, helping to create our initial proposal, and believing in it passionately.

A very special thanks to John Glusman, Vice President and Executive Editor of Harmony Books at the Random House Crown Publishing Group, for seeing the potential of *Magnificent Desolation*, embracing the project wholeheartedly, and applying his outstanding editorial skills to the manuscript. And kudos to Kate Kennedy for keeping us all on the same page.

To the numerous individuals who willingly and freely gave of their time so we could interview them, I extend my sincere thanks. You have greatly enhanced the telling of my story with your insights and information. In addition, I could not have done this without the buoy of support from my staff at StarBuzz LLC. They keep my life running smoothly and have assisted in researching many of the details and historic moments included in this book.

It is never an easy task to travel back along the roads and pathways of one's life. I especially appreciate my family, children, stepchildren, and two sisters, who shared their memories and insights. As a result, the process of writing the book has been richly rewarding and renewing.

I am deeply grateful to my wife, Lois, who has inspired me at this time in reliving and recounting the amazing journey of my life.

From the moon to the magnificence of life here on Earth, I thank the Higher Power in this great universe.